IMAGES
of America

NEWARK
PUBLIC LIBRARY

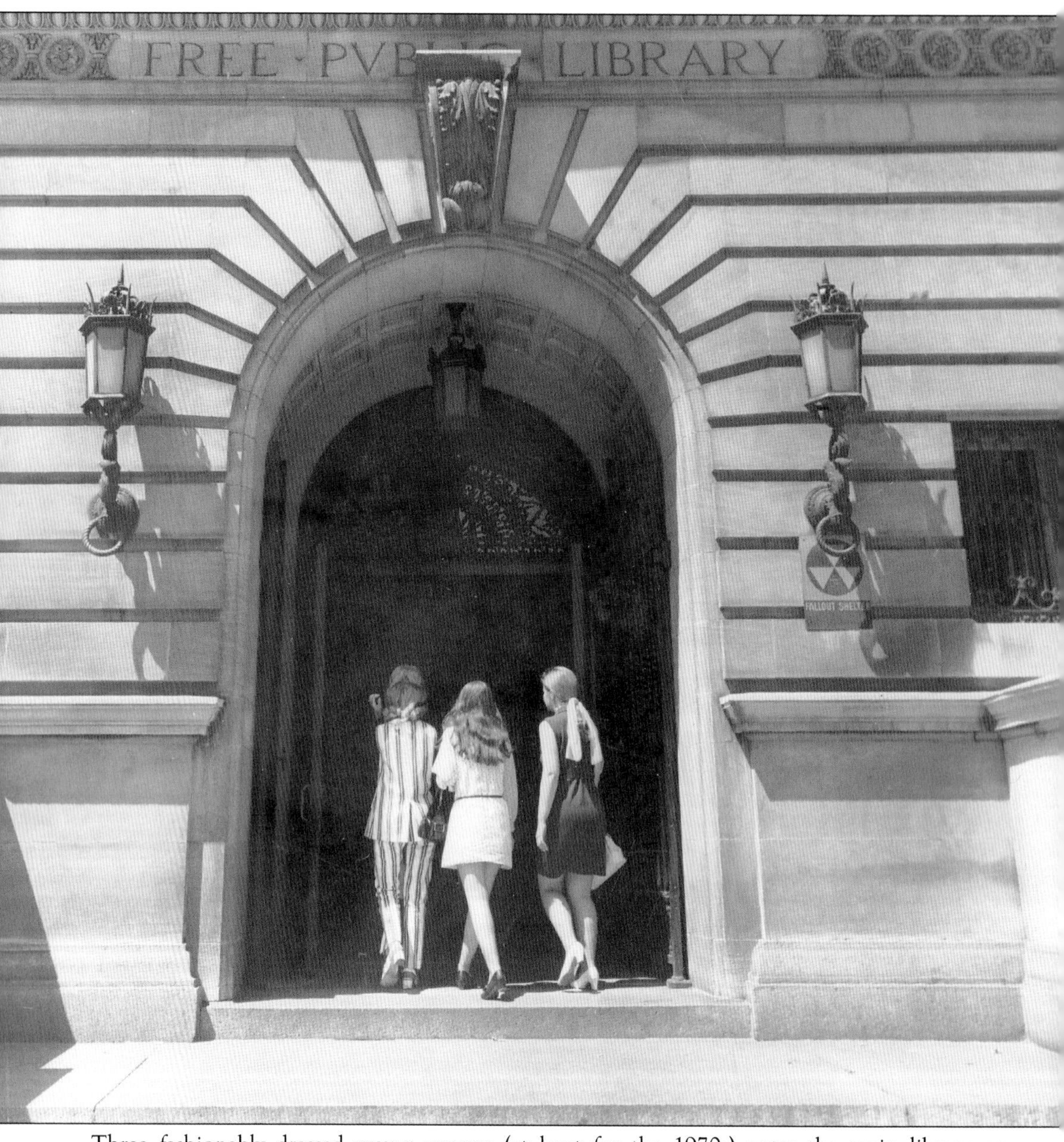

Three fashionably dressed young women (at least for the 1970s) enter the main library on Washington Street. Are they looking for the latest romance novel, the most popular music album, or the top-selling entrepreneurial manual? Whatever it is, they will find it at the Newark Public Library. (Courtesy of Van Picture Service.)

ON THE COVER: The facade of the main building on Washington Park (now Harriet Tubman Square) is enhanced by two gigantic urns. Men and women enter and exit the building, some of whom have armloads of books. (Courtesy of Laura von Schnarendorf.)

IMAGES
of America

NEWARK PUBLIC LIBRARY

William A. Peniston

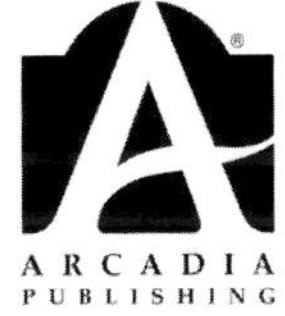

ARCADIA
PUBLISHING

Copyright © 2025 by William A. Peniston
ISBN 978-1-4671-6203-6

Published by Arcadia Publishing
Charleston, South Carolina

Printed in the United States of America

Library of Congress Control Number: 2024946798

For all general information, please contact Arcadia Publishing:
Telephone 843-853-2070
Fax 843-853-0044
E-mail sales@arcadiapublishing.com

Visit us on the Internet at www.arcadiapublishing.com

To my fellow librarians, both past and present, at the Newark Public Library

CONTENTS

Acknowledgments

I was the librarian and archivist of the Newark Museum of Art for over 25 years. For most of those years, I was a solo librarian but worked constantly with clerks, interns, and volunteers. For 13 years, I had a young, talented, very smart archivist, Jeffrey Moy, working beside me.

For all of those years, I made it a point to get together and work closely with other librarians at other institutions in Newark. At the Newark Public Library, I remember fondly Paul Stellhorn, Charles Cummings, and Bill Dane, all of whom are no longer with us. Bruce Ford, Joseph Casale, Tom Ankner, Beth Zak-Cohen, Greg Guderian, Vanessa Castaldo, and Nadine Sergejeff Giron, all at the Newark Public Library at one time or another, have also been good friends and wonderful colleagues. Paige Trapnell went over and beyond the call of duty by scanning all images for this book. Lynn Mullins and Ann Watkins at the Dana Library at Rutgers, the State University of New Jersey, Campus at Newark, were kind supporters. Ann even volunteered for me after her retirement. James Kaser and Chad Leinaweaver at the New Jersey Historical Society have remained friends long after they moved on to other institutions.

In 2013, Wilma "Bunny" Grey and Heidi Cramer gave me the opportunity to work with the Newark Public Library's archives, the Librariana Collection, from which most of these photographs come. It was in this year and a half that I became aware of the remarkable history and the lasting legacy of this outstanding institution, and I am glad to be able to share that knowledge with the public with this photographic essay. Christian Zabriskie, the current director of the Newark Public Library, has supported this project from the very beginning, and I am very grateful for his help.

All images, unless otherwise noted, are from the Newark Public Library. I have indicated the photographer, the photographic studio, or the original source of the photographs in parentheses if that information was available.

Introduction

Ever since Rev. Abraham Pierson of Bradford, Connecticut, brought his collection of 400 books to Newark in 1666, Newark has had libraries. At first attached to churches and schools, these private libraries catered to specific audiences for specific purposes; they were not open to all. The first subscription library, known as the Newark Library Society, was founded in 1797, and it charged an initial fee of $4, plus an annual fee of $1. In 1821, Moses Combs, a leading tanner and shoe manufacturer, established a library for apprentices; it merged with the Newark Library Society in 1822. Later, in 1826, the Mechanics Association was formed with a library of 650 volumes; it, too, merged with the Newark Library Society. Both of these projects indicate that civic leaders in Newark thought that the city's workers, not just the city's elites, needed access to information. Because of competition from other churches, schools, and debating societies, though, the Newark Library Society folded in 1830.

Fifteen years later, another group of civic leaders organized a new society, the Newark Library Association, in 1845, which was then chartered in 1847. It was housed in a new building on Market Street named Library Hall. The stated purpose of this new association was "to establish a library with a view to advance the interest of learning generally and to instruct and better educate the youth of Newark in science, literature, and the arts." Shares were sold for $25, and subscriptions cost $3 a year; borrowing limits were set at two books at a time. The collection grew rapidly from 1,900 books in 1848 to 7,000 in 1858, to 25,000 in 1884. Still, by this time, the idea of free public libraries supported by taxpayers had begun to grow in popularity.

In 1884, the state assembly passed "an act to authorize the establishment of free public libraries in this state." The Paterson Public Library was the first such free library in New Jersey. Newark Public Library became the seventh in 1887 when the residents voted overwhelmingly to establish a free public library. The vote was 23,994 in favor and 331 opposed. "We may state here," reported the *Sunday Call* on November 6, 1887, "that nothing Newark has done of late years has attracted more attention elsewhere or caused more favorable comment than its almost unanimous vote for a free public library."

The mayor immediately appointed a board of trustees, which then hired Frank Hill as the librarian in 1888. He had experience in libraries in Lowell and Salem, Massachusetts, and in Paterson, New Jersey. He hired a staff, selected a collection, and rented space from the Newark Library Association's new building on West Park Street. Because of his work and the work of his assistants, the collections grew and, more importantly, circulation grew. In the later part of the 1890s, he oversaw the construction of the grand, palace-style building on Washington Street, which has since been the headquarters of the Newark Public Library for over a century.

The second director, John Cotton Dana, expanded the outreach of the library in multiple ways. In addition to books for all citizens, young and old, native-born or immigrant, he established nine branches in the city's neighborhoods and a Business Branch for the bankers, lawyers, insurance executives, department store owners, and factory owners as well as the office workers and laborers, both skilled and unskilled, who worked in those industries. A brilliant promoter of the library, he once said that libraries were "a means for elevating and refining tastes, for giving greater efficiency to every worker, for diffusing sound principles of social and political action, and for furnishing intellectual culture to all." They were, in his opinion, indispensable for an advanced industrial democracy.

Other leaders were to follow in Hill's and Dana's footsteps, and other staff members were to contribute to the overall success of the public library through their dedication to its services and its collections. These leaders, both the directors and the trustees, will be the subject of the first chapter. The staff, the topic of the next chapter, were indispensable to the remarkable achievements that the library has obtained over the course of the last 130 years. They acquired, cataloged, and repaired books, developed outreach services, and built outstanding collections, both of which (services and collections) will be the subject of the following two chapters.

Services from the ordinary, like cataloging and bookbinding, to the extraordinary, like outreach to adults, children, and teenagers as well as to various ethnic and racial groups, will be the topic of the third chapter. The first collection in the Newark Public Library included both fiction and nonfiction books selected from the Newark Library Association's collection. From this modest selection, the library grew to include well-rounded collections in the fine arts, humanities, and social sciences. Over the years, special subject areas were developed in Newark and New Jersey history, politics, and culture, African American studies, and Latin American heritage.

Along the way, the library expanded beyond its walls on Washington Park (now Harriet Tubman Square) to include several delivery stations and many branches at different times and places throughout the city. By the 1930s, the Newark Public Library had eight neighborhood branches and 33 extension libraries in other institutions. Bookmobiles and traveling vans were introduced in the 1930s and then again in the 1950s. Today, it has only six branches.

In the concluding chapter, the legacy that has maintained the library for over a century and a third will be highlighted. That legacy consists of dedicated staff, who provide excellent services and inspiring programs based on unique collections, with strong community support.

Rev. Abraham Pierson (1611–1678), the elder, came to Newark from
Branford, Connecticut, to be the first minister of the Congregational
church in 1666. He brought with him his 400-volume library of
religious materials, and he lent them out to his parishioners. His son
Rev. Abraham Pierson (1646–1707, pictured), the younger, inherited
his pulpit and his library. Hence, he was Newark's second minister and
second "librarian."

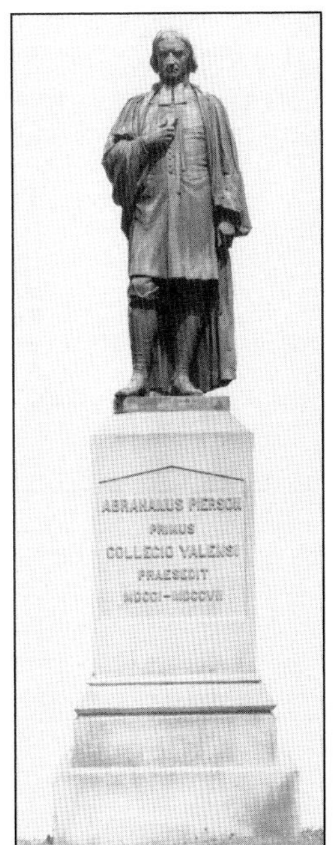

Reading and writing were central to the faith of these early Puritans
who believed that all good Christians should be able to read the Bible.
Their early schools struggled to survive, but in 1774, the Newark
Academy built its first school on the Upper Commons (now Harriet
Tubman Square), not far from the present main library. Like other
early schools, it, too, had a small collection of books for its students.

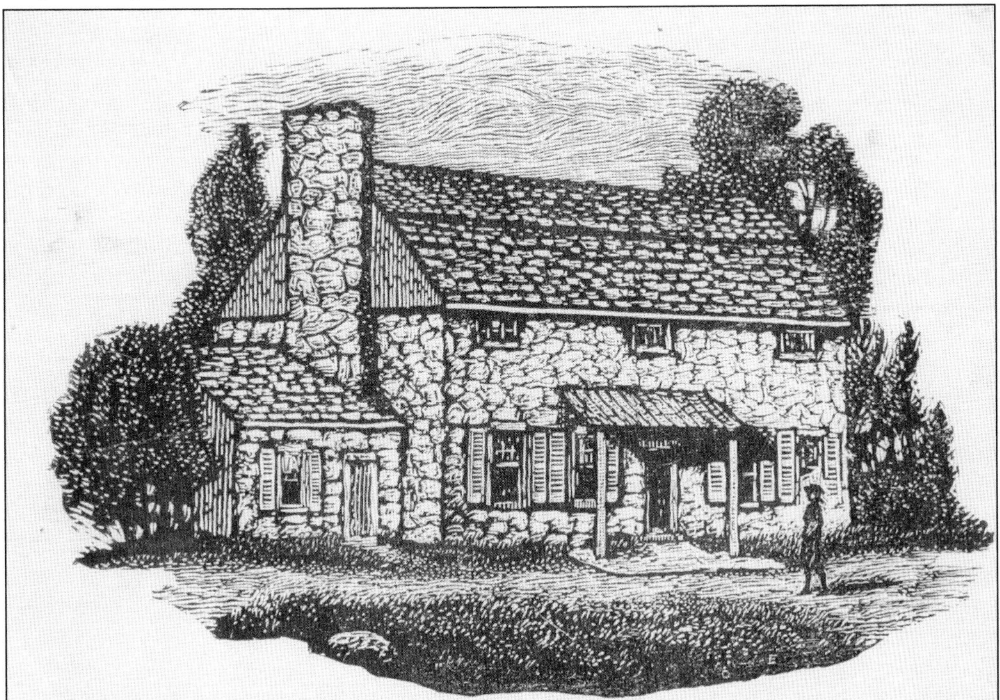

1774—Washington Park

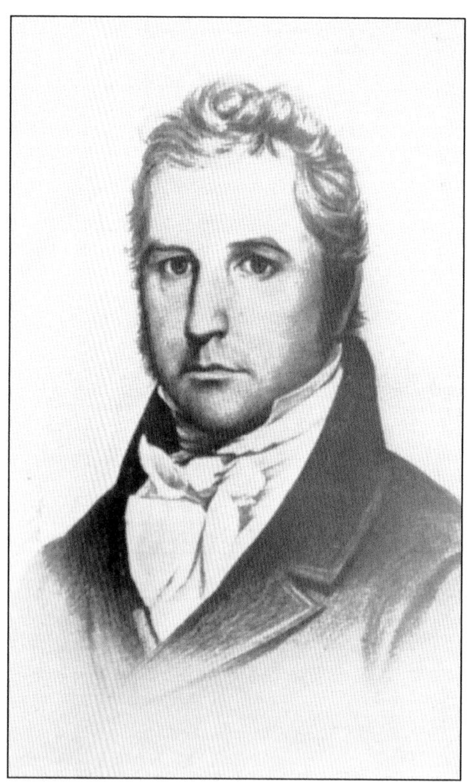

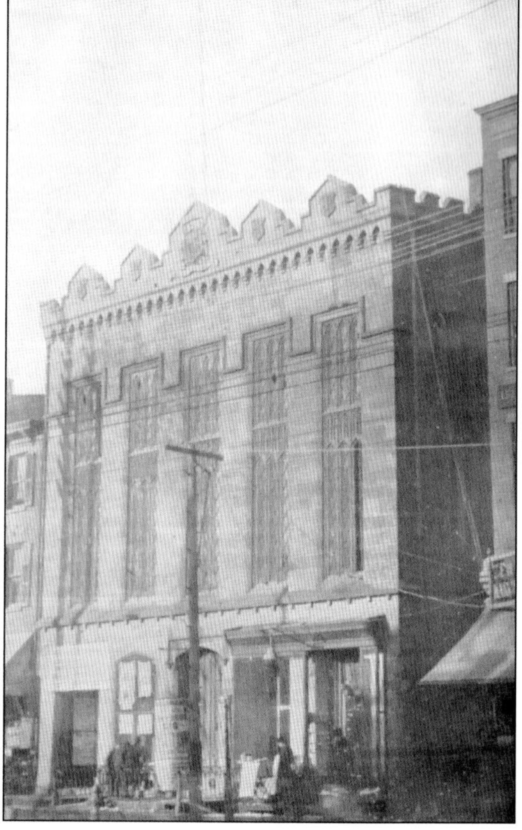

William Halsey (1770–1843), a prominent lawyer in the city, was the "librarian" for the Newark Library Society, which operated from 1797 to 1830. It had grown out of a debating society, and by the time of its demise, it had over 12,000 volumes. Halsey later became the first mayor of Newark in 1836 when it was incorporated as a city.

Library Hall on Market Street was the first home of the Newark Library Association. Erected in 1847, it was a three-story building with a reading room and space for books on the second floor. The first floor was rented out to businesses and offices. The Newark Board of Education and the New Jersey Historical Society had offices on the third floor. In the back was a concert and lecture hall.

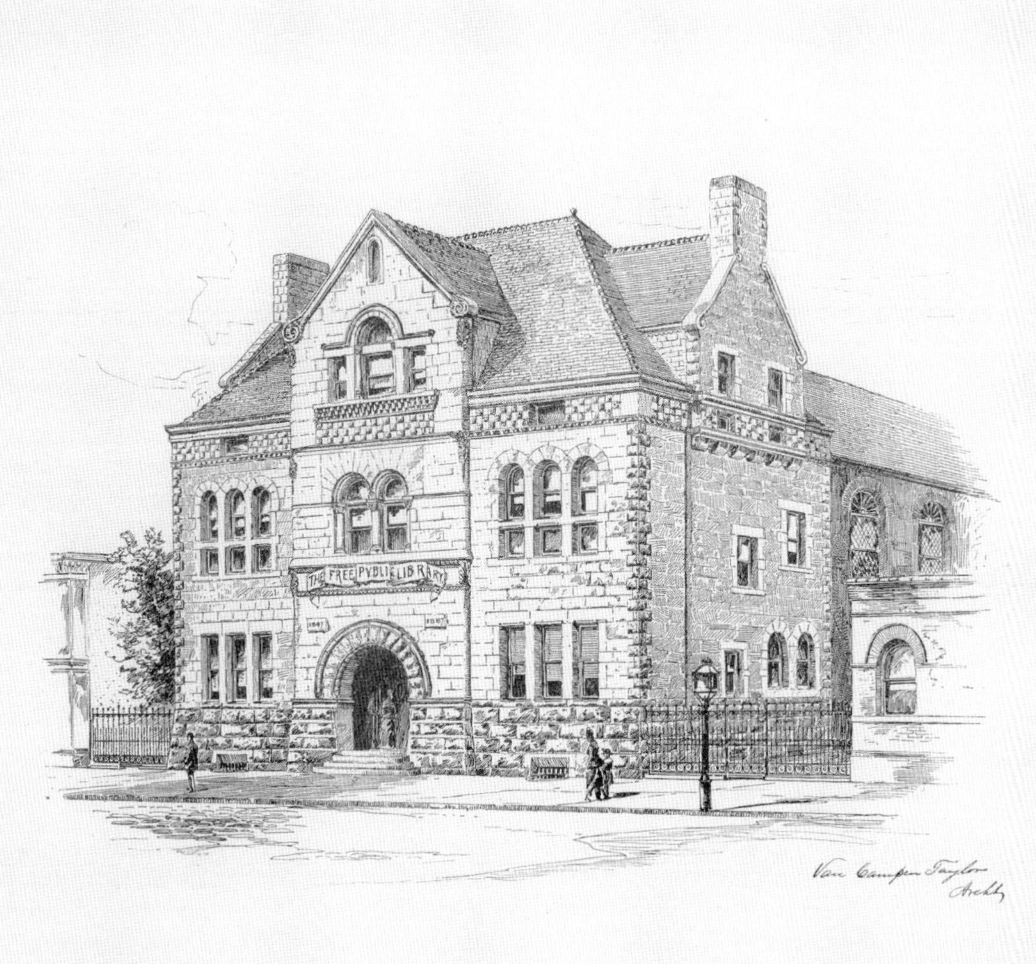

Originally a church and then a theater, this building on West Park Street was purchased by the Newark Library Association, remodeled, and leased to the newly established Newark Public Library in 1889. Made of Belleville stone in the Romanesque style, the first floor consisted of the catalog room and a room with book stacks and wall cases in alcoves and balconies. The women's reading room was discreetly tucked away in a corner. On the second floor, the main reading room was spacious with high ceilings and bright windows. Its oak tables and chairs sat 150 visitors, who had access to newspapers, magazines, and books. The top floor was set aside for the use of pupils from the public schools and their teachers.

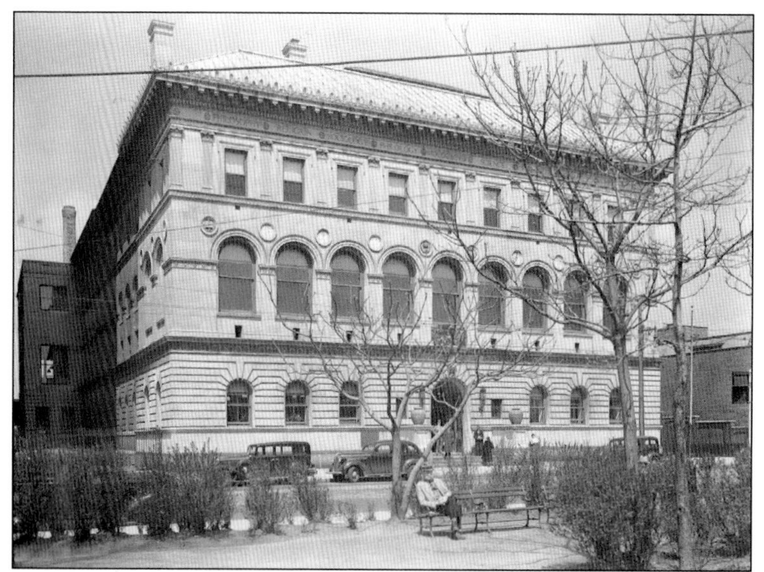

Opening in 1901 and modeled after the Palazzo Strozzi in Florence, the main library was designed by Rankin and Kellogg, a prominent architectural firm in Philadelphia, in the Beaux-Arts style. It is a four-story brick building with a limestone facade. Arched windows enhance the first and second floors, and rectangular windows frame the third floor. (William F. Cone.)

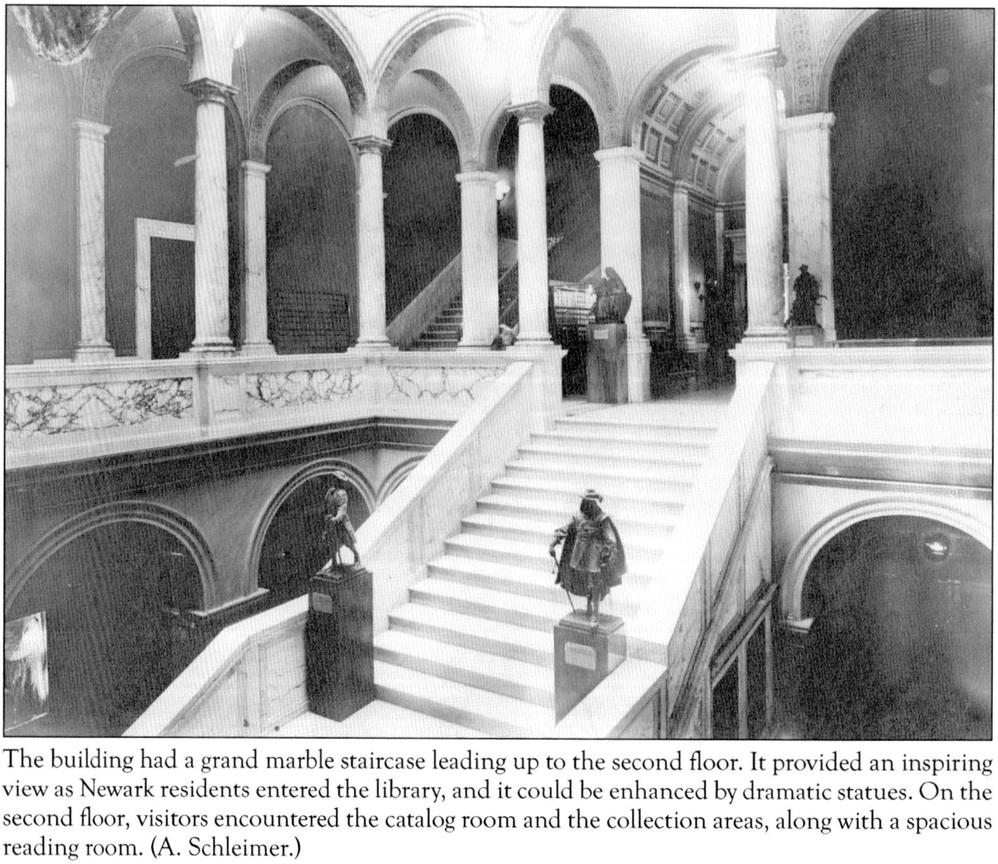

The building had a grand marble staircase leading up to the second floor. It provided an inspiring view as Newark residents entered the library, and it could be enhanced by dramatic statues. On the second floor, visitors encountered the catalog room and the collection areas, along with a spacious reading room. (A. Schleimer.)

One

LEADERS

On Tuesday, November 1, 1887, the citizens of Newark, New Jersey, voted to establish a public library in the city. The mayor, Joseph E. Haynes, promptly appointed a board of trustees, which included the superintendent of schools and five citizens, mostly lawyers and politicians, along with one businessman. They hired Franklin Pierce "Frank" Hill as the first "librarian," a man with almost a decade of experience in public libraries in Massachusetts and New Jersey. He was instrumental in hiring the staff, selecting the collection, cataloging it, and making it available to the public, both young and old, men and women, businessmen, professionals, and workers, native-born and immigrant. He also oversaw the construction of the new building on Washington Park (now Harriet Tubman Square).

John Cotton Dana succeeded him and brought to the role of the librarian an amazing aptitude for promoting the library. He had his staff print bookplates, broadsides, booklists, and pamphlets, while he wrote numerous articles in library journals and local newspapers. As the foremost librarian in the country at the time, he made the Newark Public Library an example of what public libraries could do for their communities.

Dana was succeeded by his very capable assistant, Beatrice Winser, who had also served as the assistant librarian under Hill. She guided the institution through the Great Depression and into the first year of World War II. Together, these three directors established the Newark Public Library on a solid foundation. Their successors adapted the library to the changing needs of the city. John Boynton Kaiser instituted civil service reforms; James E. "Ned" Bryan expanded the building and the services in the 1950s and 1960s; Bernard Shein, William "Bill" Urban, and Thomas J. Alrutz initiated technological changes in the 1970s and 1980s; and Alex Boyd and Wilma Grey responded to the changing demographics of the city in the second half of the 20th century, building on collections in African American and Hispanic and Latino art, literature, and culture and improving services to those communities. All have made the Newark Public Library a space for lifelong learning; explorations in the arts, humanities, and sciences; and a place to connect with other members of the diverse communities that make up the city.

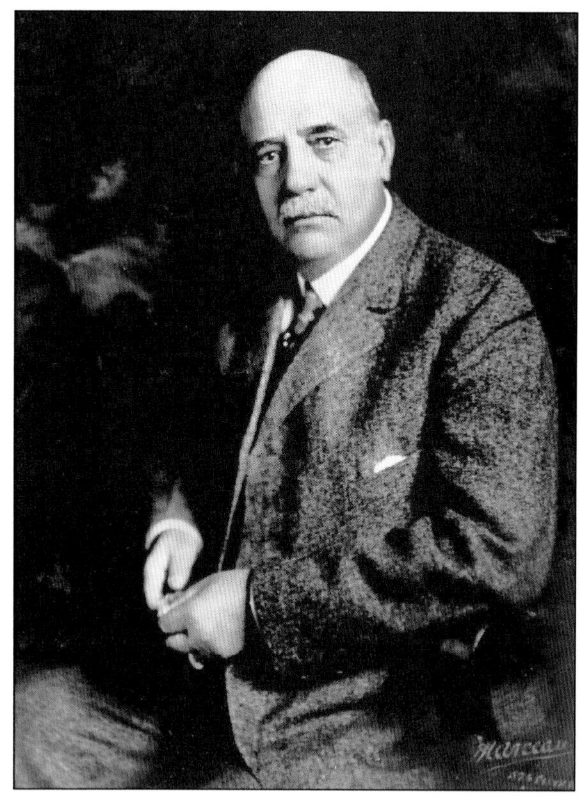

As established by law, the board of trustees of the Newark Public Library was originally composed of seven members: the mayor, the superintendent of schools, and five citizens appointed by the mayor. These men (and they were only men at that time) supported the development of library services to the community by establishing policies, advocating for funding, approving expenditures, and most importantly, hiring a competent, professional librarian, who oversaw the overall administration of the library. Pictured here are board members J. Franklin Fort, a lawyer and politician (later governor of New Jersey, left) and L. Spencer Goble, a prominent insurance businessman and civic leader (below).

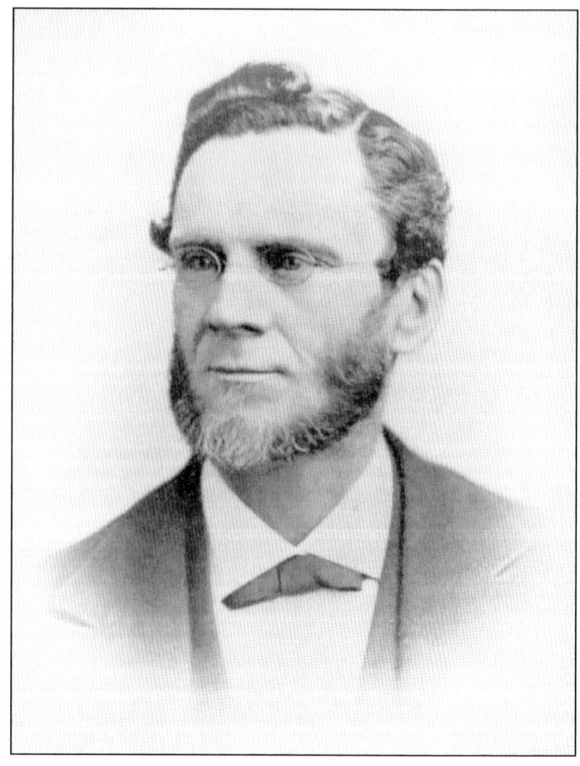

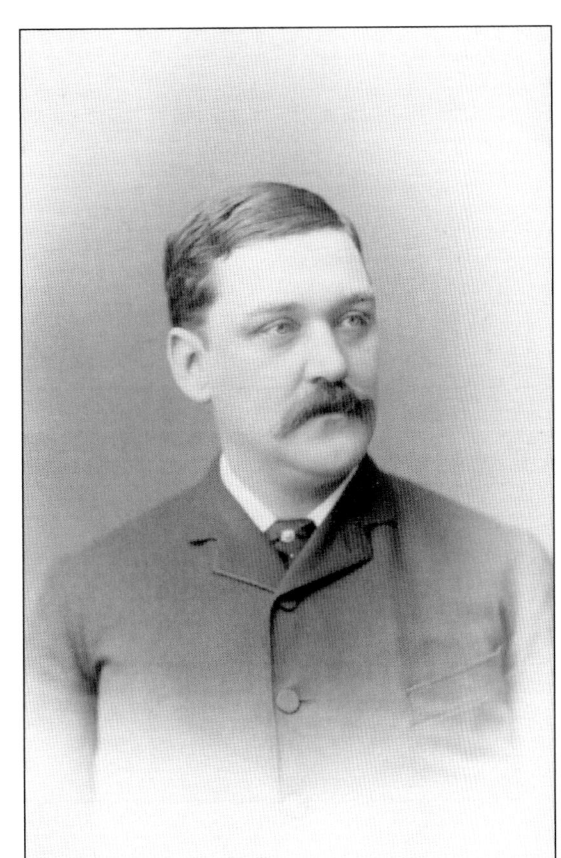

In addition to Fort and Goble, the first board of trustees included Mayor Joseph E. Haynes, a former principal and later, a postmaster; William N. Barringer, the superintendent of schools; George S. Duryee, another lawyer active in politics (right); Frederick H. Teese, yet another lawyer and politician (below); and Samuel J. Macdonald, a scholar, lawyer, and city councilman.

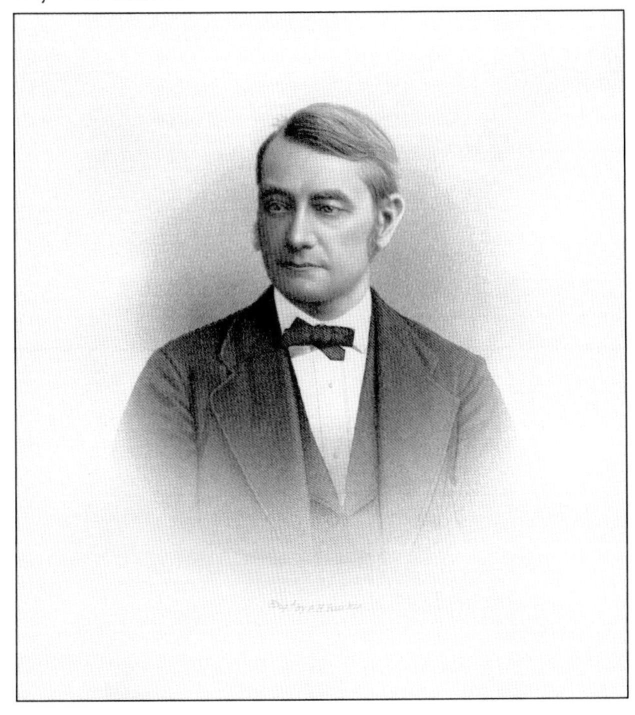

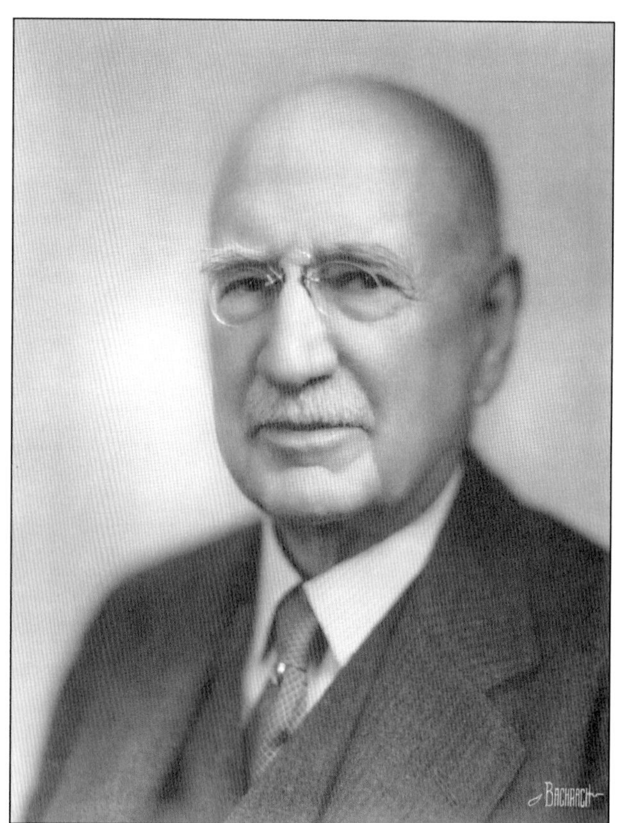

A graduate of Dartmouth College, Franklin Pierce "Frank" Hill (1855–1941) began his library career in Lowell, Massachusetts (1879–1884), then at Paterson, New Jersey (1885–1887), the first public library in the state, and finally, at Salem, Massachusetts (1888). He was hired as the librarian of the Newark Public Library in 1888, started in 1889, and resigned in 1901. He finished his career as the librarian at the Brooklyn Public Library. (Fabian Bachrach.)

Hill immediately set about hiring the staff, selecting 7,000 volumes from the defunct Newark Library Association, cataloging them, making the nonfiction books available to the public in open, browsable stacks (the third library in the country to do so), setting aside specifically designated areas for women (right) and children, buying books in foreign languages for immigrants, and distributing books by horse-drawn wagon to schools, firehouses, and other delivery stations throughout the city.

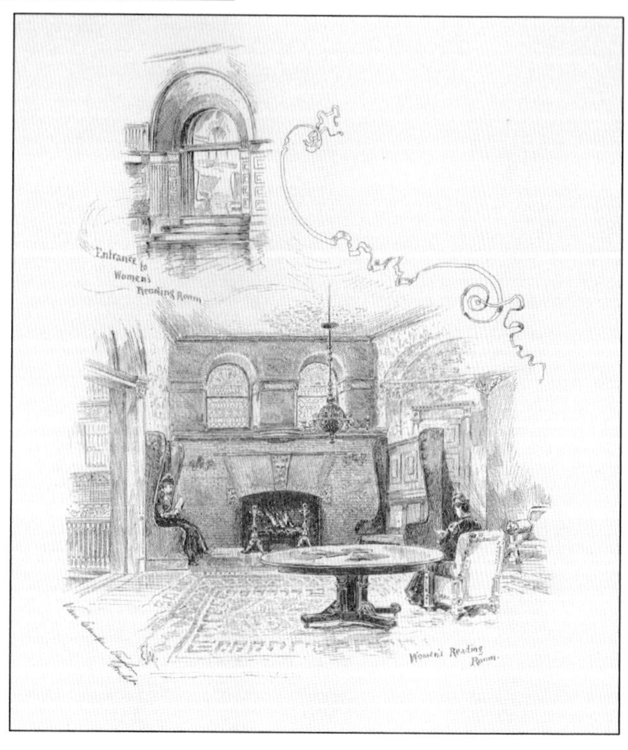

Professional journals, trade journals, and literary magazines as well as local, regional, and national newspapers provided men, women, and children with current information on a variety of topics. Hill expressed his philosophy in the following way: "We do not purchase every new book, published, be it good, bad, or indifferent, but strive to gather a library useful to students, interesting to readers, and profitable to all."

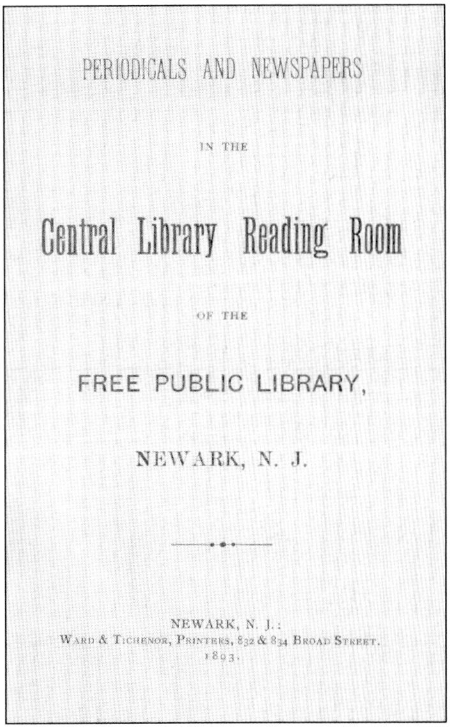

In addition, under Hill's direction, the new main library building at 5 Washington Street was planned and erected. Construction began in 1898, and it opened to the public in 1901. It cost the city $315,000, the largest public works project of its era. Ironically, Hill inhabited the librarian's office for only a few months.

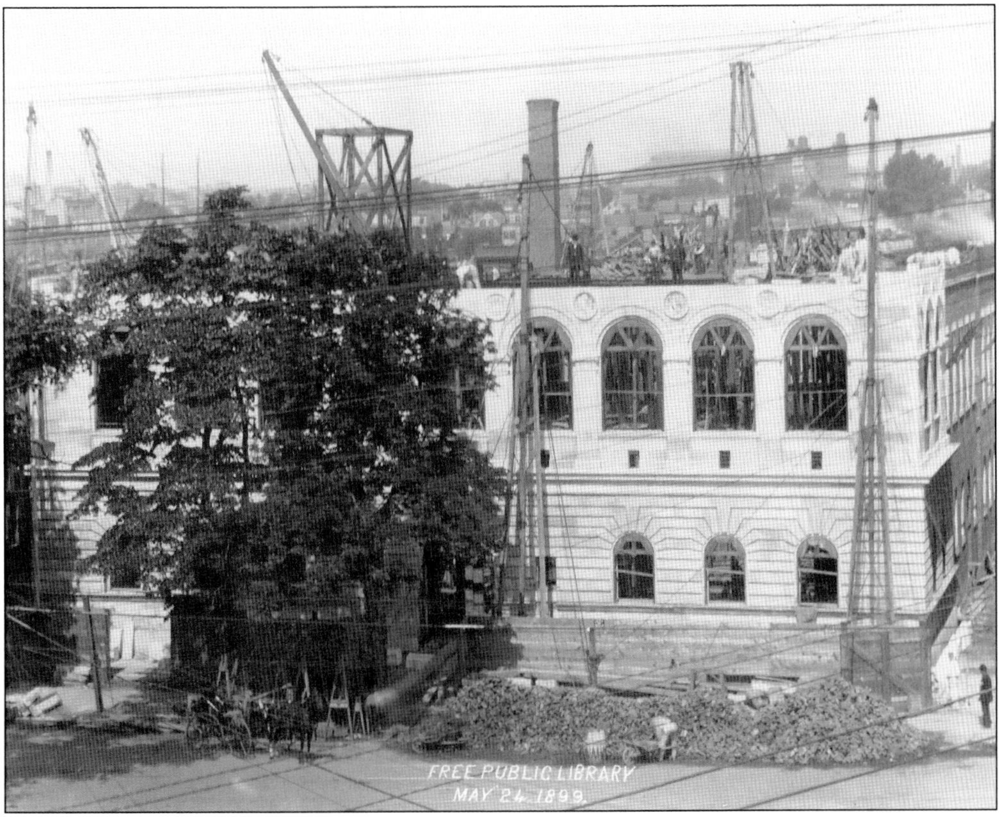

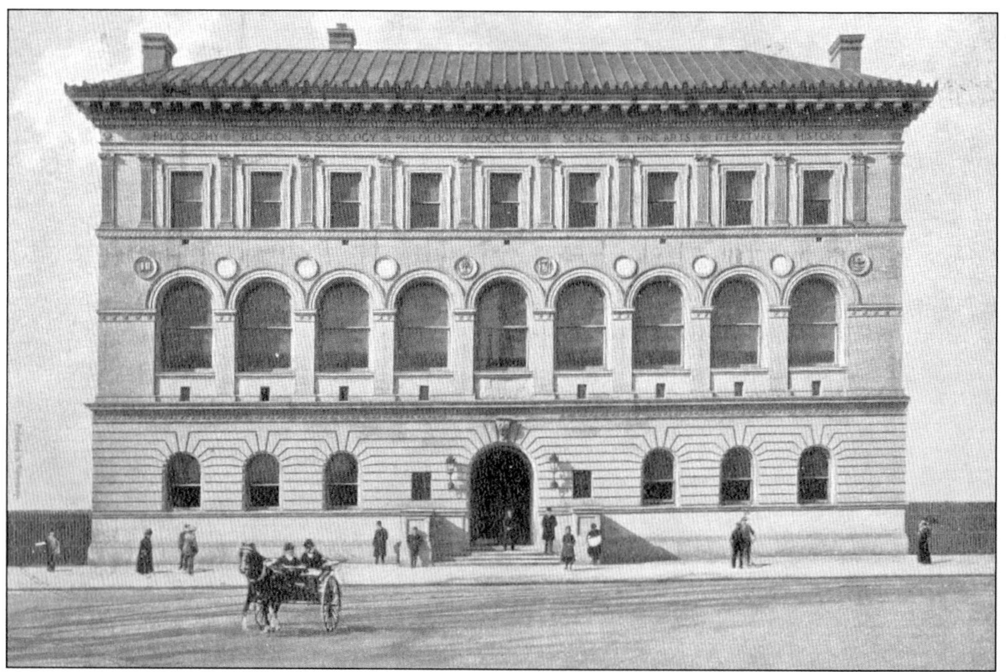

The iconic building on Washington Street became a favorite subject for postcards. This one features a horse-drawn carriage, which was still common in 1901, and several pedestrians. It stands alone in this image, which it does not in reality. (Raphael Tuck & Sons.)

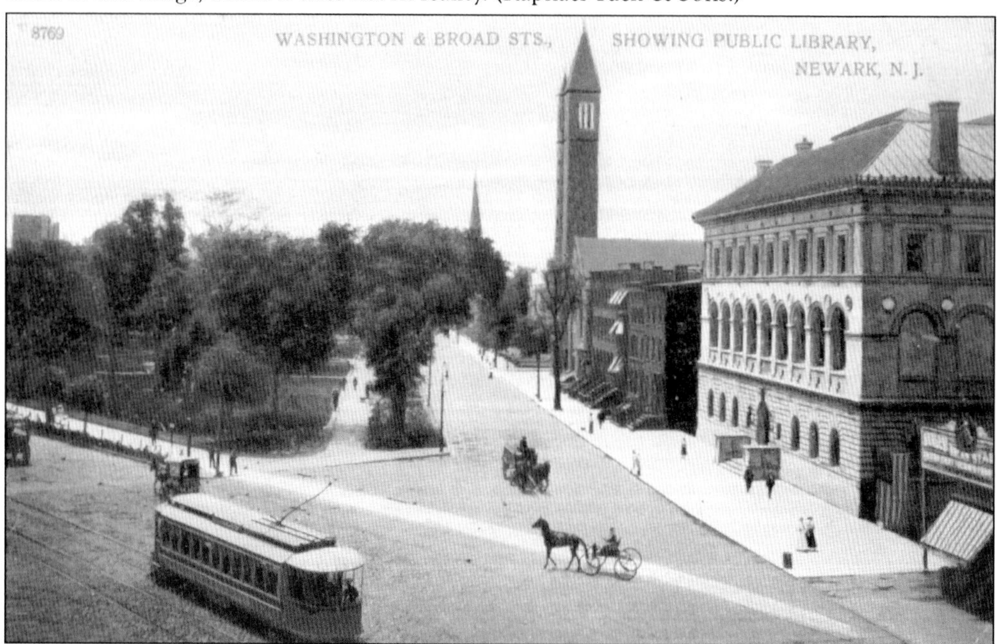

This aerial view provides an overview of the neighborhood. The library dominates the corner of Washington Street and Broad Street, with the bell tower of the Second Presbyterian Church ("the holy smokestack") piercing the sky (this church burned in the 1930s and was replaced by the existing building). The steeple of St. Patrick's Cathedral (now just a parish church) is in the distance. A trolley heads out toward the suburbs. (A.C. Buselman & Co.)

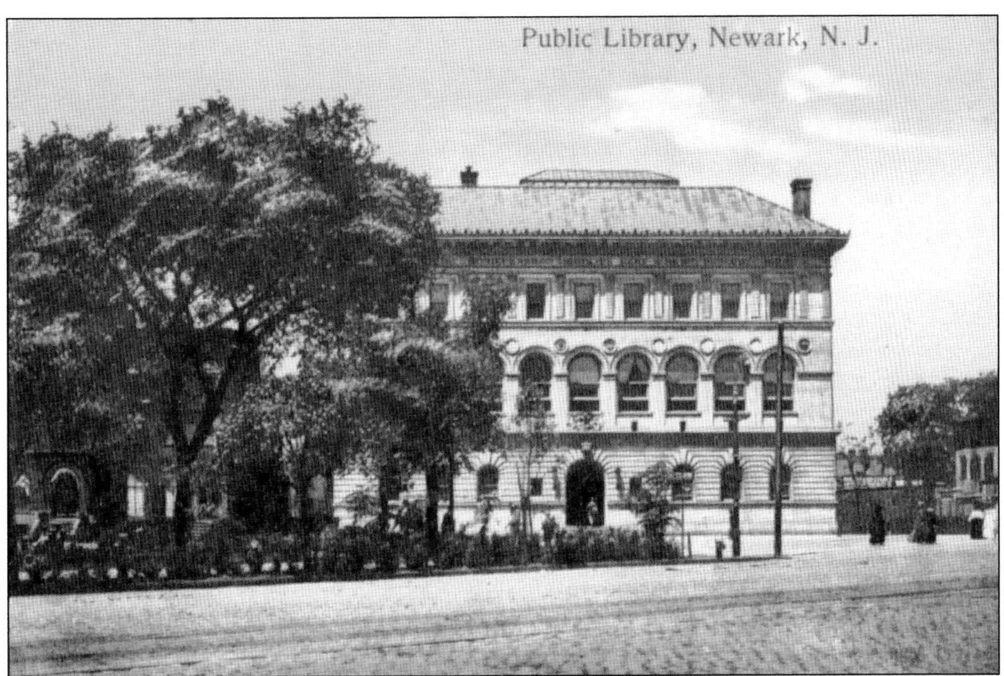

In this postcard, the trees and shrubs of Washington Park (now Harriet Tubman Square) complement the contemplative nature of the library. The major classifications of the nonfiction collection—philosophy, religion, sociology, philology, science, fine arts, literature, and history—are engraved underneath the eaves of the roof. (US Postal Service.)

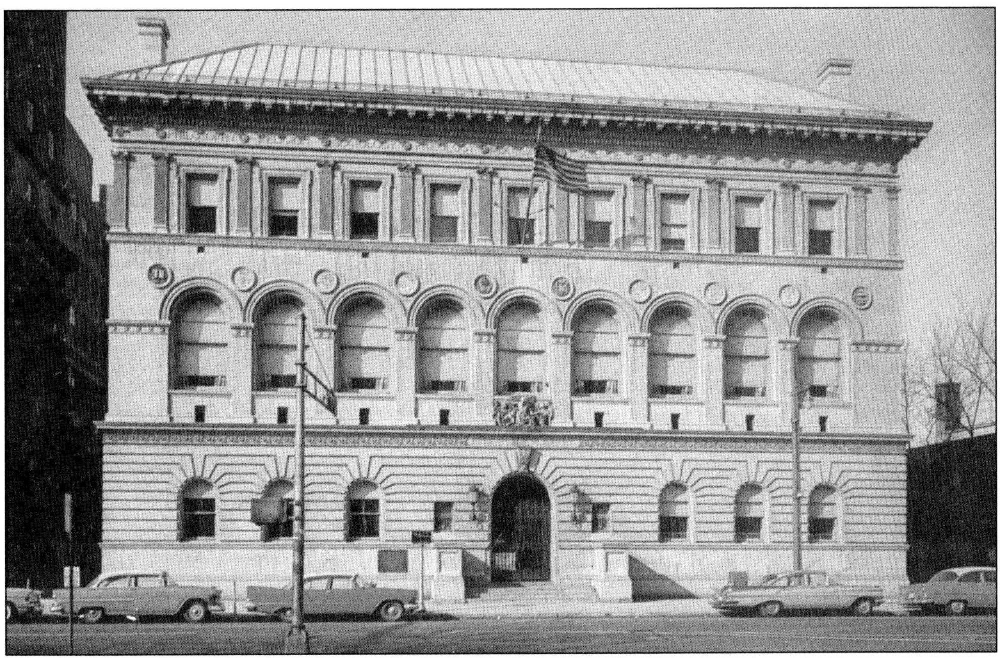

In this postcard, "What's good for General Motors" is good for the Newark Public Library. The facade of the library was unchanged from the time of its construction, but renovations in the back had increased the size of the building in the 1950s. (Deluxe Greeting Card Co.)

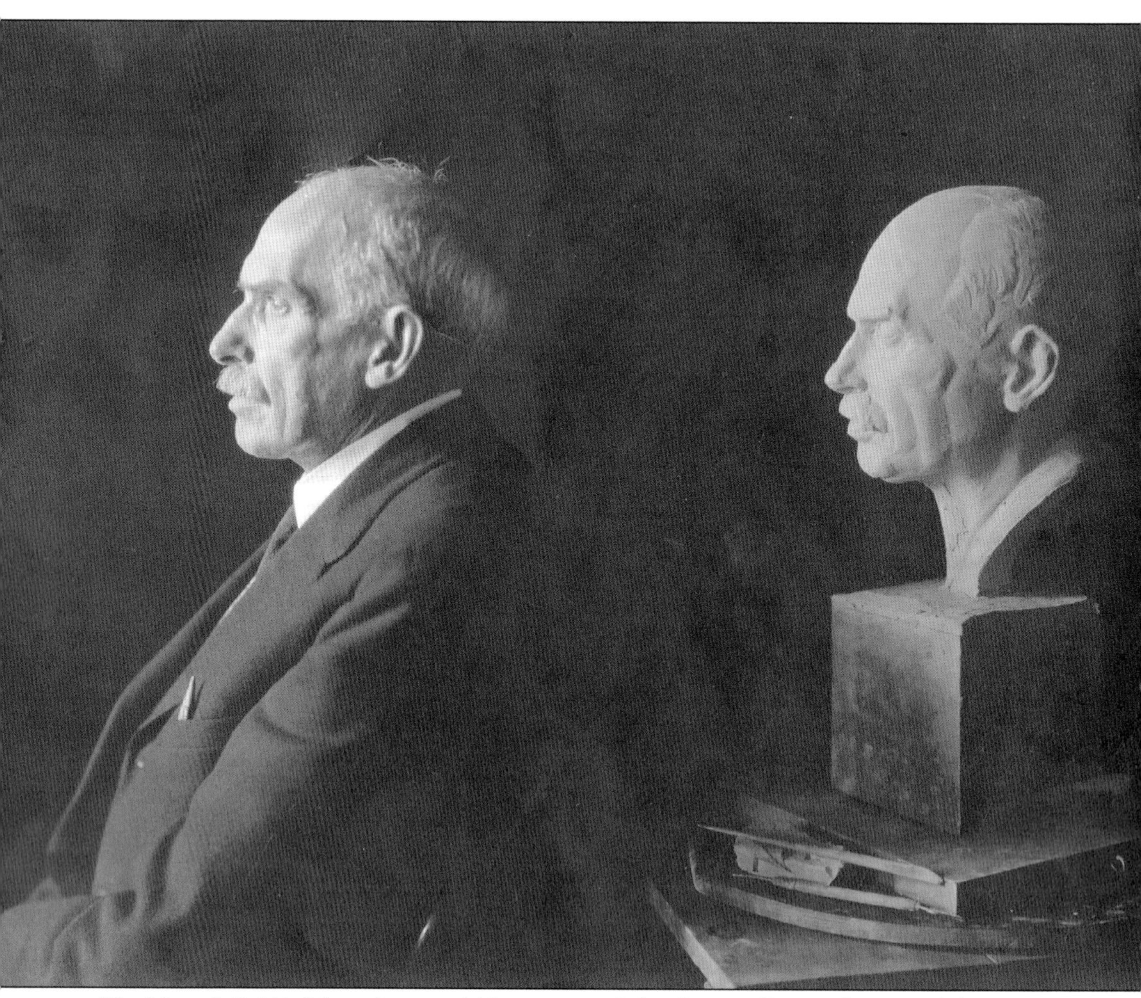

The Newark Public Library's second librarian was John Cotton Dana, who served from 1902 to 1929. He was a miner, a surveyor, a rancher, a lawyer, a journalist, and a Unitarian minister (at least for one month) before he became the librarian at the Denver Public Library at the age of 33. As a librarian, he found his vocation as a thinker, a critic, and an educator. "What does a public library do for a community?" Dana asked his patrons, and in answer, he wrote, "It supplies the public with recreational reading; it supplies books on every profession, art, or handicraft; it helps in social and political education—in training citizens; it promotes culture, the diffusion of good reading among people in giving tone and character to their intellectual life; it is the ever-ready helper of the school-teacher; and it aids the work of reading circles and other home-culture organizations."

In 1907, Dana purchased a printing press for the Newark Public Library, and from then on, he and his staff printed countless broadsheets, leaflets, pamphlets, and other materials, all promoting the library and its activities. In this photograph, he inspects a poster right off the press, while a library assistant looks on.

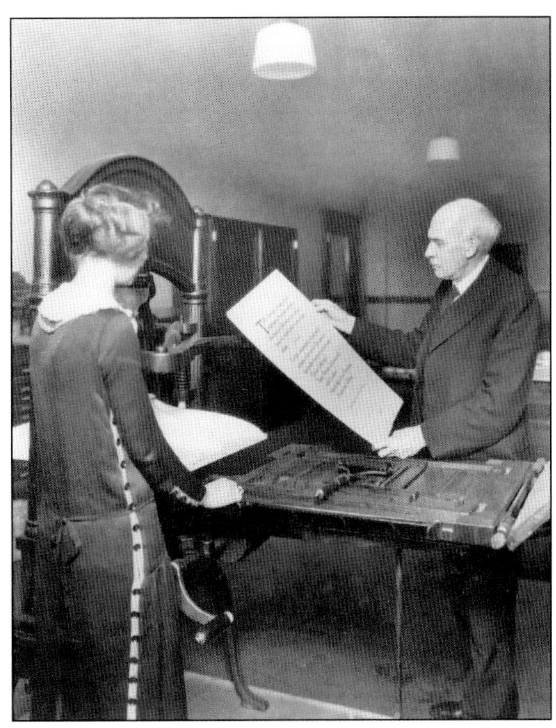

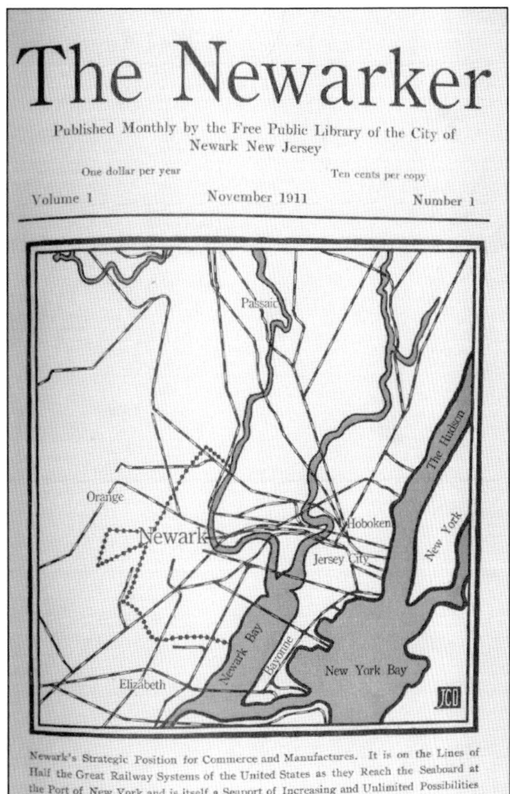

Newark's Strategic Position for Commerce and Manufactures. It is on the Lines of Half the Great Railway Systems of the United States as they Reach the Seaboard at the Port of New York and is itself a Seaport of Increasing and Unlimited Possibilities

Printed on the library's press, the *Newarker* was "a journal published to introduce a city to itself and its public library." It ran from 1912 to 1916, and in its final year, it became the official organ for the 250th anniversary of the founding of the city. It covered historical topics as well as issues of current concern. It was relaunched in 1936 to celebrate the centennial of the city's charter.

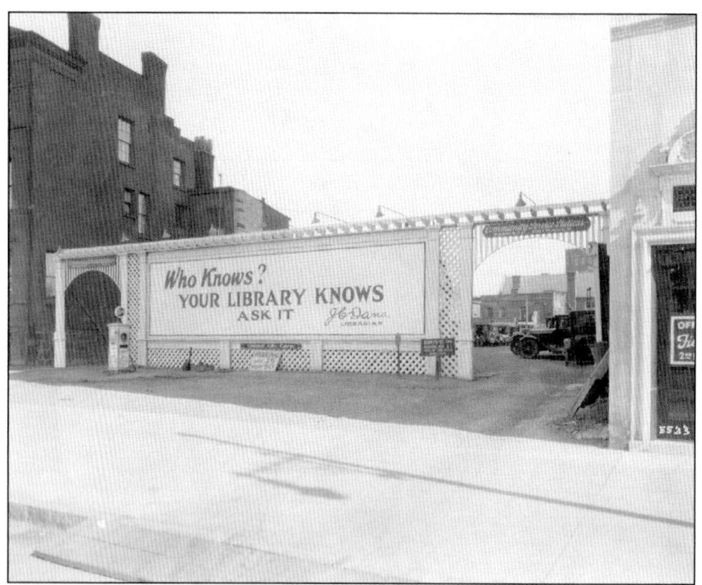

Dana wanted the citizens of Newark to know that the library was the source of useful information; all they needed to do was "ask it." Billboards, like this one, were a way of getting the public interested in the library, getting them through the doorway, and getting them involved. (United Advertising Corporation.)

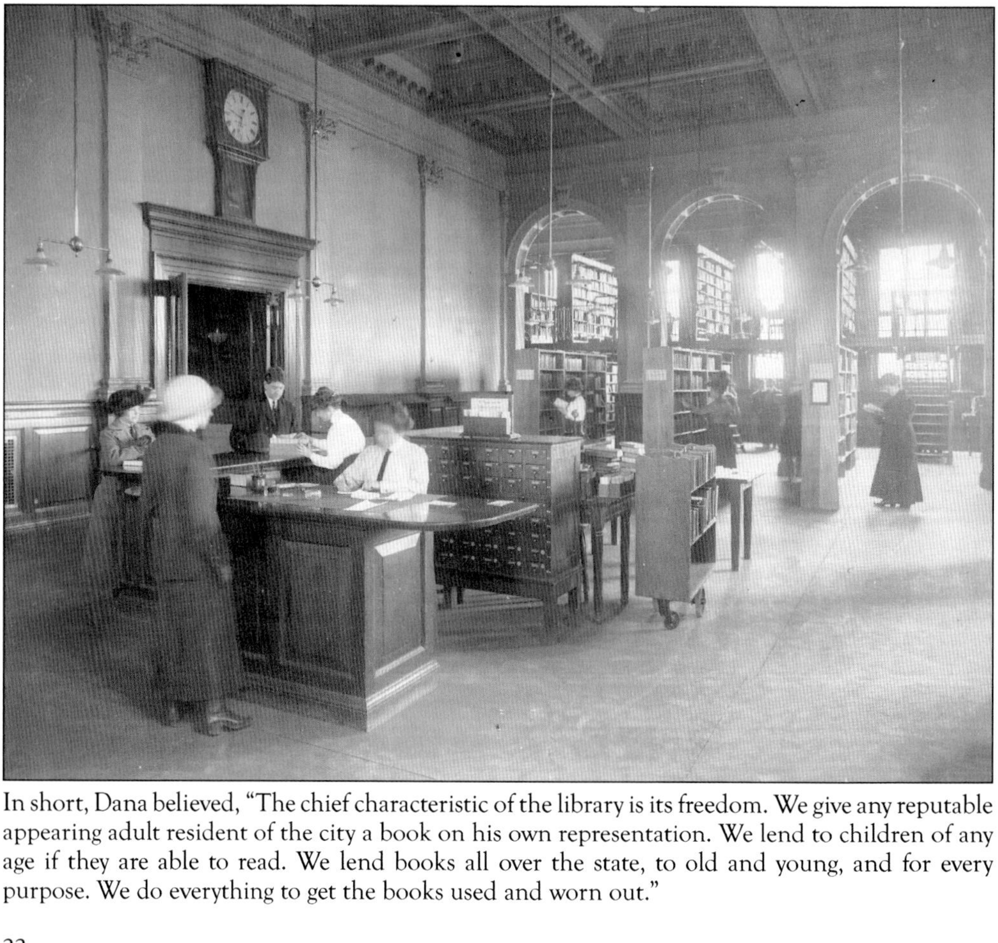

In short, Dana believed, "The chief characteristic of the library is its freedom. We give any reputable appearing adult resident of the city a book on his own representation. We lend to children of any age if they are able to read. We lend books all over the state, to old and young, and for every purpose. We do everything to get the books used and worn out."

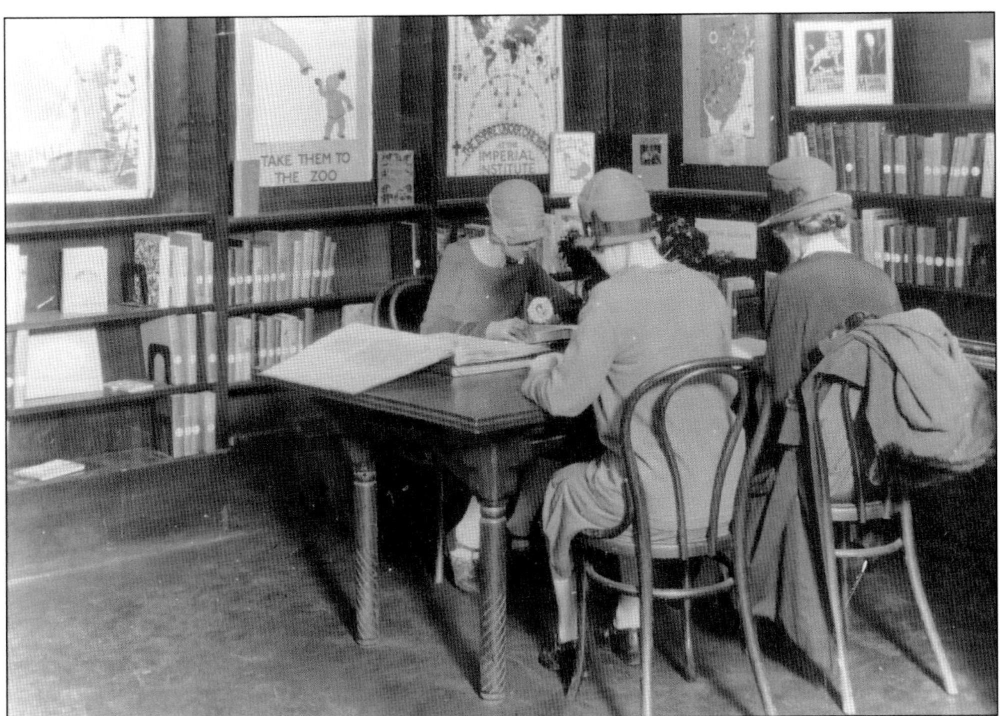

Dana wrote that there were five kinds of patrons: the adult student, who looked to supplement his or her own knowledge; the dilettante or amateur, who wanted just enough information for a social club or a political meeting; the serious-minded reader, who alternated between Macaulay, Darwin, and Fielding; the indiscriminate reader, who wanted "just anything good you know"; and the person who does not read, whom the library should be trying to recruit. Which categories do the young ladies pictured above fall into? And which category do these boys below belong to?

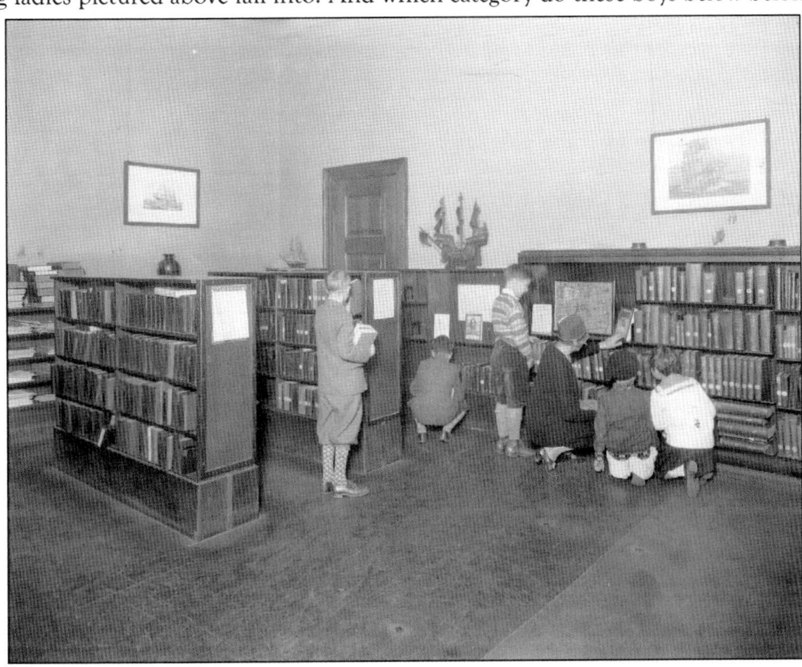

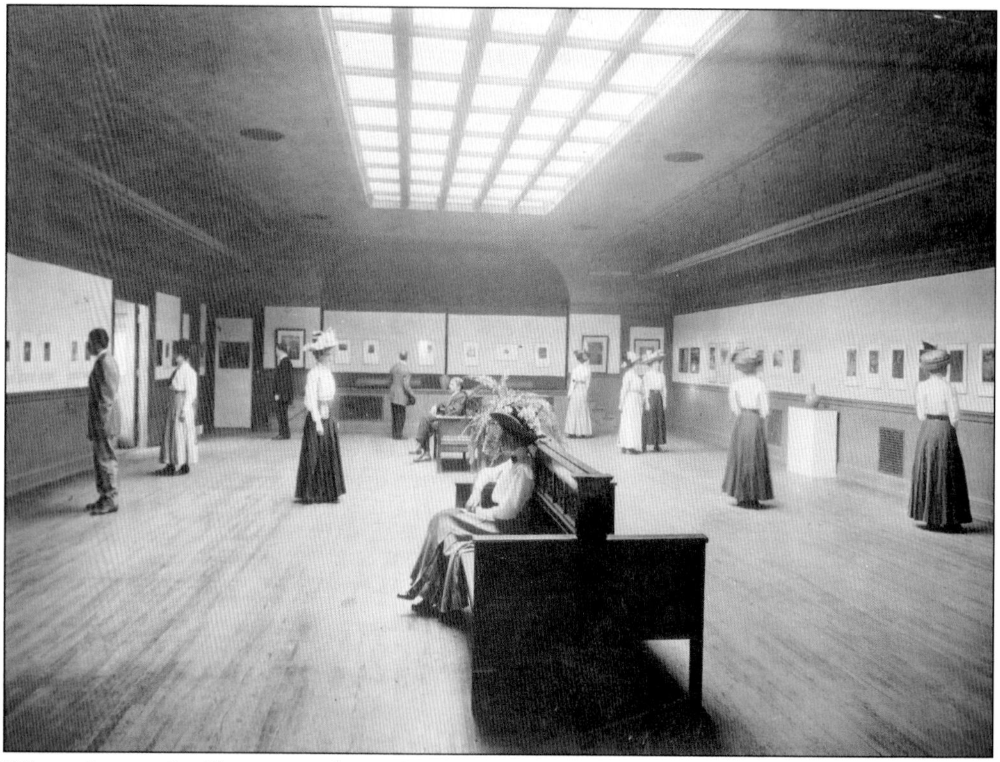

When the new building opened in 1902, Dana found two rooms and an auditorium on the fourth floor that were underutilized, so he began to display objects of fine arts and decorative arts on one side and specimens of natural science on the other side. By the end of 1908, a total of 56 exhibitions had been held, and 266,181 people had visited them. (The Newark Museum of Art Library and Archives.)

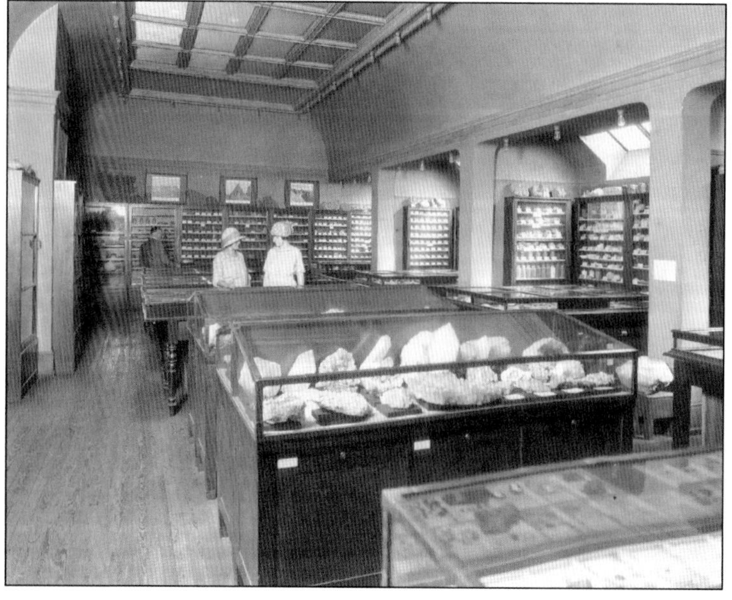

The previous photograph shows an exhibition devoted to prints in the art gallery in 1911, and at left is one of the science collection in 1904, which consisted of rocks, minerals, plants, and animal specimens. These exhibitions were so successful that in 1909, Dana founded the Newark Museum Association as a complement to the library's educational mission. (The Newark Museum of Art. Library and Archives.)

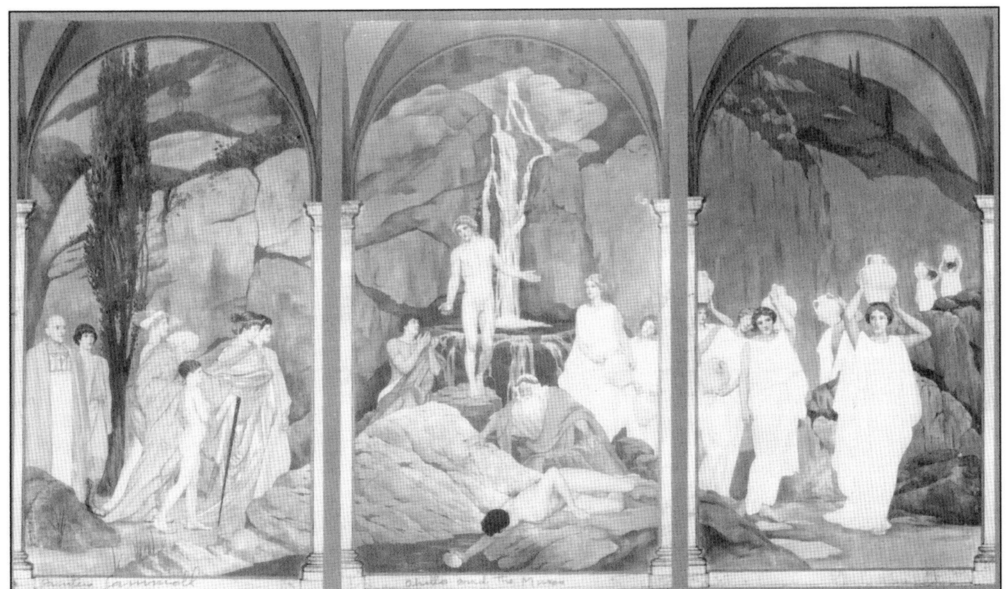

Depicting the Nine Muses, the daughters of Zeus and Mnemosyne, along with Apollo and a group of sages, youths, and women imbibing from *The Fountain of Knowledge*, this mural was commissioned by the Friends of the Newark Public Library in 1927 to celebrate Dana's 25 years of service. Painted by Robert Hales Ives Gammell, a member of the group known as the Boston Painters, it was installed on the east wall of the second-floor gallery. The man at the far left is a representation of Dana himself (details seen right). In the prudish years of the 1950s, it was judged to be of questionable taste, perhaps because of the nudity of some of its figures; it was covered up in that decade and remained so until the centenary of the library in 1989. (Both, Peter A. Juley & Sons.)

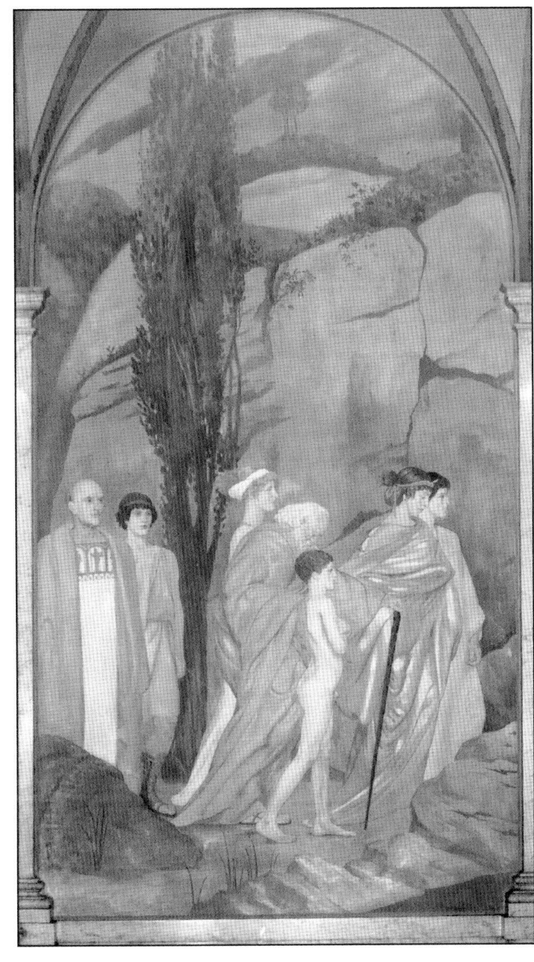

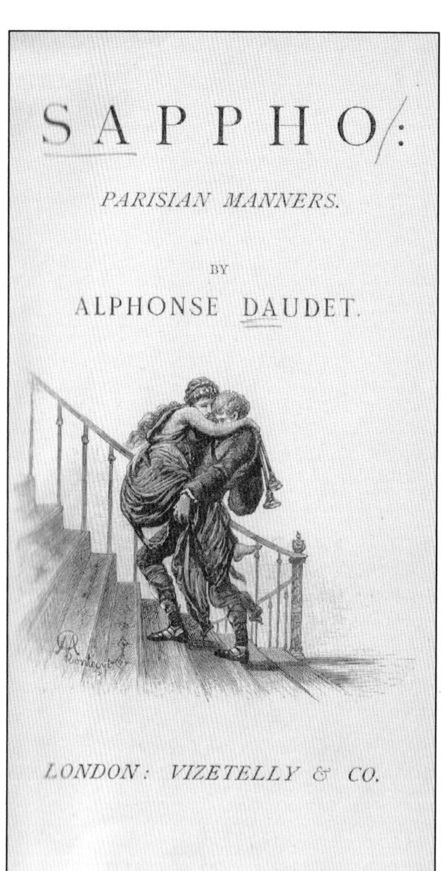

All public libraries have faced criticism from time to time for what they have added to their shelves. Frank Hill was criticized in 1900 for adding Daudet's *Sappho*. He defended the library's policy by stating that it did not make sense to banish this popular French novel when newsboys were hawking cheaper editions on every street corner.

In December 1917, in the midst of the hysteria over World War I, a self-appointed group called "the Vigilantes" demanded that Dana remove eight books that, they believed, were sympathetic to Germany. He refused. "I came to the conclusion many years ago," he declared, "that liberty of thought is a very desirable thing for the world and that liberty of thought can only be maintained by those who have free access to opinion."

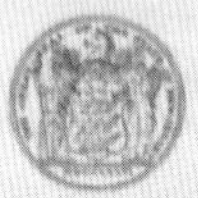

Trained as a librarian at Melville
Dewey's library school at Columbia
University (before it moved to
Albany), Beatrice Winser was one
of the first employees of the Newark
Public Library in 1889. She quickly
became indispensable, becoming
assistant librarian under Frank Hill
in 1894, a position she retained
under John Cotton Dana. She
succeeded the latter upon his death
in 1929 and resigned in 1942 after
53 years of service.

During Winser's tenure, the
book collection doubled, and
circulation reached an all-time
high. Minor attempts at expansion
led to the rental of space at the
Newark Museum's addition for the
children's department and the art
and music department (pictured
here). These departments remained
there until the modernization of
the main building in the 1950s.
(Laura von Schnarendorf.)

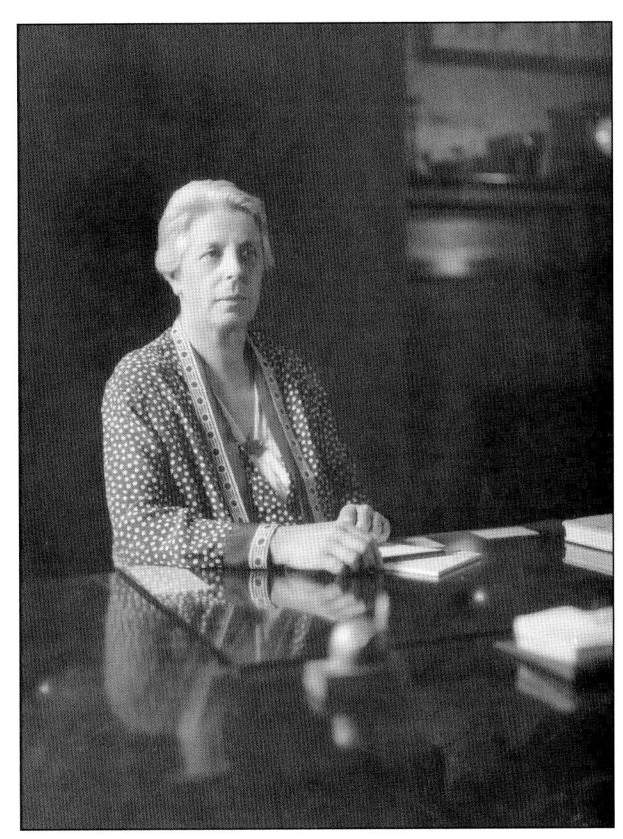

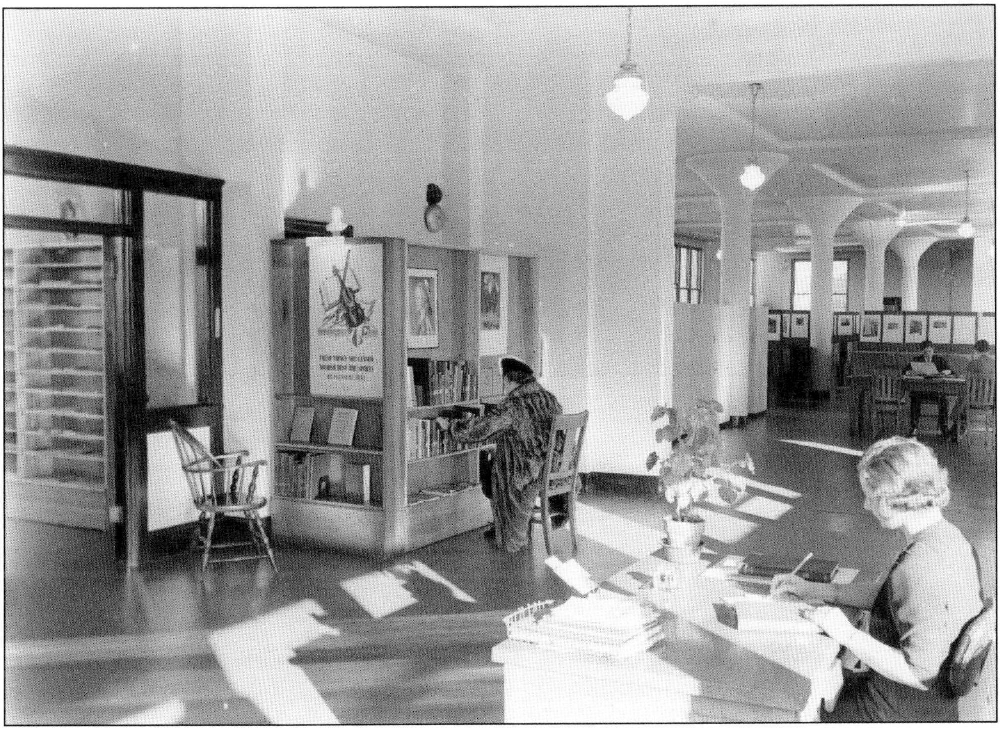

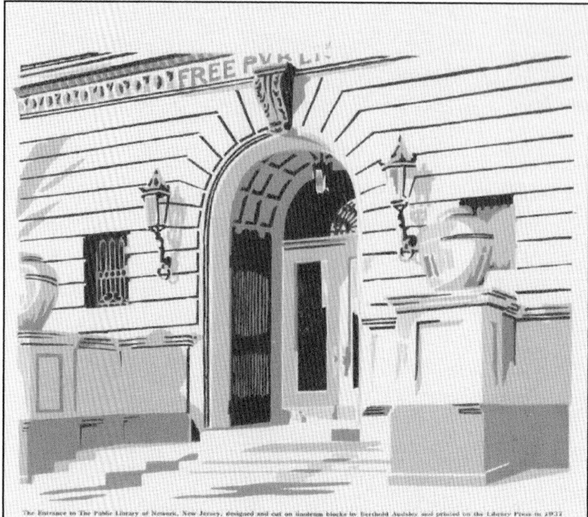

Like Dana before her, Winser was proud of the work that she and her staff were doing, and she was not shy about broadcasting it. She felt strongly that the Newark Public Library was a good example of librarianship, not only to the residents of Newark and New Jersey, but also to the people of the United States. In 1937, for a local and regional audience, she mounted an exhibition on The American Library Yesterday and Today, in which she emphasized that the Newark Public Library was one of its pioneers. The same theme she took to a national audience in a series of placards on display at the American Library Association's annual conference across the river in New York City that June. She was not afraid to use humor to get her points across.

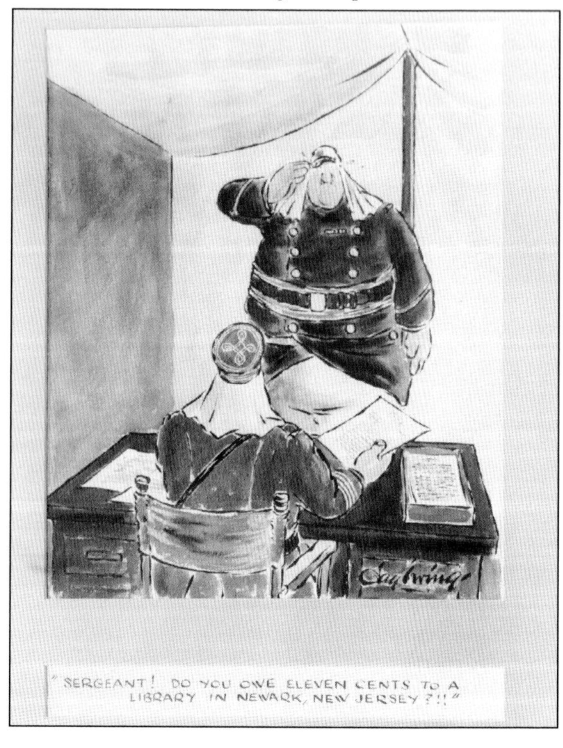

As assistant director under Dana, Winser
headed up a book drive for soldiers
and sailors during World War I. She
also campaigned aggressively in public
and private for women to serve as head
librarians at military camps against the
wishes of Secretary of War Newton
Baker and librarian of Congress Herbert
Putnam. Eventually, women were allowed
to serve.

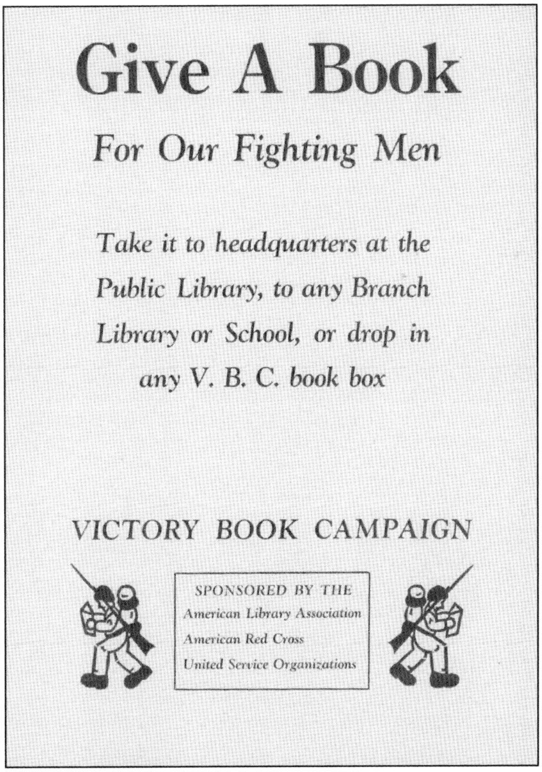

In World War II, Winser again headed
up a book drive that supplied thousands
of books to the members of the armed
forces both at home and abroad. She
also established a War Information
Center at the library that provided books,
pamphlets, and newspaper articles to the
public so that they could keep informed
of the war's progress. Her successor
maintained this work.

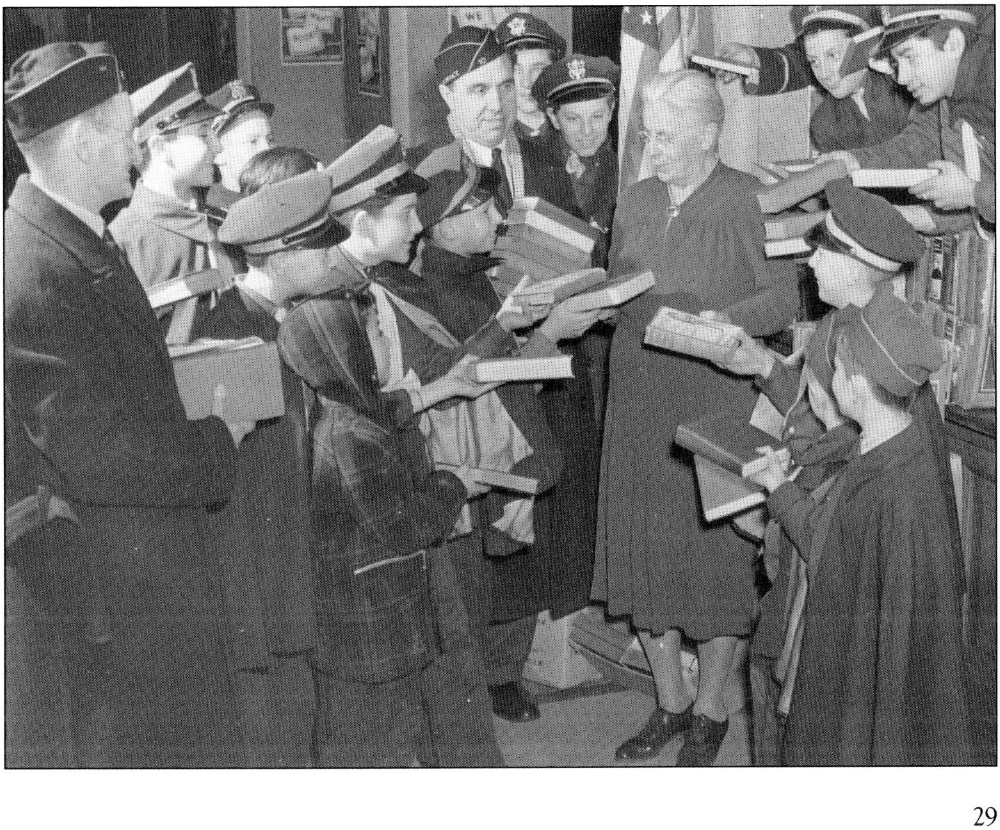

Give A Book

For Our Fighting Men

*Take it to headquarters at the
Public Library, to any Branch
Library or School, or drop in
any V. B. C. book box*

VICTORY BOOK CAMPAIGN

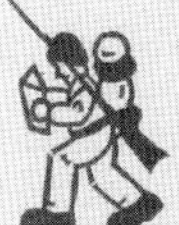
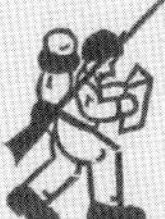

SPONSORED BY THE
American Library Association
American Red Cross
United Service Organizations

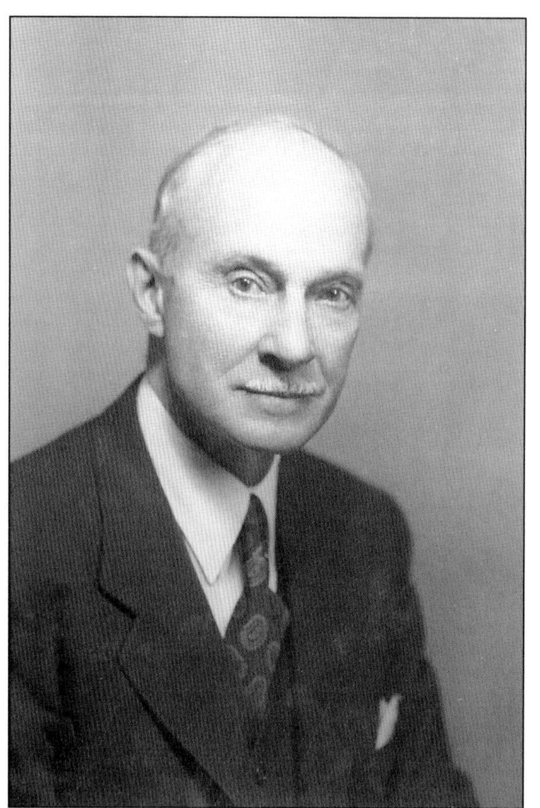

In 1942, Mayor Vincent J. Murphy (1941–1949) appointed Regina D. Hagerty, Augustin J. Kelly, Peter Yablonsky, and Dr. Raymond L. Russomanno to the board of trustees. Dr. Samuel L. Hamilton (left), a carryover of the previous administration, remained chairman of the board. Concerned about her high-handed management of the staff, they forced Winser out as the director of the library. (Potter Studio.)

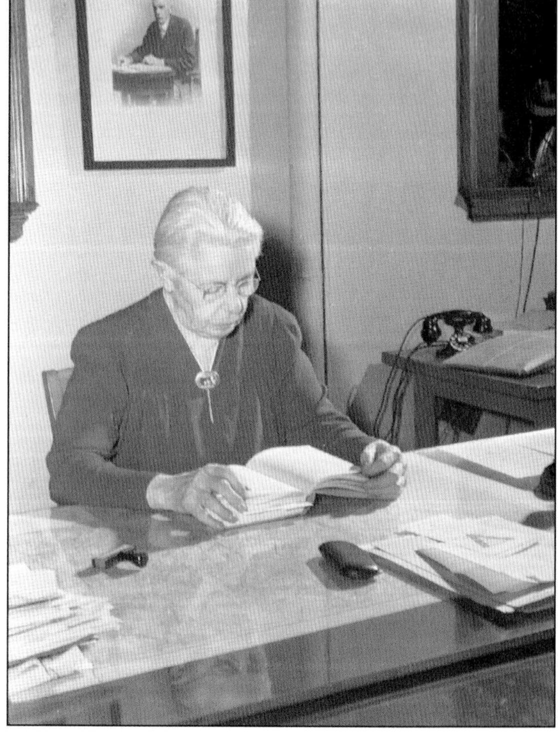

Winser did not go quietly. She released a statement to the press accusing the board of being less interested in the library and its work than the management of its personnel. The three local papers covered the controversy extensively, and leading professional journals printed editorials of support. In frustration, Dr. Hamilton stated that "the furor has been a distinct disservice to the city."

30

A graduate of the New York State Library School
in Albany, New York, John Boynton Kaiser had
extensive experience in law libraries (New York State
Library and Texas State Library), academic libraries
(University of Illinois and University of Iowa), and
public libraries (Tacoma Public Library and Oakland
Public Library). Known for his formal, impersonal,
and objective approach to administrative problems, he
was the perfect candidate to oversee personnel reform.
(Fabian Bachrach.)

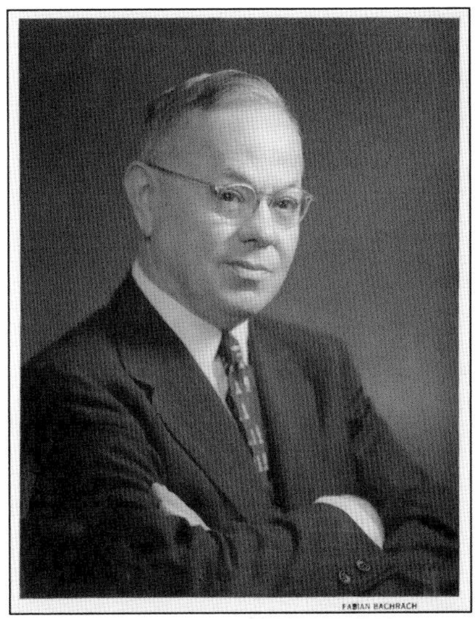

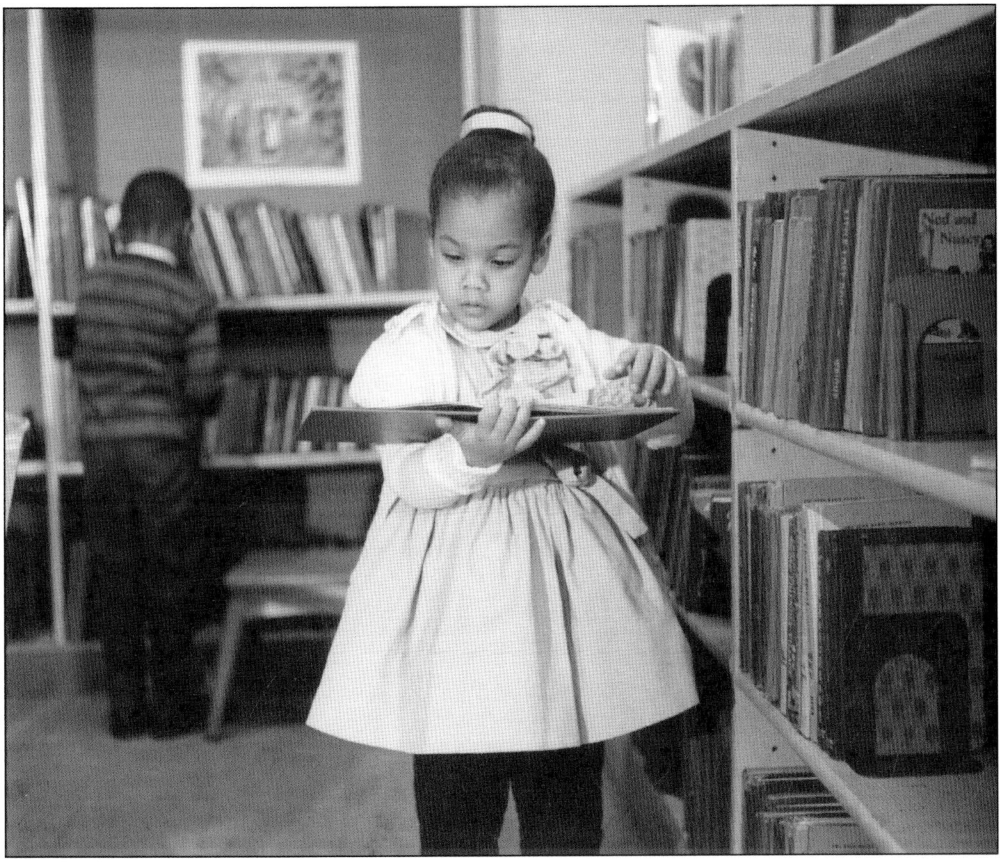

Kaiser instituted a new personnel classification plan that distinguished librarians with professional
responsibilities from library assistants with clerical duties; he undertook a "work simplification
survey" that streamlined operations; and he made three reports to the community, *The Power of
Print* (1946), *More Power* (1953), and *At Your Service* (1958), about the library and its activities. Seen
here is the cover photograph for *At Your Service*. (Ann Zane.)

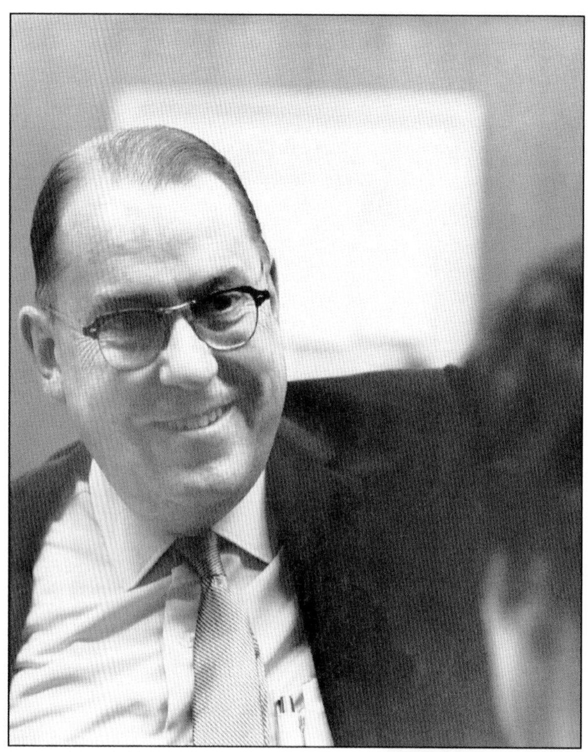

James E. "Ned" Bryan came from the Carnegie Library of Pittsburgh to Newark in 1943 to be the assistant director, a position he held until 1958 when he became the director. He was extremely active in professional organizations, like the New Jersey Library Association, the Public Libraries Association, and the American Library Association, making the Newark Public Library a leader in the field. He retired in 1972. (Ann Zane.)

As Kaiser's assistant, Bryan managed a modernization of the main building on Washington Street. The renovations included the removal of the grand central staircase, which left a large open space on the first floor where a new information desk was installed. In the back, to the right was an elevator, and to the left were stairs. (Public Service Electric Corporation.)

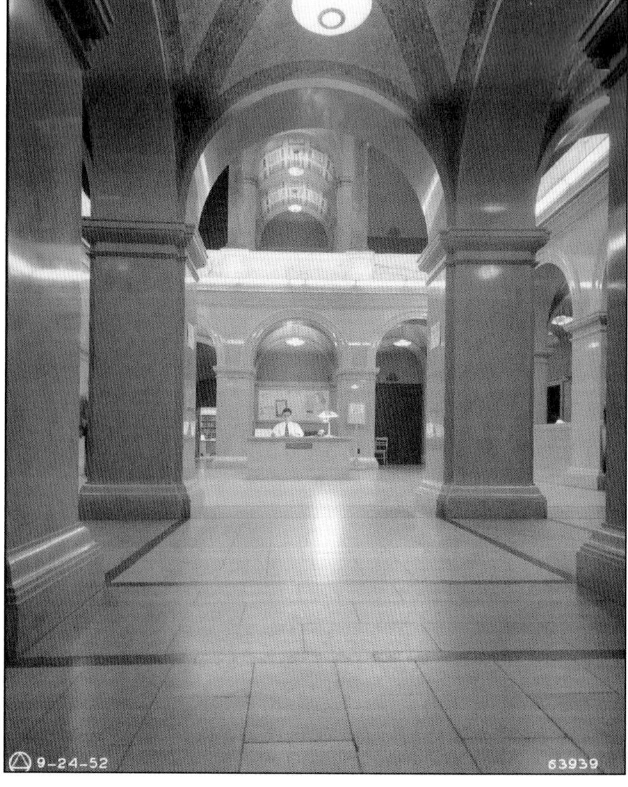

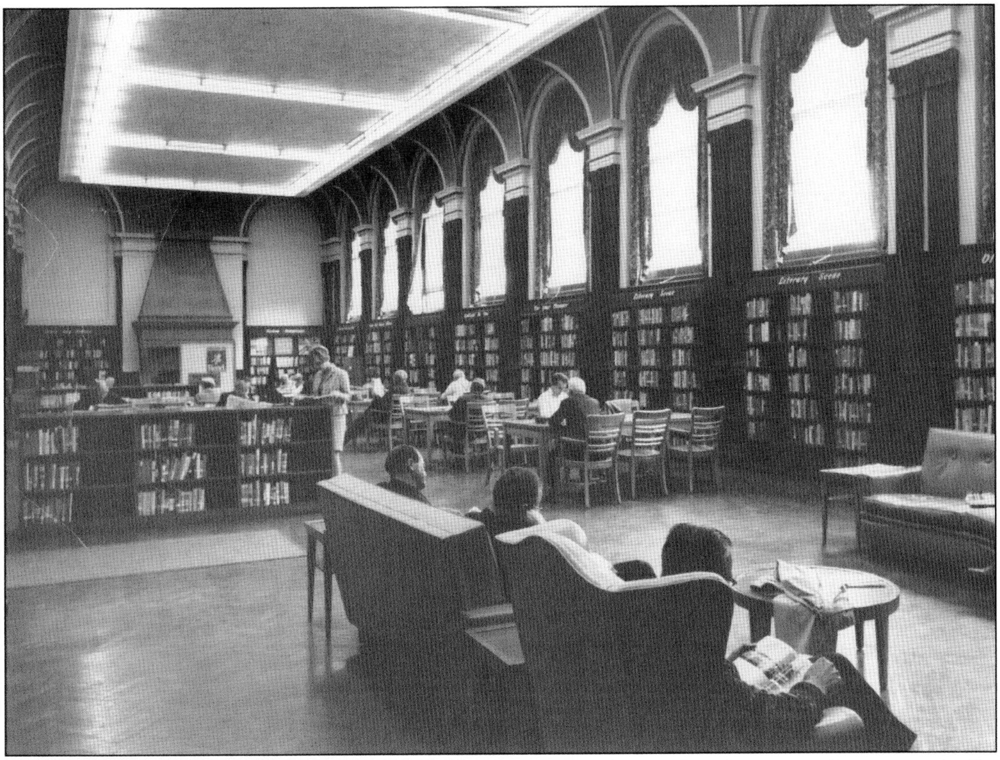

In order to improve lighting in the main reading room, a dropped ceiling with fluorescent bulbs was installed, but it obscured some of the finer features of the original room. In 1989, for the library's centennial, it was removed, and Centennial Hall, as it came to be known, became a space for large programming. (C.B. Crawford.)

In the back of the library on the second floor, the reading room was renovated, providing easy access to reference works on various topics on open shelving. New open stacks, still a priority in the 1950s, were also accessible from this area. In total, the new stacks stored up to 200,000 books, and the new seating areas accommodated 400 visitors. (Ann Zane.)

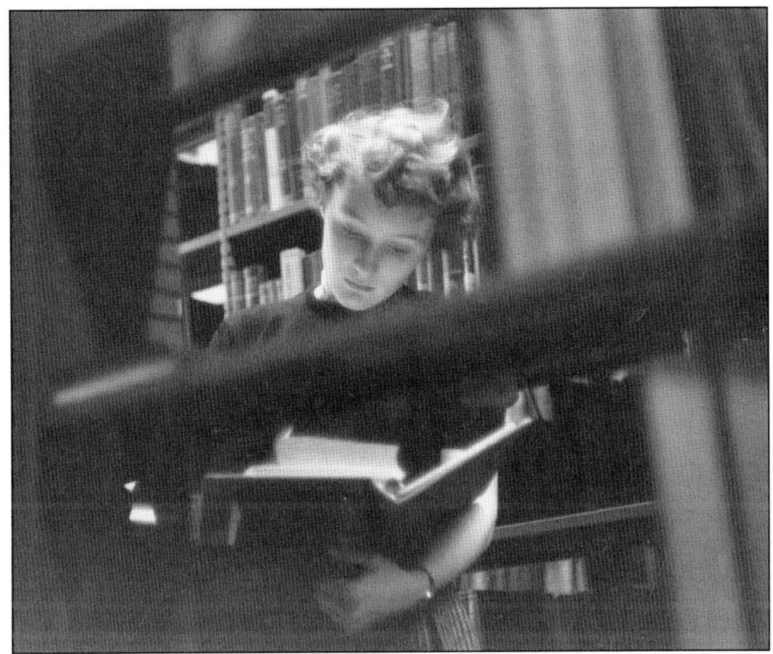

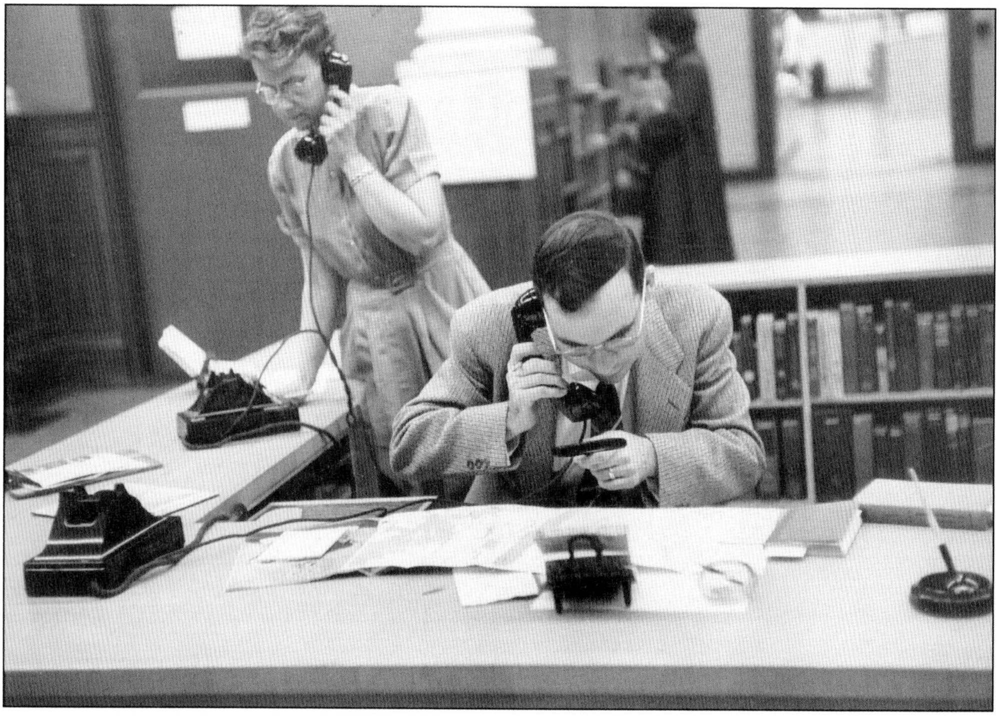

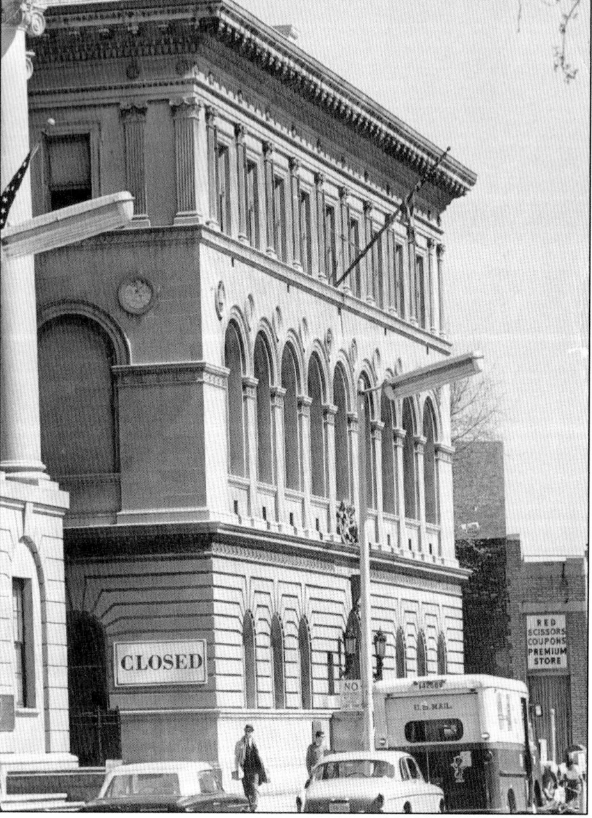

As the largest public library in the state, the Newark Public Library became a statewide resource center for information for all residents of New Jersey in 1964. Designated one of the four research libraries in the state, it took on increased responsibilities for interlibrary loans, photocopy services, and extended reference work.

This doctored photograph of the facade of the main building features an overly large "closed" sign. It was taken in 1969 when the city threatened to cut off funding to the library. In the end, the State of New Jersey came to the rescue in exchange for increased statewide outreach for library services. The optimism of the 1950s had turned into the pessimism of the 1970s following the civil disturbance of 1967.

Bernard Schein joined the staff in 1930 and served in various positions before becoming director from 1972 to 1977. After an equally long career at the Newark Public Library, William "Bill" Urban followed Schein as director from 1977 to 1979. Unlike Schein and Urban, Thomas J. "Tom" Alrutz (pictured here) came from outside the state, and he brought a new perspective to the library as the director from 1979 to 1987.

All three of them—Schein, Urban, and Alrutz—were responsible for moving the library into the modern age by using technology to streamline procedures and provide patrons with more effective services. As a member of OCLC, beginning in 1979, the Newark Public Library improved its ability to catalog and classify new books and participate in interlibrary loans.

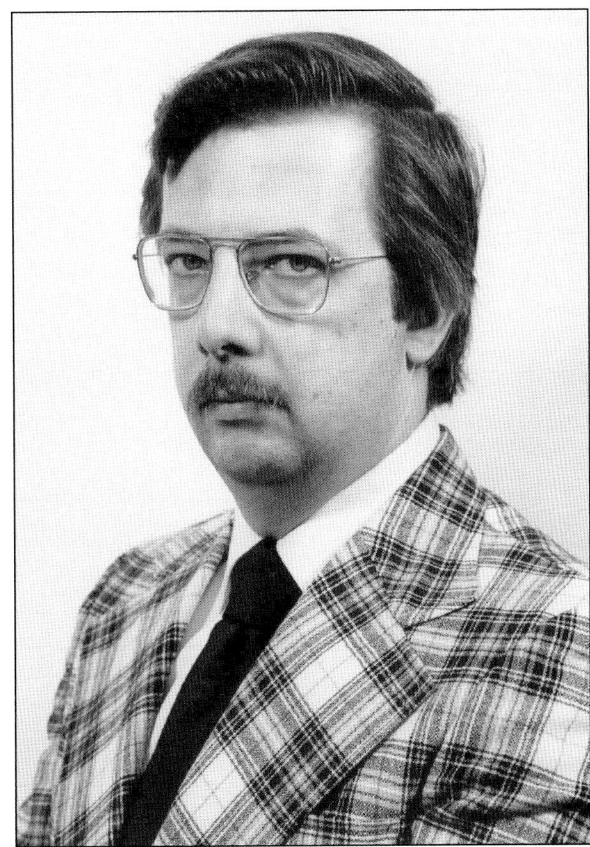

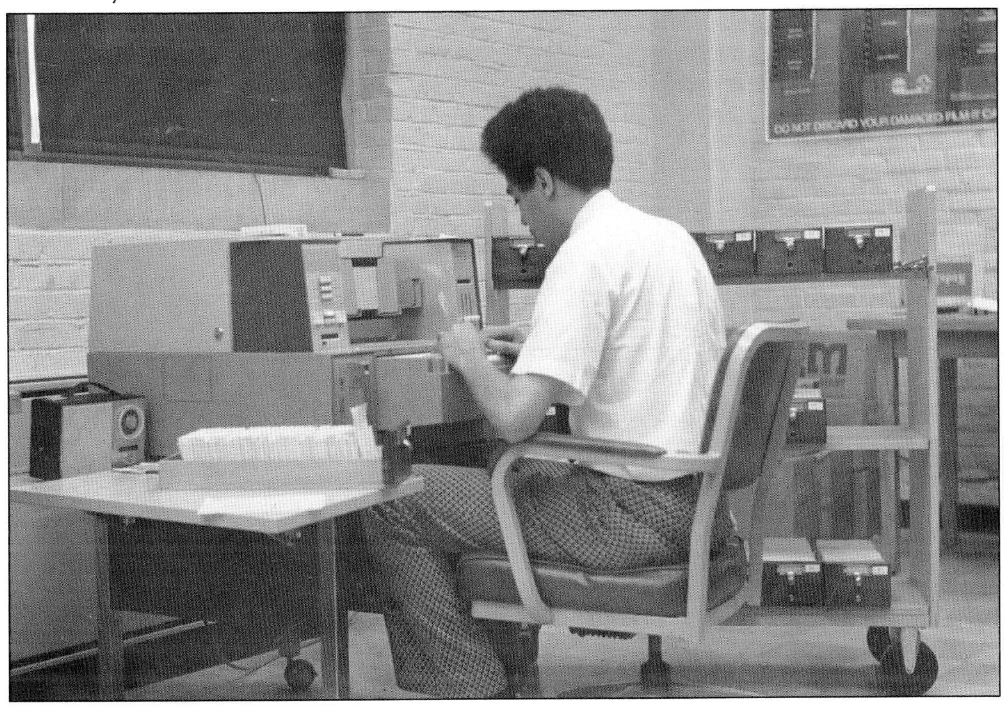

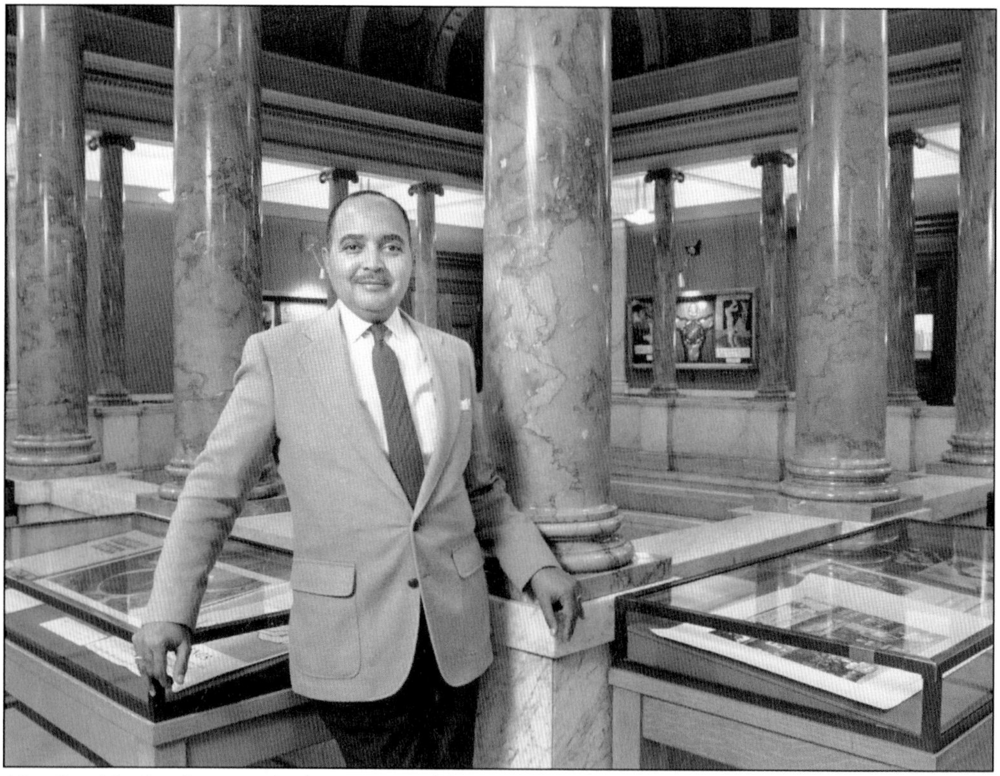

Alex Boyd had a distinguished career as a librarian in academic and public libraries in the South and the Midwest, as a bibliographer in Afro-American studies, as an instructor in librarianship, and as an assistant director of planning and development. He was director of the Newark Public Library from 1988 to 2004. He believed that the library could help "individuals make a difference" in their own lives and in their communities. (The *Star-Ledger*.)

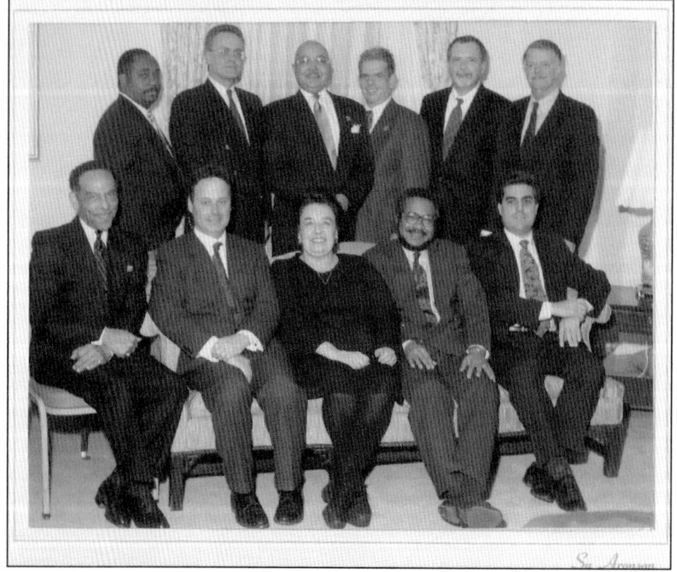

Director Alex Boyd (second row, center) is surrounded by his senior leadership team and the board of trustees. Pictured are, from left to right, (first row) Howard Caesar, Miles Berger, Betty Rufalo, Clement Price, and Mark Santangelo, all educators, businessmen, or civic leaders serving as trustees; (second row) Gerald Fitzhugh, facilities; Paul Stellhorn, development; Boyd, director; Joseph Casale, finance; Bruce Ford, technical services; and Charles Cummings, special collections.

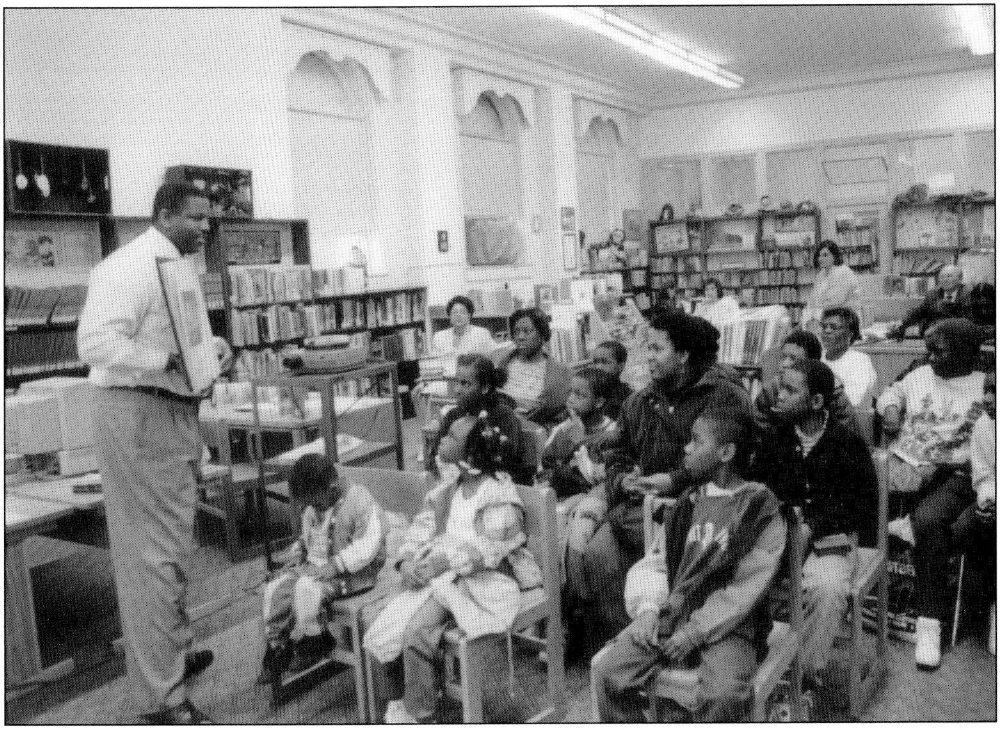

As one of the founders of the Black
Caucus of the American Library
Association, Boyd was instrumental
in expanding the library's outreach
to the African American community
without neglecting the Hispanic, Latino,
Portuguese, and other communities
within the city. In this undated
photograph, Michael Bryant, a well-
known African American children's
book illustrator, presents a program
on his methods and ideas at a special
children's program.

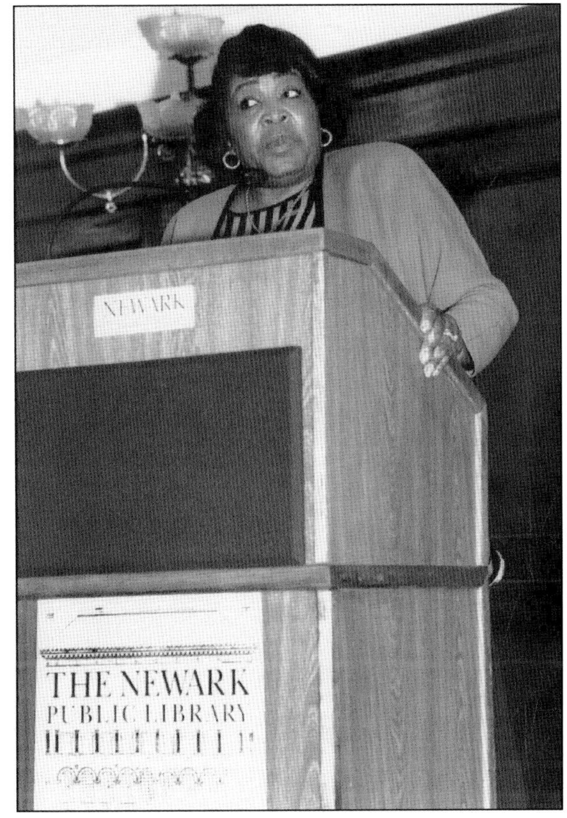

Like his predecessors, Boyd did not
shy away from current events, even
if some of them might have proven
to be controversial. In this undated
photograph, Betty Shabazz, the
widow of Malcolm X, discusses her
husband's relationship to Martin Luther
King Jr. and its impact on the civil rights
movement. The celebration of Black
History Month became an important
part of the library's annual calendar.

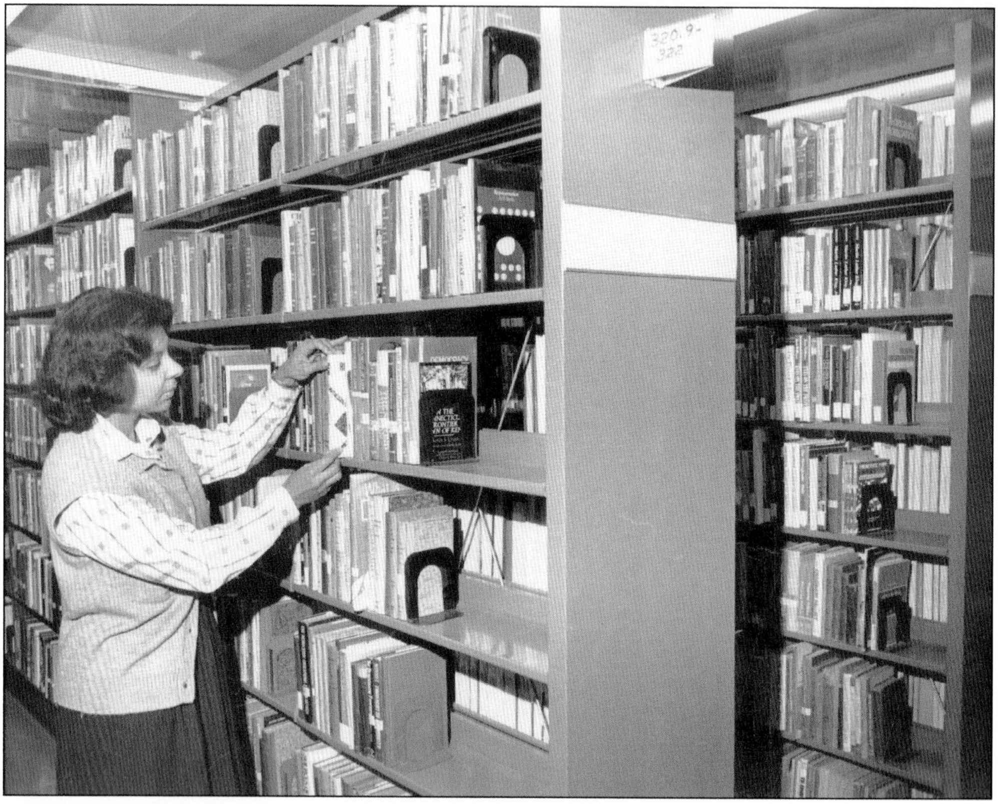

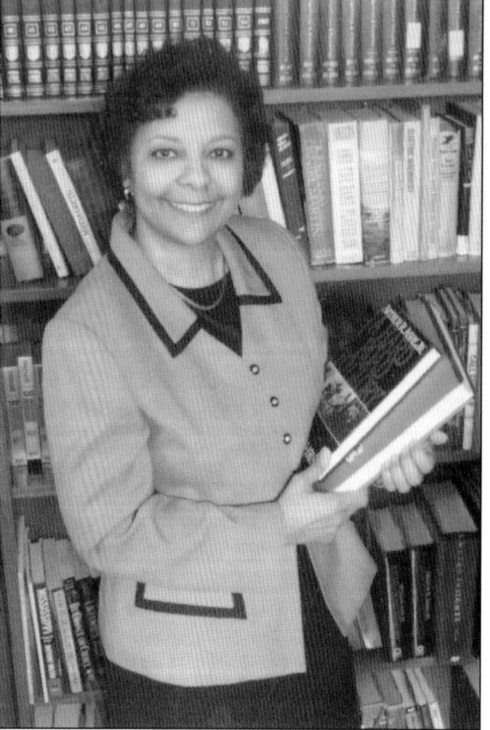

Wilma "Bunny" Grey grew up in Newark where she discovered a world of books and ideas at her local library, the Roseville Branch. A summer job in 1969 led to a 46-year career at the Newark Public Library. Before she became the director from 2005 to 2015, she had been assistant director for statewide outreach, among other positions.

Literacy was one of Grey's primary concerns. She became a great supporter of the Newark Literacy Campaign, which was given space for its activities at the main library, and working with that organization, she helped expand literacy programs to diverse communities within the city and the state.

Two

STAFF

The director oversees the administration of the institution—and he or she usually receives the bulk of the credit—but it is the staff who does the work, from the ordinary, like acquiring, cataloging, and repairing books, to the extraordinary, like developing outreach services or building up outstanding collections, both of which will be the subject of the following chapters. This chapter will briefly examine the history of the staff from a tight-knit team of selectively chosen assistants to a cohort of over 100 librarians, assistants, and support staff. Several individuals stand out for their contributions to specific areas, but their stories will be told briefly in the third and fourth chapters.

In 1890, at the end of the library's first year of service, Frank Hill, the librarian, was aided by a small group of assistants. By 1895, the staff had grown to include 24 employees: four night messengers, six day messengers, one stenographer, two assistants at circulation and registration, four delivery assistants, two reading room attendants, one reference librarian, two catalogers, one assistant librarian (Beatrice Winser), and one librarian (Frank Hill). When the main library opened on Washington Park in 1901, the staff had increased, and it was better paid. The assistants worked seven hours a day and half a day every other Saturday in the summer. They received 20 vacation days and 12 sick days. At the time, John Cotton Dana commented, "Work is better done by a few efficient, experienced, zealous, well-paid persons than by a large number of persons of indifferent skills."

During the Depression, the staff took salary reduction of up to 15 percent over the course of four years (1932–1936). Nevertheless, thanks to various New Deal programs, additional staff was hired to perform special projects, such as newspaper clipping of local information, indexing of business literature, developing a guide to illustrations in books about New Jersey, updating cardholders' information, and managing the information files. Perhaps the most important work to come out of these relief programs was the WPA guide to New Jersey compiled by the Federal Writers' Project. Salaries began to increase in 1936, but it took the postwar years of prosperity to bring library salaries up to competitive levels.

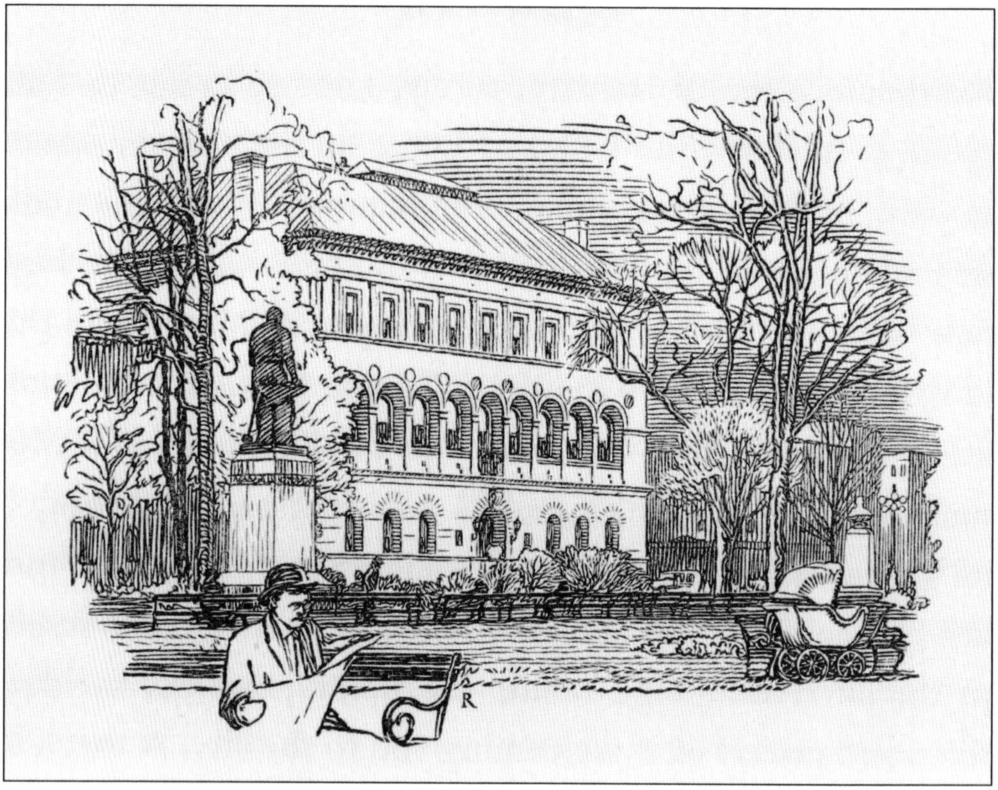

Dana used Rudolph Ruzicka's engraving of the Newark Public Library as the frontispiece for his series of pamphlets, *Modern American Library Economy*, which accompanied his training program in librarianship, a 10-month course in the history and theory of libraries as well as hands-on experience in library work. The first class in 1907 had six applicants. (Carteret Book Club.)

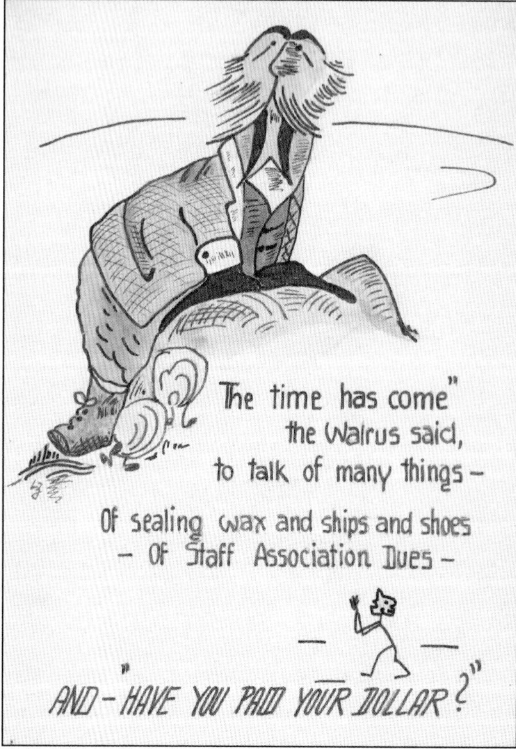

A staff association was organized in 1937. Its purpose was to boost morale, but it also addressed personnel issues, such as salaries and benefits. Eventually, it was replaced by an affiliation with the American Federation of State, County, and Municipal Employees. Today, the union has 80 members and focuses on working conditions for librarians, assistants, maintenance workers, and specialists. Pictured is a placard reminding staff members to pay their dues.

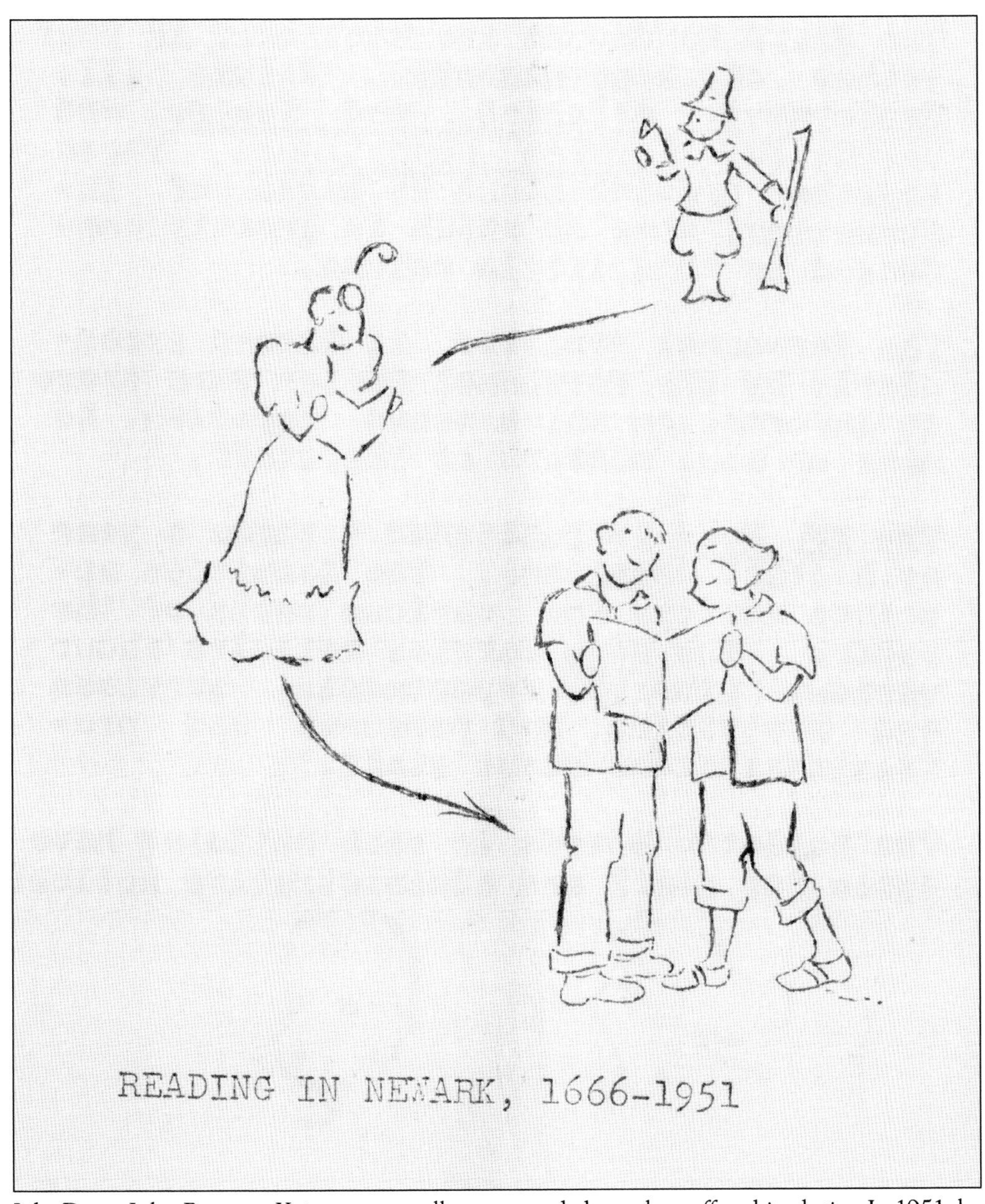

Like Dana, John Boynton Kaiser was equally concerned about the staff and its duties. In 1951, he issued a little mimeographed handout, in which he discussed the library's reputation, which he pointed out rested on the "good job" of all employees: "Your work, if well and cheerfully done, contributes to making friends for the library." The handout also outlined the facilities and services for the staff, like the staff handbook and the staff newsletter; the staff's responsibilities, like hours, attendance, recordkeeping, and other such personnel issues; and facts about civil service, such as appointments, classification, salaries, promotion, and grievances. The supervising librarian for the art and music department, Julia Sabine, illustrated it with a few whimsical drawings.

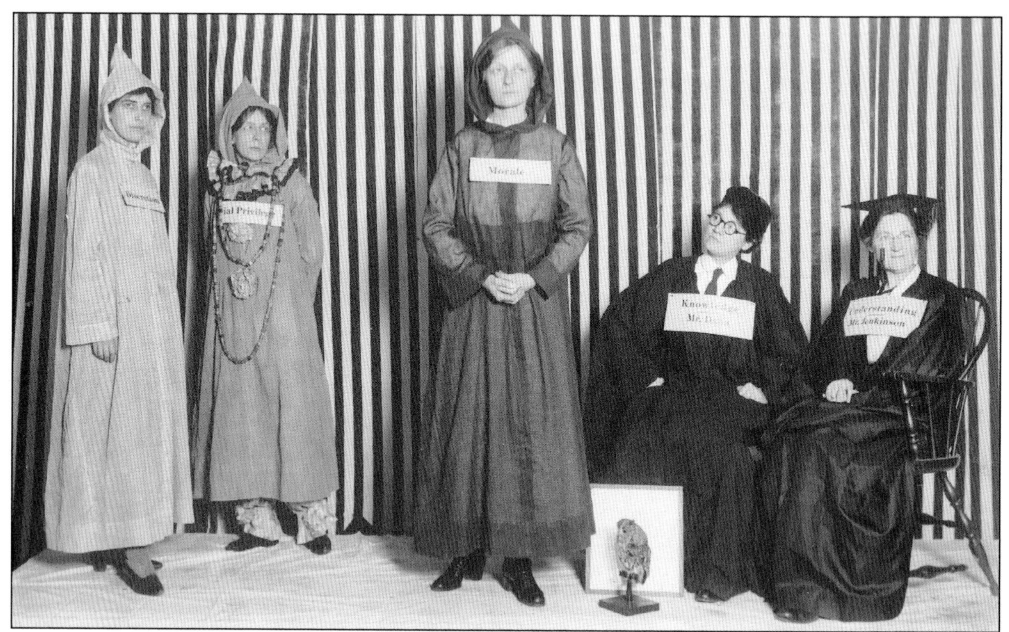

At the annual New Year party during the Dana years, "a satirical spirit prevailed," in historian Ezra Shales's words. The staff wrote and performed skits that both celebrated and parodied their work as library employees. In the above photograph, the women represent such virtues as perfection, accuracy, and efficiency that were deemed necessary for library work. (Koenig.)

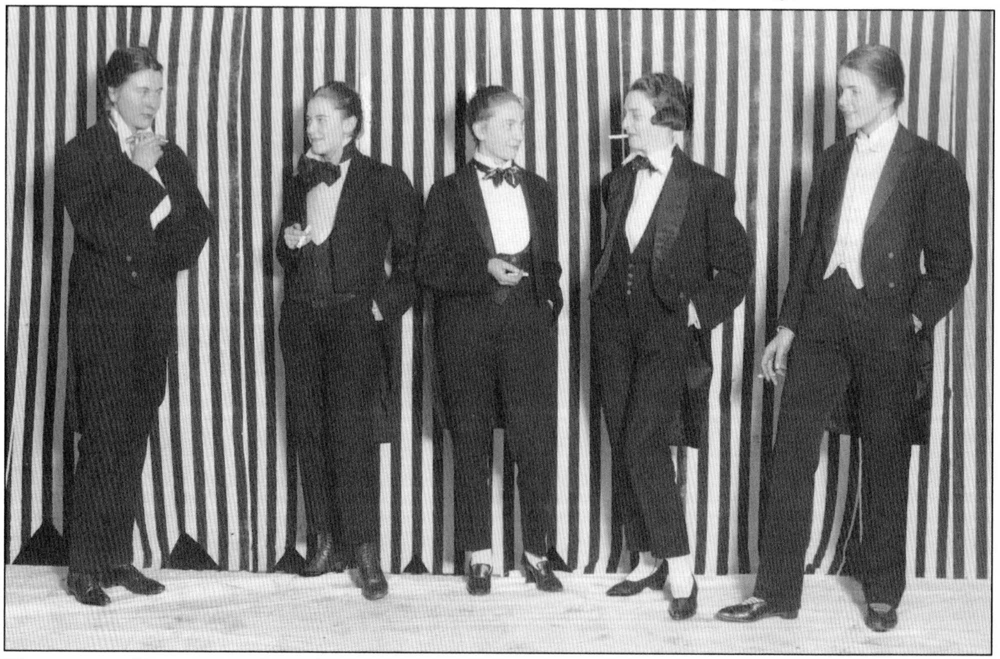

There was a "bitter irony" in these plays since these virtues were coded as "manly" at the time, and yet these women were expected to embody them in their work, which was promoted as a civic ideal, but they themselves were not full-fledged citizens. As Shales puts it, "The carnivalesque plays inverted the relations of power and sense and the dogma of the institution in word and image." (Koenig.)

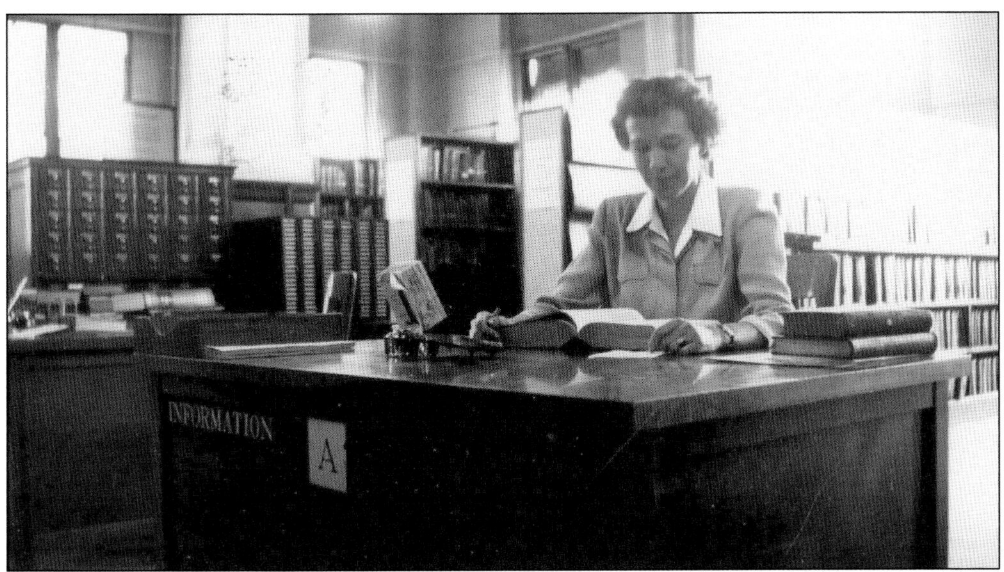

In the early 1940s, a series of snapshots were taken of the staff in action. In this one, Zelta Norcross searches a thick volume for an answer to a reference question from a patron at the Information Desk. To her left is the engineering index, and to her right is part of the extensive reference collection.

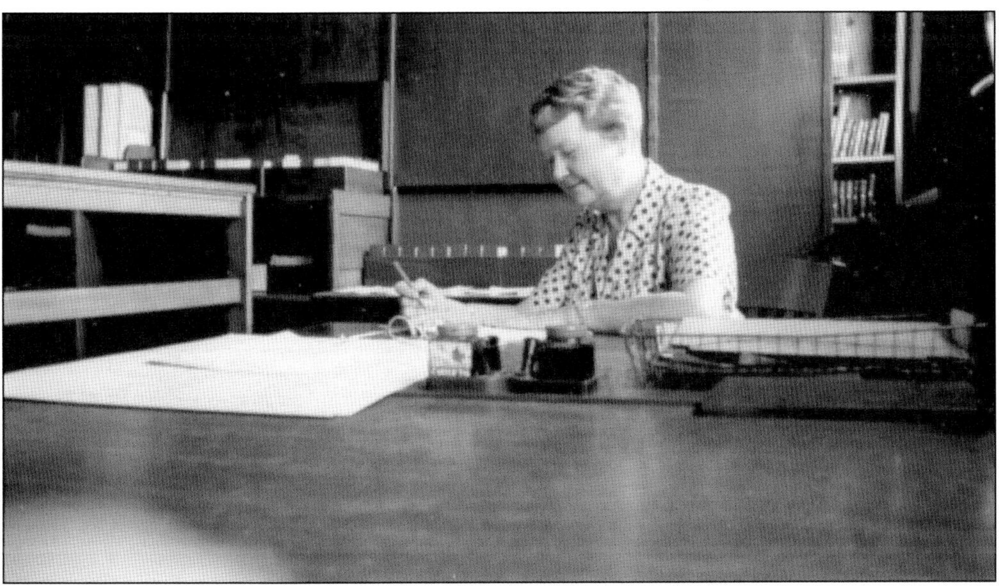

Formerly the librarian at Barringer High School, Emma Alberta Grady was in charge of the reference books. Behind her is "the Cage," a locked case in which "books that have a tendency to be stolen" were kept. Some of these books were "sex books," which may have been kept there because of their sensitive topic.

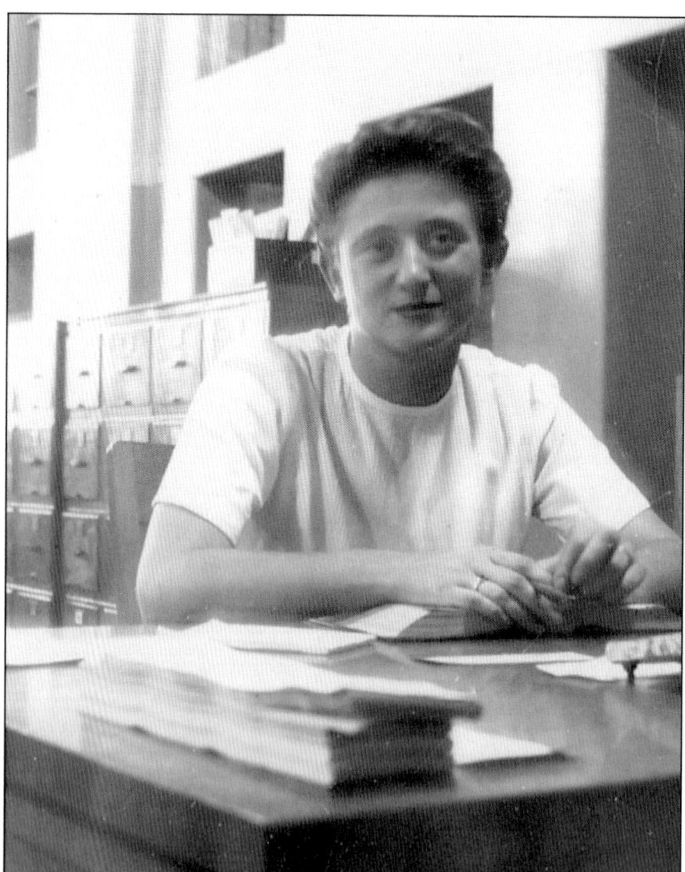

Ester Lerner was a war refugee who took a job as a clerk in the library when she first arrived in this country. She and her husband eventually resettled in Buffalo.

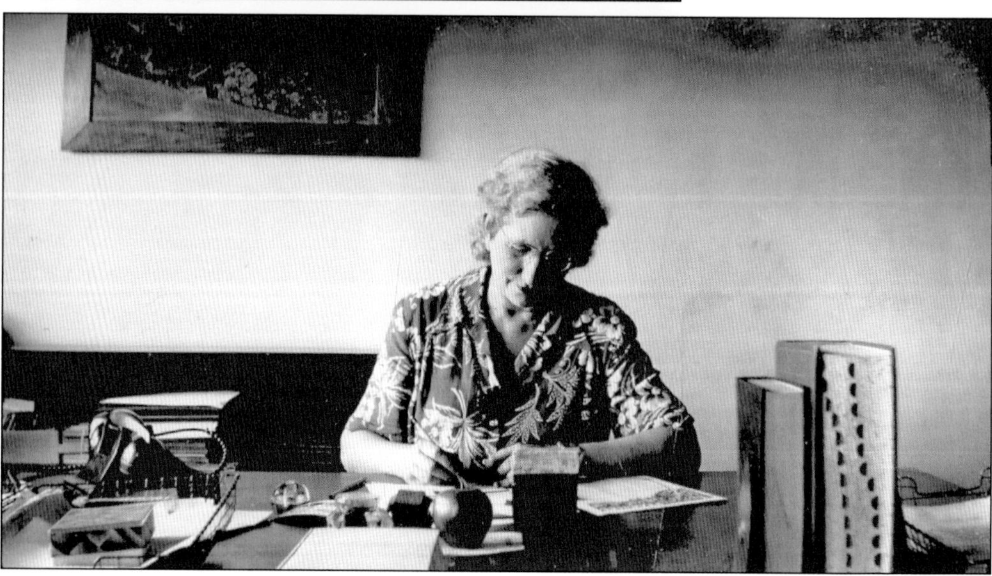

Anna Borden started out as a clerk at the age of 16 and worked with periodicals, business information, and reference sources. Eventually, she became the chief librarian for the lending and reference department. She retired in 1955 after 43 years of service.

Helen DeVita was the librarian in charge of
government documents in the 1940s. She was credited
for getting them out of the "gobbledygook" stage
and into a more readily accessible condition. During
the war and afterward, she claimed that patrons
increasingly used this collection.

Education librarian Mildred Lockett Lipscome assists
a young man in 1952. Is he a student looking for
information about a future career or a good book to
read for entertainment? Or is he a teacher looking
for materials to use in his classroom? Lipscome was
the third African American librarian hired by the
library in 1946. She remained at the library until her
retirement in the 1980s. (Ann Zane.)

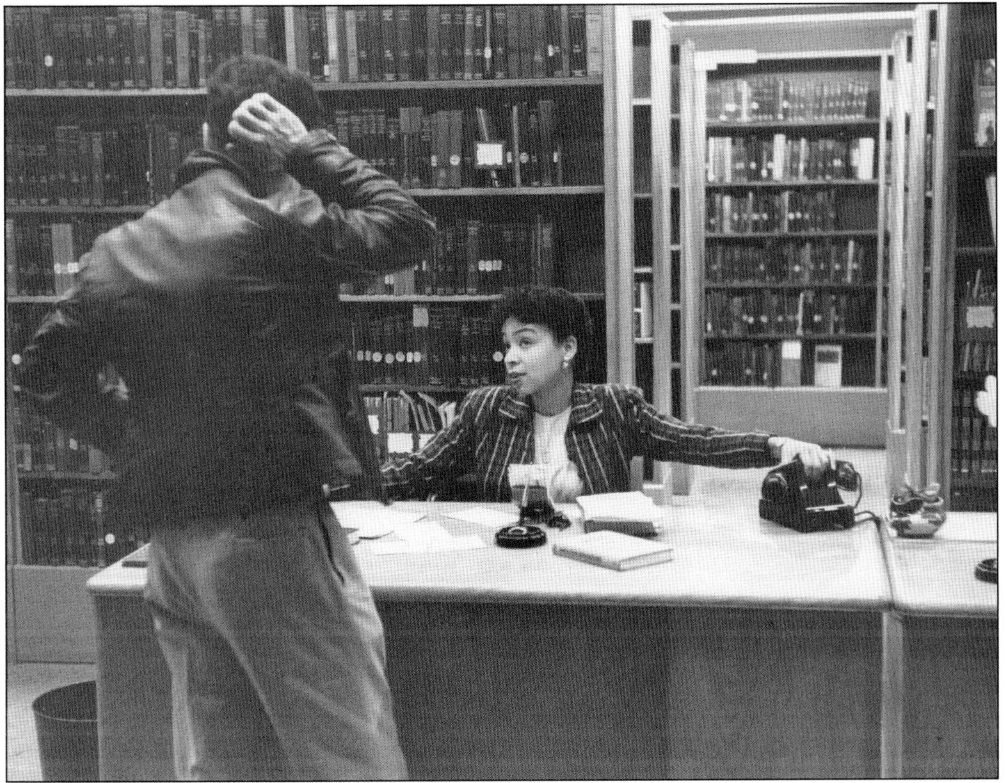

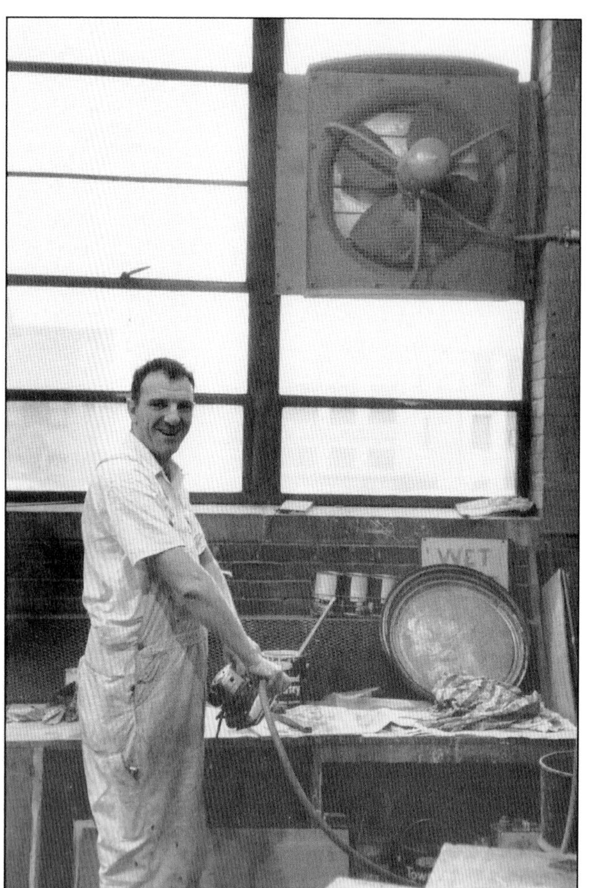

Simon Kaiser Printer worked in the maintenance department in the 1950s. Keeping the main library and its branches neat, clean, and presentable was as important as assisting patrons with their information needs. Repairing shelves, tables, and chairs was also part of the job of the men and women who worked in maintenance. (Ann Zane.)

A busy day at the Business Branch in 1954 required librarians Jessica Doty (sitting) and Helen Buzzell (standing) to assist patrons with their questions about personnel management, cost of living statistics, public relations, and accounting. In addition to their professional duties, Doty was involved in the Library's Staff Association, and Buzzell was active in the Special Libraries Association. (Ann Zane.)

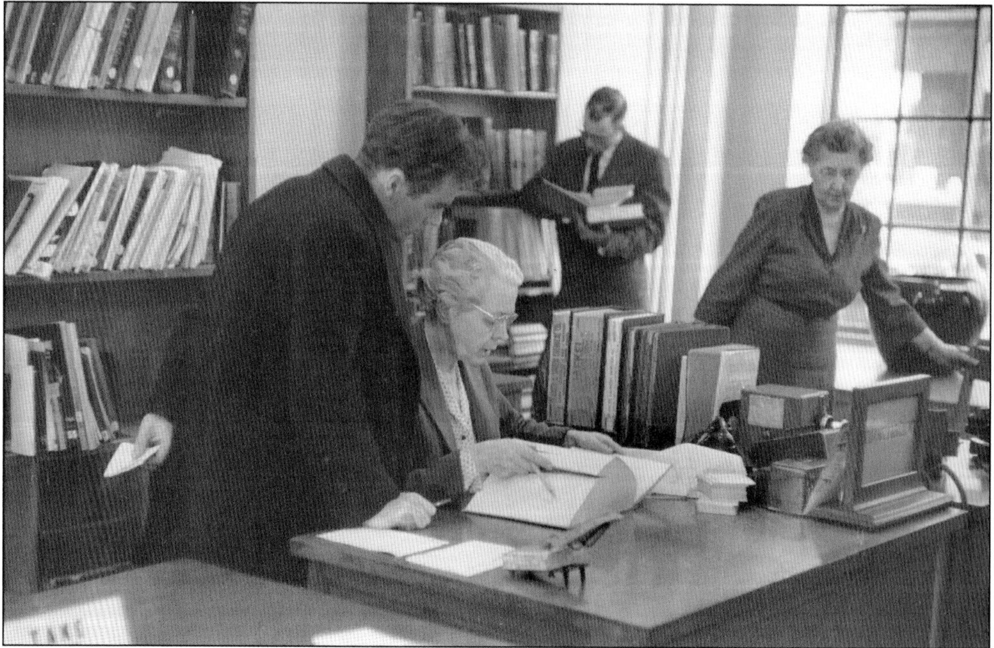

Children's librarian Lemoyne Wilson engages preschoolers in storytelling and creative play at the Weequahic Branch of the Newark Public Library in 1961.

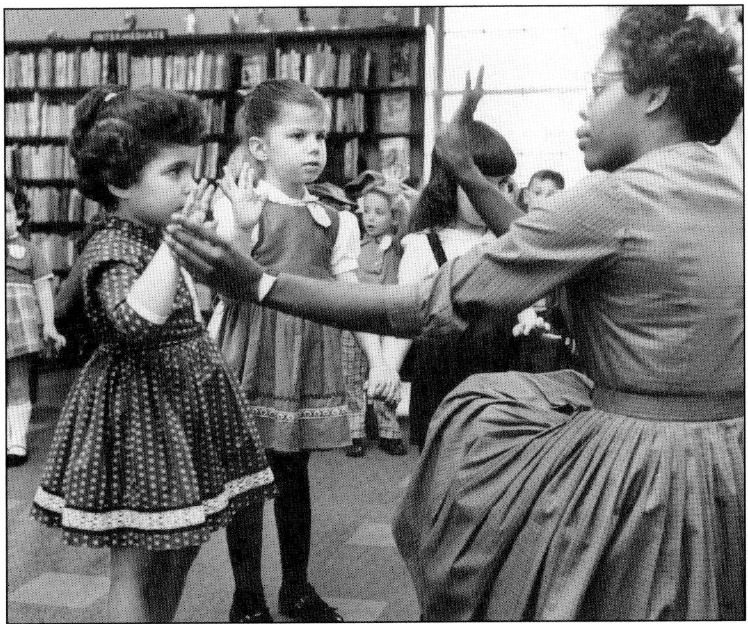

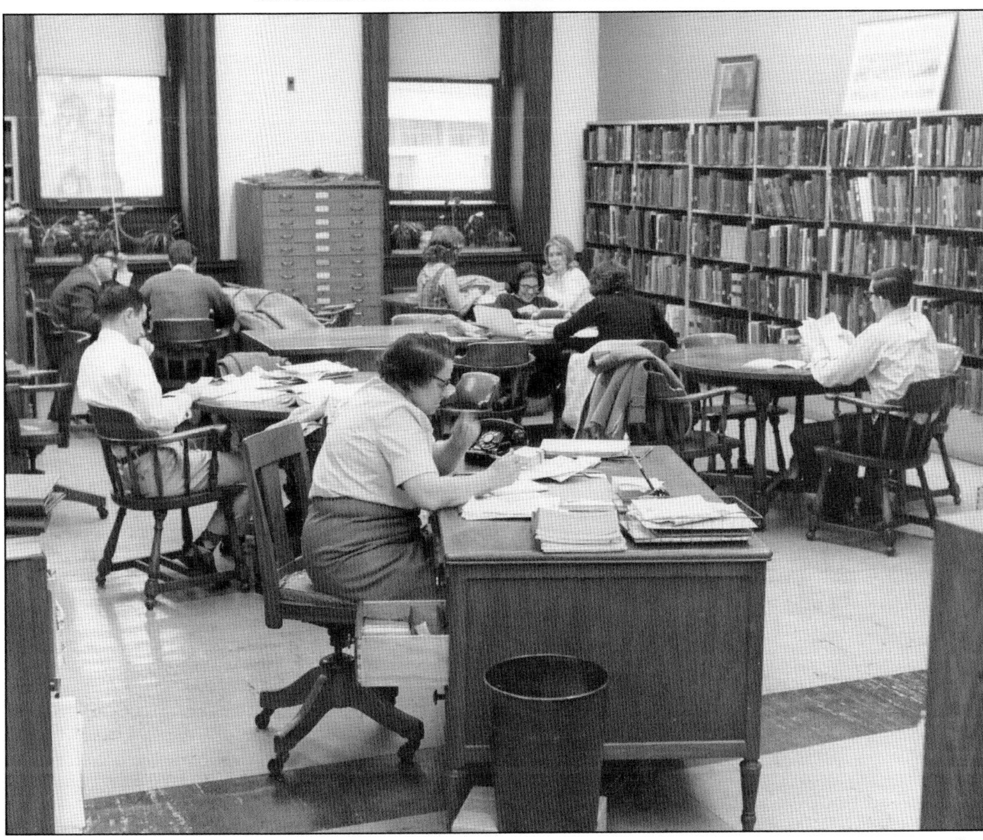

Librarian Gertrude Cahalan researches questions from some patrons, while others pursue their own interests in the New Jersey Room in 1962. In total, Cahalan spent 40 years working for the Newark Public Library, from 1936 to 1976. (C.B. Crawford.)

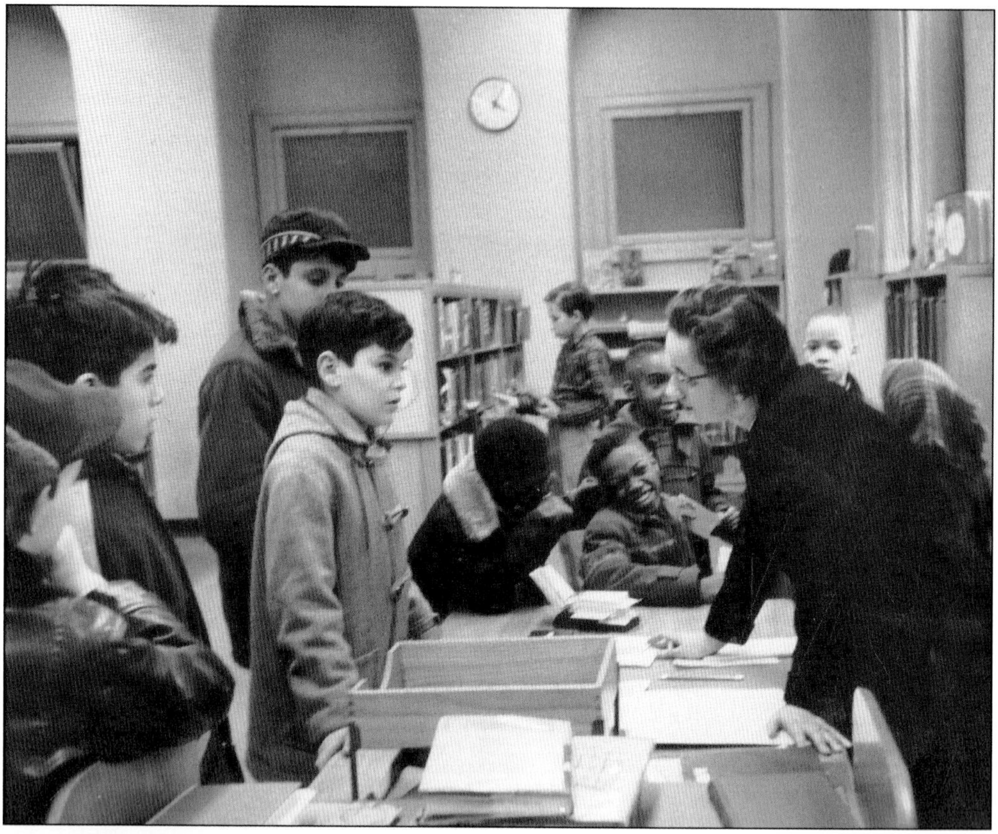

Clara Kircher was the supervising librarian for the children's department in 1963, overseeing the juvenile collections at the main library and the branches. On the back of this photograph is written the following: "'Finding out' is serious business in the Children's Room of the Newark Public Library." (Ann Zane.)

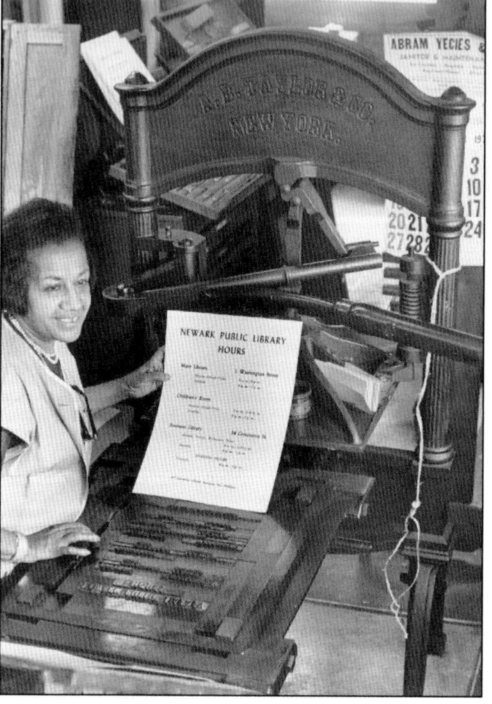

The 1907 printing press was still operating in the 1970s, still turning out posters, leaflets, brochures, and other small items of information. Rose Thompson was the printing specialist from the 1950s to the 1970s. In a newspaper interview, she said, "It's artistic to me and I like it."

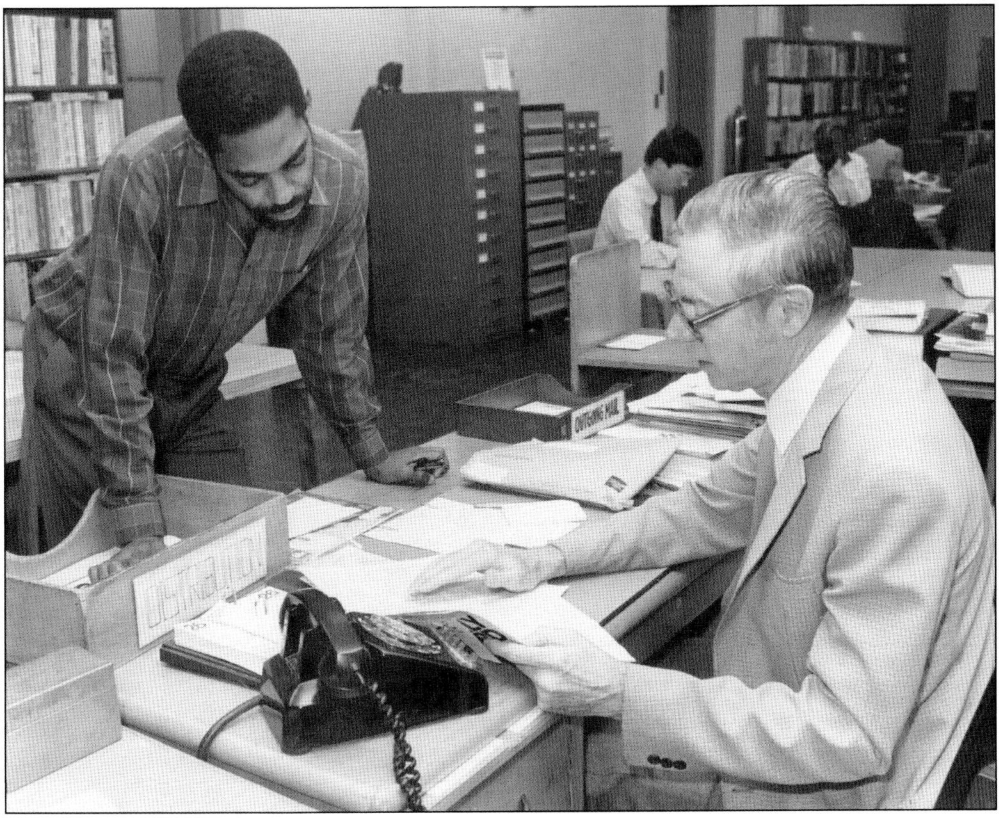

Principal librarian Leslie Rupprecht at the Business Branch assists Walter Phipps of Newark with a question about business practices within the city in the 1970s. In addition to his desk duties and administrative responsibilities, Rupprecht frequently gave book reviews to audiences at the branches. (The *Star-Ledger*.)

Stephen Crook, a junior librarian in the lending and reference department, shows off the new video instruction equipment in 1982. He explains how it is used to prepare adult patrons to take the high school equivalency examination. (Photograph by John A. Gibson Jr.; courtesy of the *Star-Ledger*.)

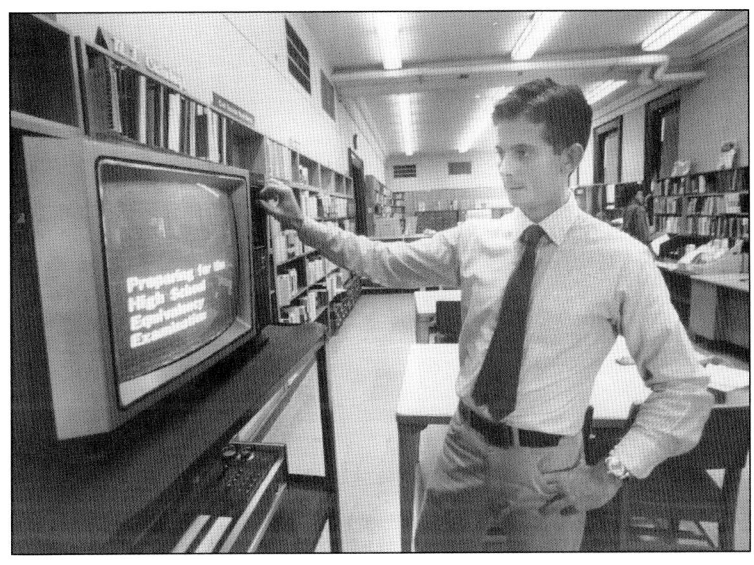

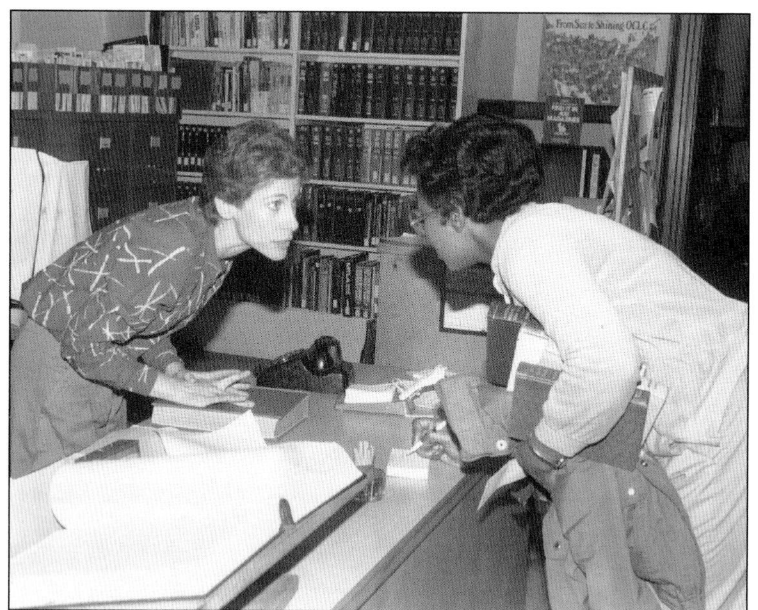

Leslie Kahn, a reference librarian from 1981 to 2021, assists a patron with a question at the humanities desk. The caption on the reverse of this photograph states, "This help gives the library its 'user-friendly' reputation."

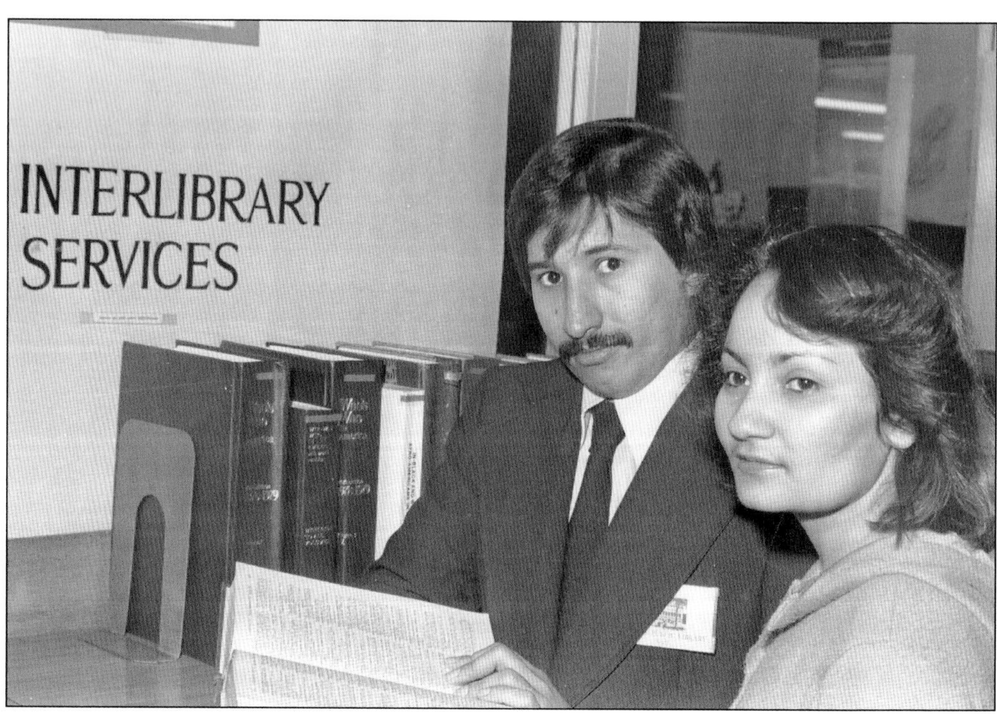

Danilo Figueredo, the reference librarian in charge of the bilingual program for adult services, and Mercedes Mendez, a junior library assistant in the same program, discuss how to make Spanish-language resources at the Newark Public Library easily accessible to other patrons throughout the state through Interlibrary Services.

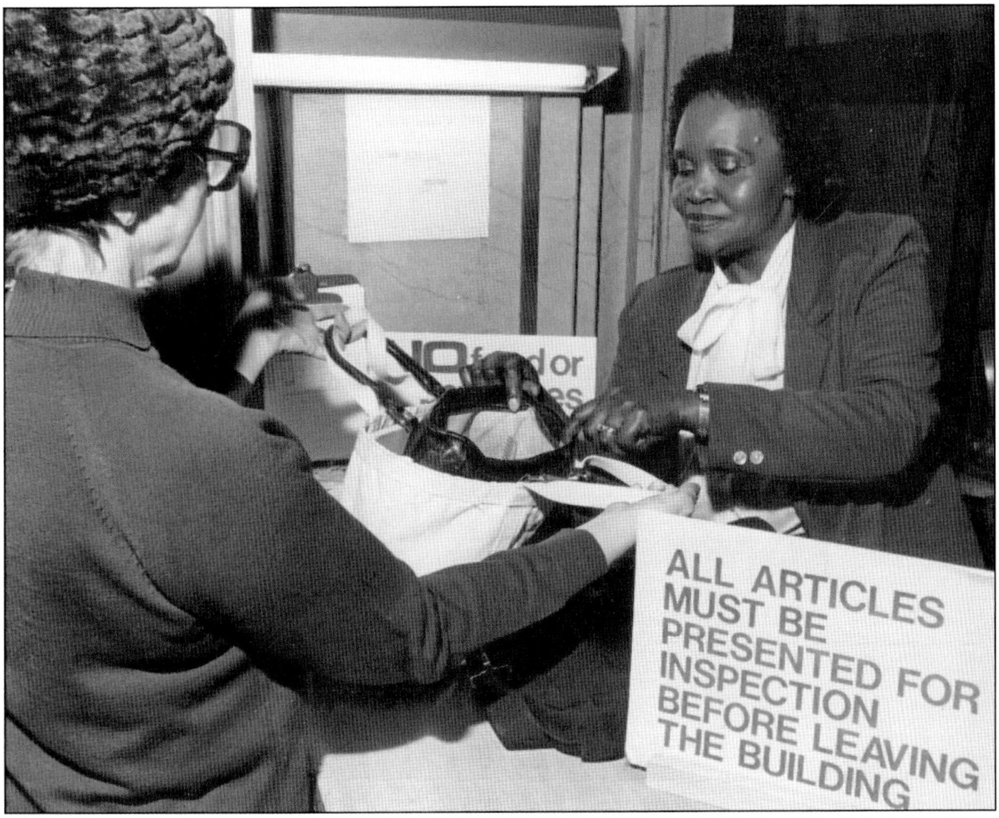

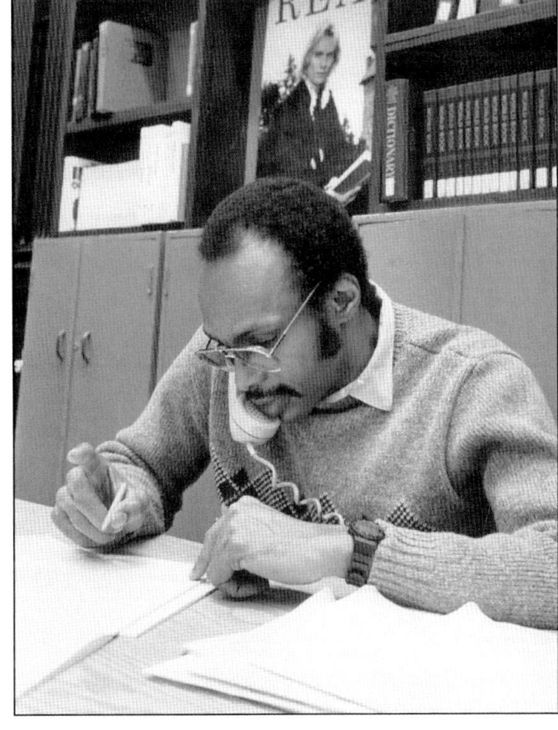

Della Crawford, a library clerk, inspects a patron's handbag at the security desk in 1986. Theft and vandalism have always been a concern at the Newark Public Library, and employees took measures to protect the books—and the users. (The *Star-Ledger*.)

Phil Johnson, the coordinator of the Homework Hotline, discusses an assignment with a caller in 1986. Providing personal services to high school students remained important into the 1980s, whether in person or by telephone. (The *Star-Ledger*.)

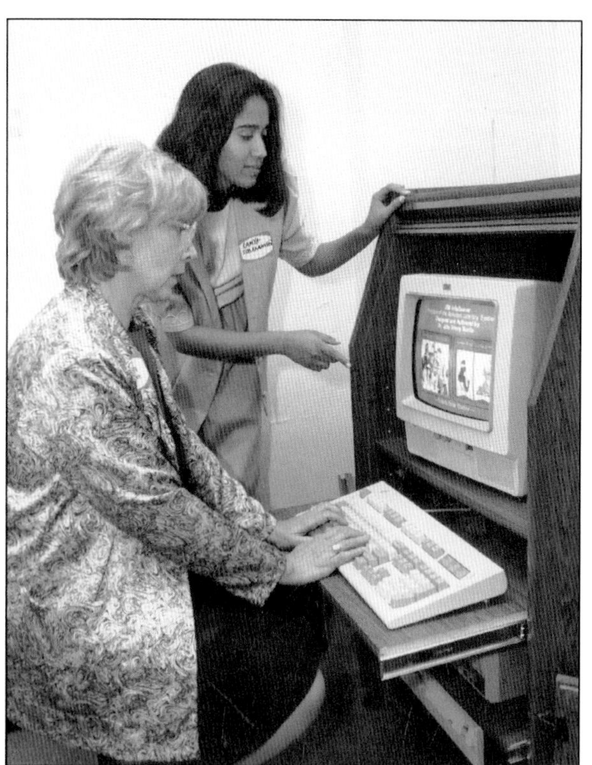

Ramya Subramanian, center, the coordinator for the Action Center for Reading and Learning, assists Frances Wingren (left), a teacher's assistant, with a research inquiry on the computer in 1990. (The *Star-Ledger*.)

Daniel Schnur, an independent exhibition designer, worked on exhibitions for the library for decades on an on-call basis. In consultation with the librarians, he would take their ideas and design an aesthetically pleasing display in table cases or wall cases. (The *Star-Ledger*.)

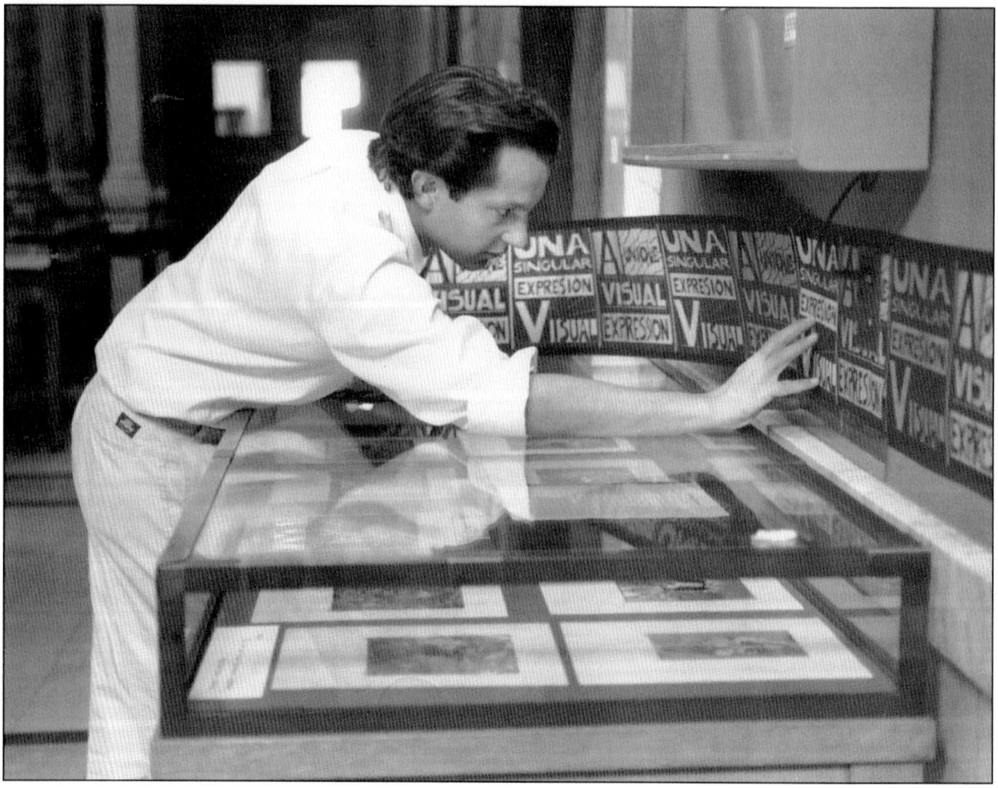

Senior reference librarian James Osbourn stands in front of a photograph of the original Prudential Insurance Company. Librarians often doubled as curators and interpreters for the many exhibitions that the library mounted throughout the years. (The *Star-Ledger*.)

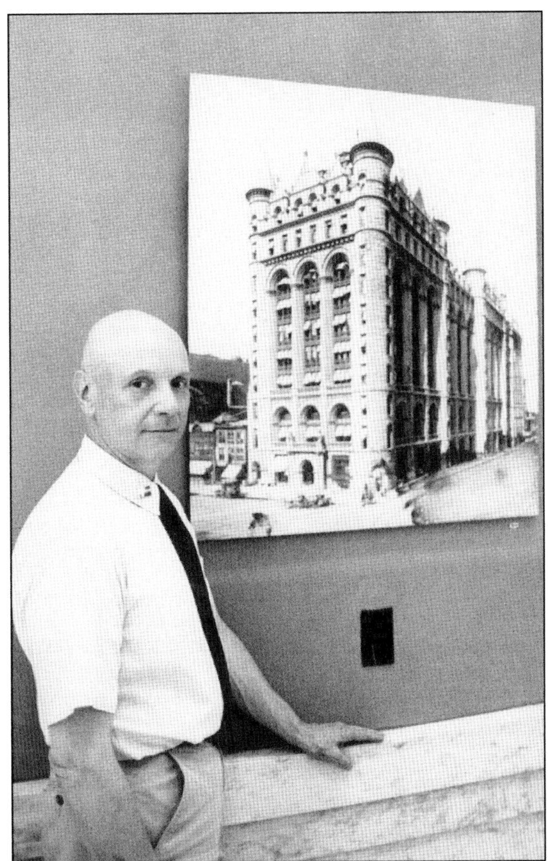

Dale Colston, the assistant director for special collections, speaks at the celebration for Martin Luther King Jr. Day in 2020. Like many staff members, she has had a long and distinguished career at the Newark Public Library.

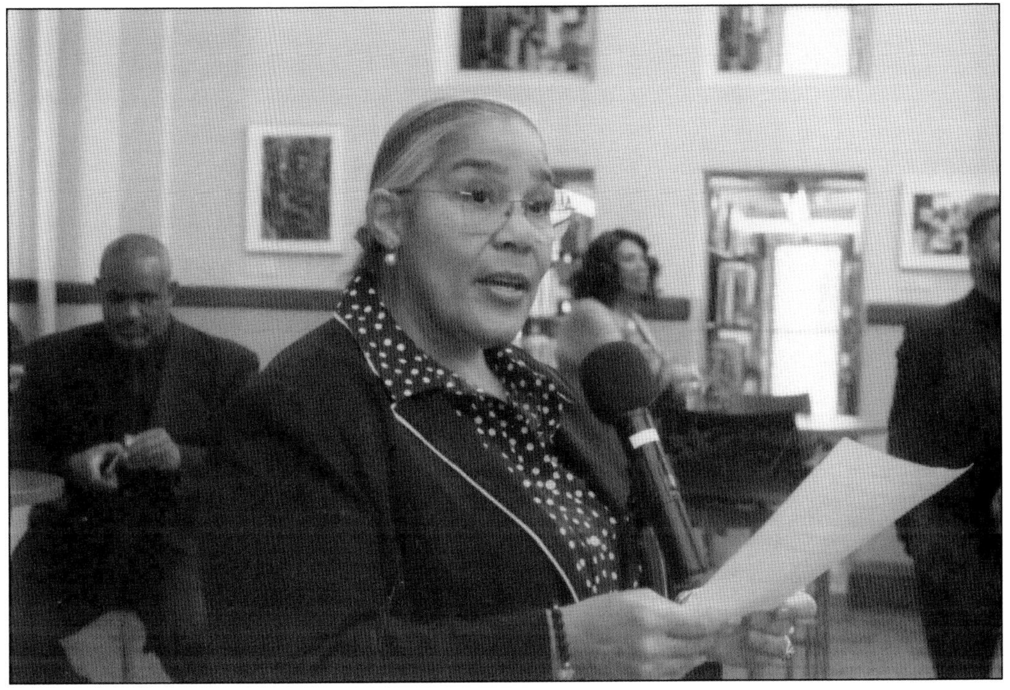

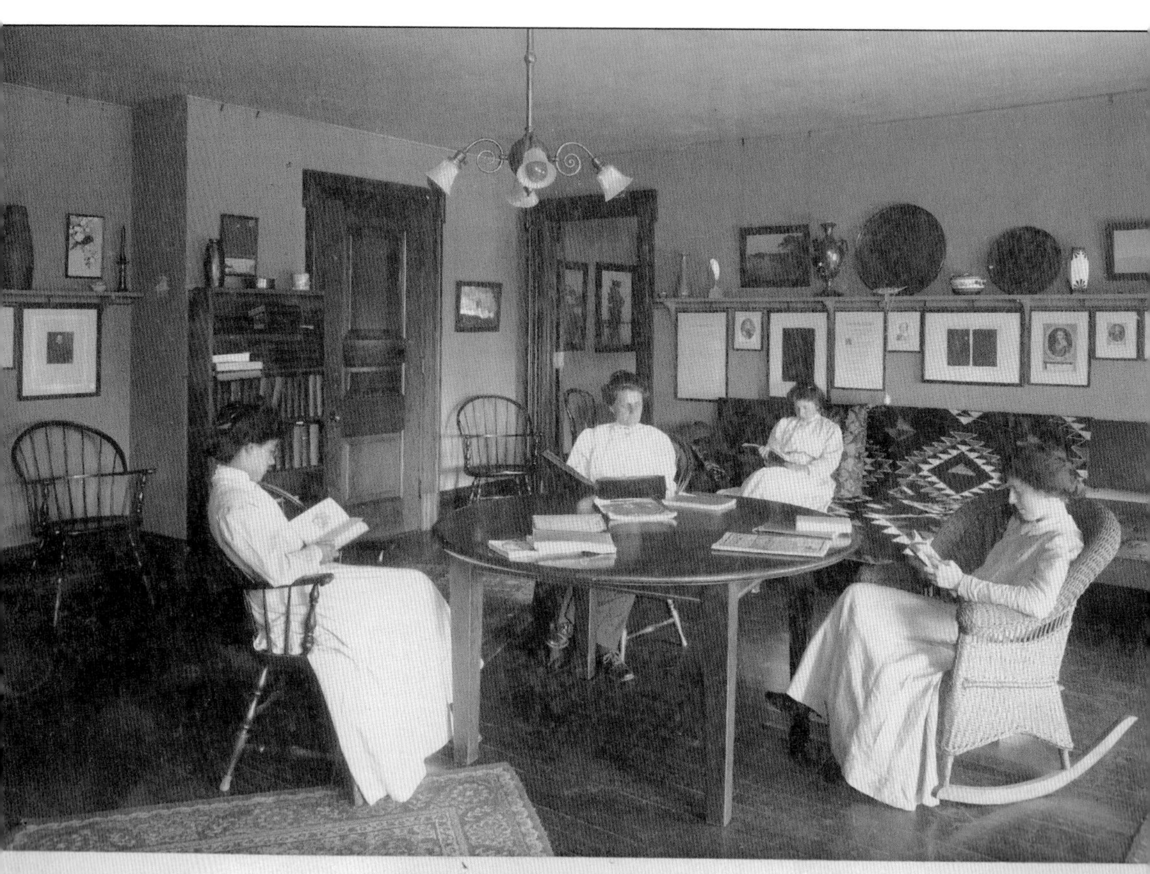

Rest Room for the Staff.

The hardworking staff of the Newark Public Library deserved a break from time to time, and from its very beginnings, a special room was set aside for them, first in the building on West Park Street, and then in the new structure on Washington Street. In this 1909 photograph, with prints and objects to enliven the space, four library assistants relax in the "rest room." And how do they relax? By reading, of course!

Three

SERVICES

Librarians and their assistants acquire books, pamphlets, and periodicals by purchase or donation; they catalog them by author, title, and subject in an attempt to make them easily retrievable (today, keyword searching is used); they classify them so similar books on the same subject are grouped together on the shelves, another means of making the materials more easily browsable; and they preserve the items through various direct and indirect means.

More importantly, though, they assist readers with their informational needs by helping them find the right book, pamphlet, or article on the topic that they are researching. Referring to this last task in 1889, the librarian Frank Hill wrote, "The duty of the attendant at the Bureau of Information is to answer, or try to answer, all questions; to give assistance to readers and students; where possible, to guide the reading of the young, and in general, to see that no one leaves the library in a dissatisfied frame of mind."

In a manual on librarianship that John Cotton Dana published in three editions in 1899, 1909, and 1920, he, too, articulated his view of the duties of librarians. "As librarians," he wrote in *A Library Primer*, "we can slowly persuade our fellows to make library buildings central, ample, and convenient for those who use them. We can help to make the book-collections in schools, colleges, and business and industrial plants more complete, more comfortably housed, and better managed. We can learn to be sympathetic toward scholars, students, and investigators, of whom we have too few. We can explore new fields of library work as they are suggested by our more inventive friends. . . . We can try to get so broad a view of all kinds of work with print—I mean the collecting and mastering of all kinds of it for all possible purposes—that we can sympathize with each and every kind and be hostile to none."

Throughout the century and a third that the Newark Public Library has existed, its services have changed and adapted, but fitting the needs of its patrons has always been paramount.

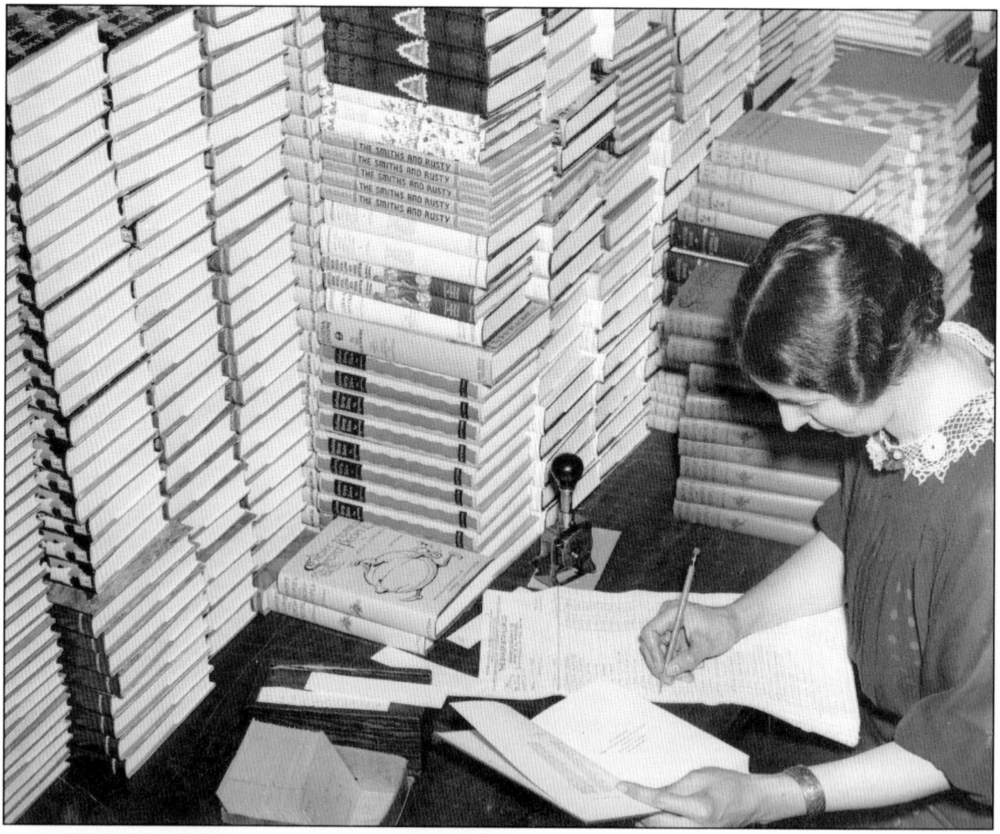

In 1938, the *Newark Sunday Call* published a full-page photographic article entitled "The Life of a Newark Public Library Book." This is a photograph of the order department with the caption "When a shipment of new books arrives from the publisher, it goes to the order department, where library workers check each volume with the order record." (*Newark Sunday Call.*)

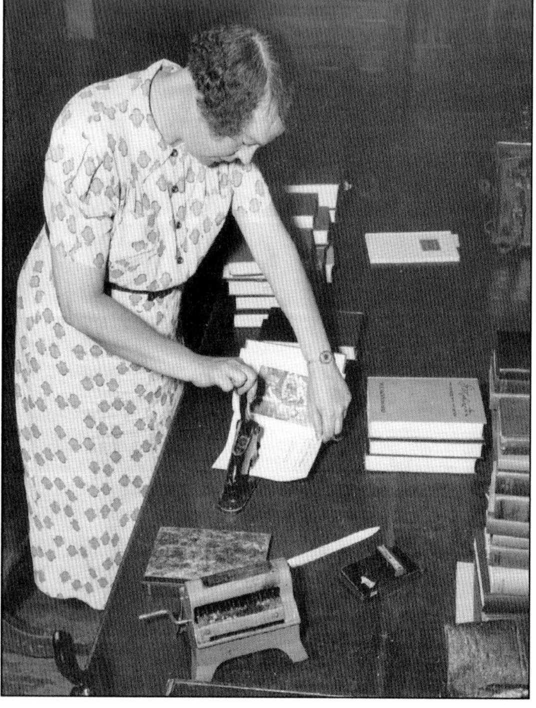

The newspaper further states, "Books go next to the catalog department (pictured), where they become officially part of the library collection. Each volume is stamped, numbered, and equipped with a pocket to hold the borrowing record slip." (*Newark Sunday Call.*)

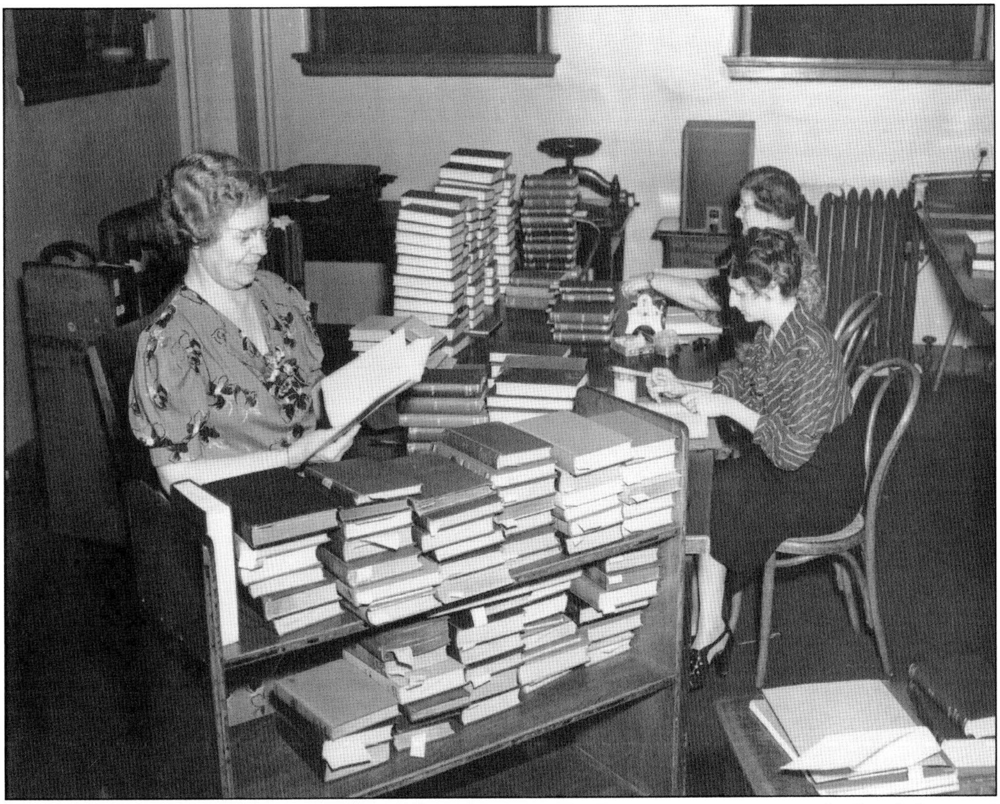

The caption for this photograph reads, "Books in need of minor repairs go to the book hospital on the library's first floor, where a special staff is kept busy mending torn pages, cleaning soiled covers, erasing pen and pencil marks, and performing a score of other minor operations." (*Newark Sunday Call.*)

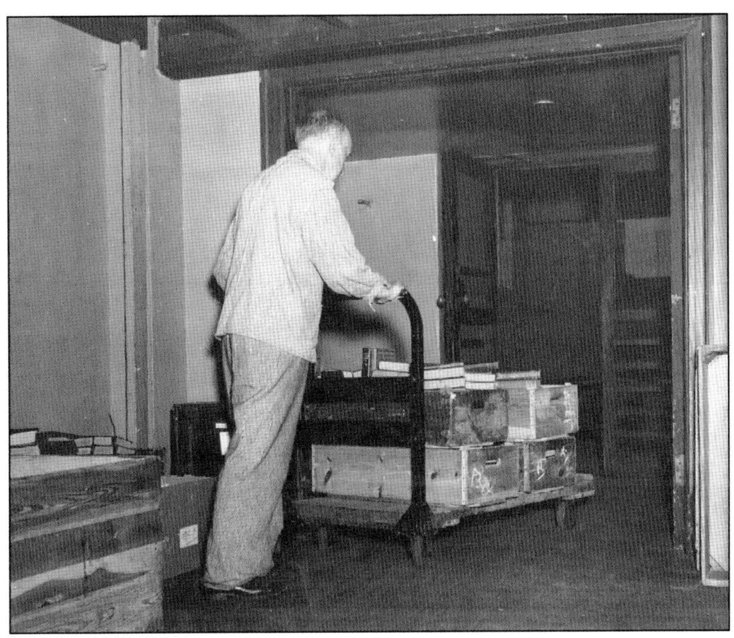

In its "last mile, the book goes into discard" if it is "worn and broken beyond repair" or if it has "illegible print" and "pages missing." Therefore, if a book is "of no further use," it can be safely withdrawn from the collection, sold at a library book sale, or recycled. (*Newark Sunday Call.*)

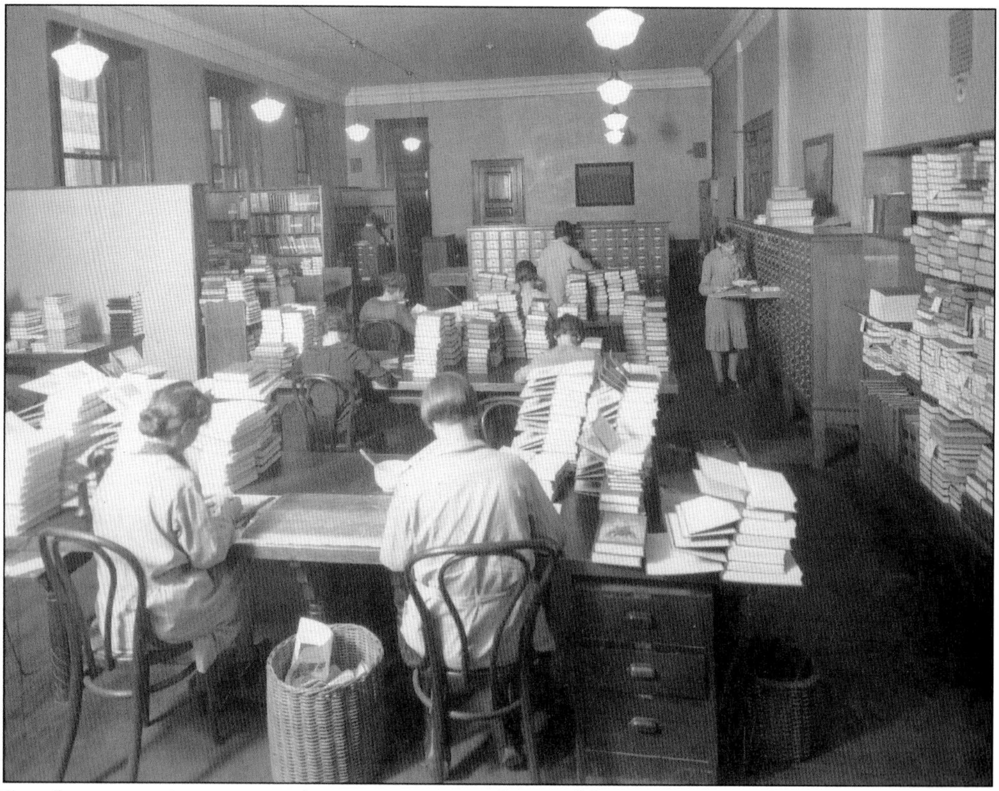

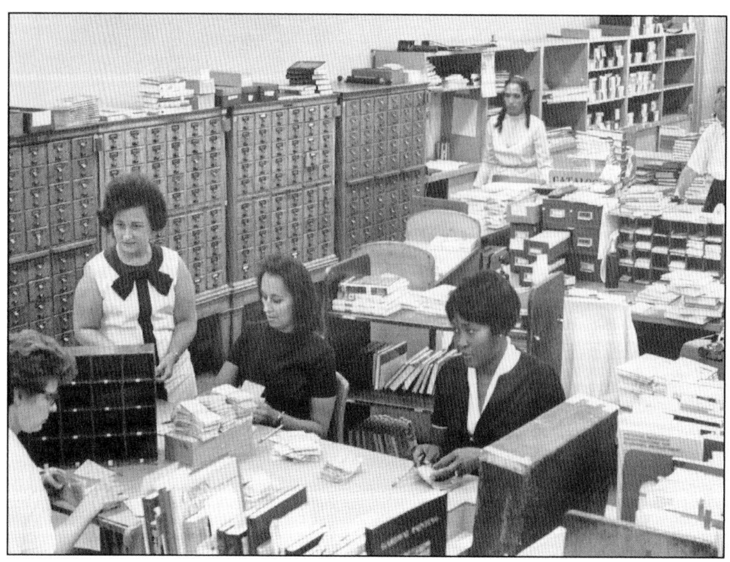

Based upon reviews in popular magazines, professional literature, or trade journals, librarians selected new books for acquisition. Sometimes, they followed the recommendations of patrons. After arriving at the library and being checked in, the new books were then sent to the cataloging department (seen here in 1910).

The cataloging department (pictured in 1970) described the books bibliographically so that patrons could find them easily by author, title, or subject. It also assigned classification numbers to them so that patrons could browse the shelves in search of books on similar topics. Accuracy was crucial, but the most important point was to help patrons find books.

Bibliographic records were originally produced by hand on three-by-five index cards in what was known at the time as the "library hand." Later, they were typed or printed in multiple copies so that they could be filed by author, title, and subject. They were filed in card catalogs, like the one here.

In the 1970s and 1980s, catalogers developed a new format known as "machine readable cataloging records" (MARC). One record could be searched by multiple access points (author, title, subject, and now keyword). Computers slowly but surely replaced the old card catalogs. (Photograph by John A. Gibson Jr.; courtesy of the *Star-Ledger*.)

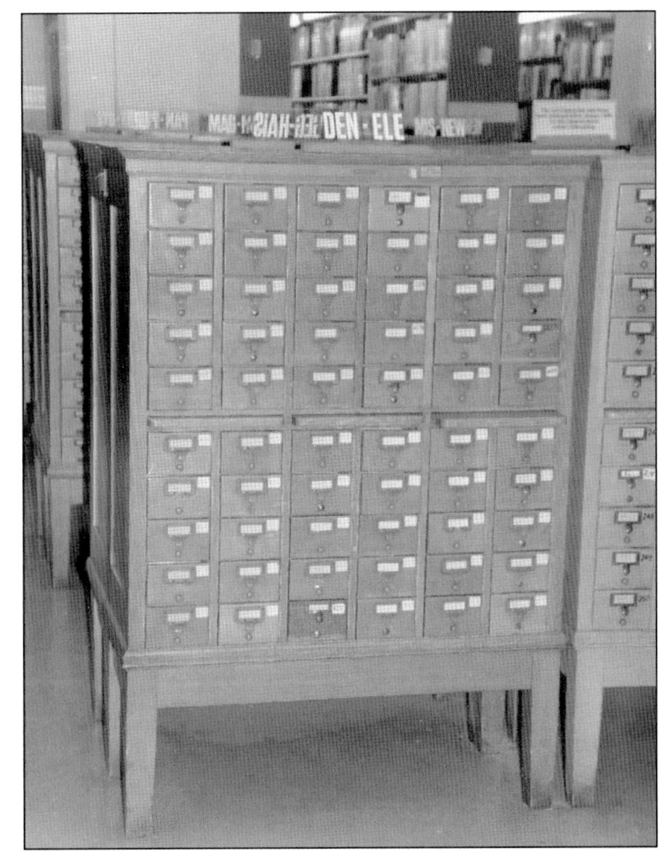

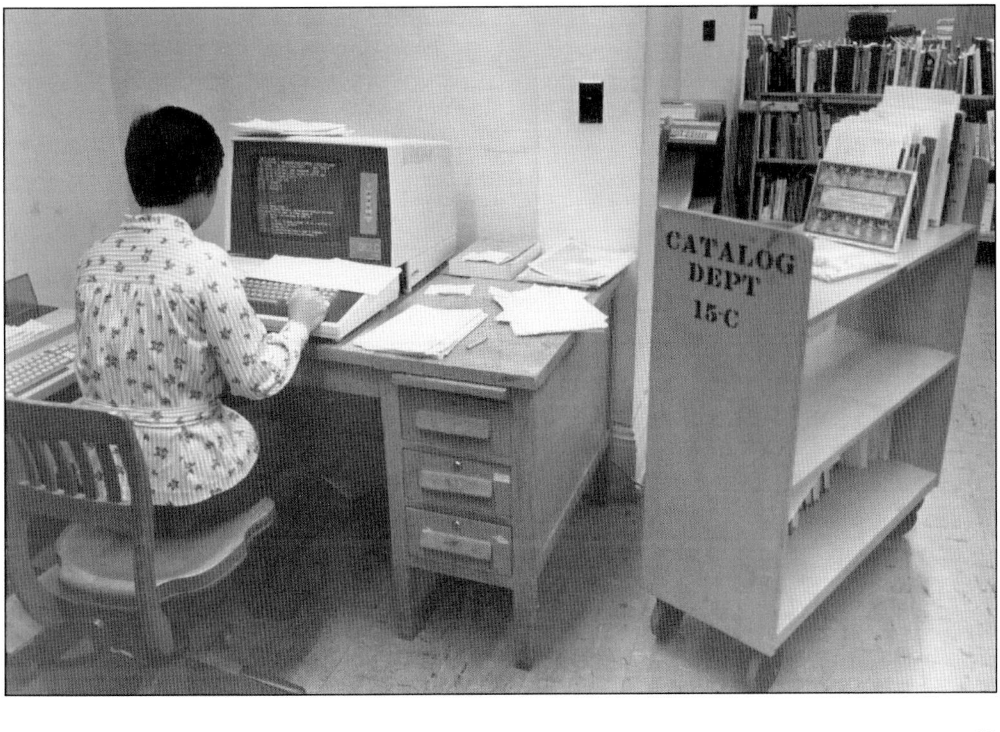

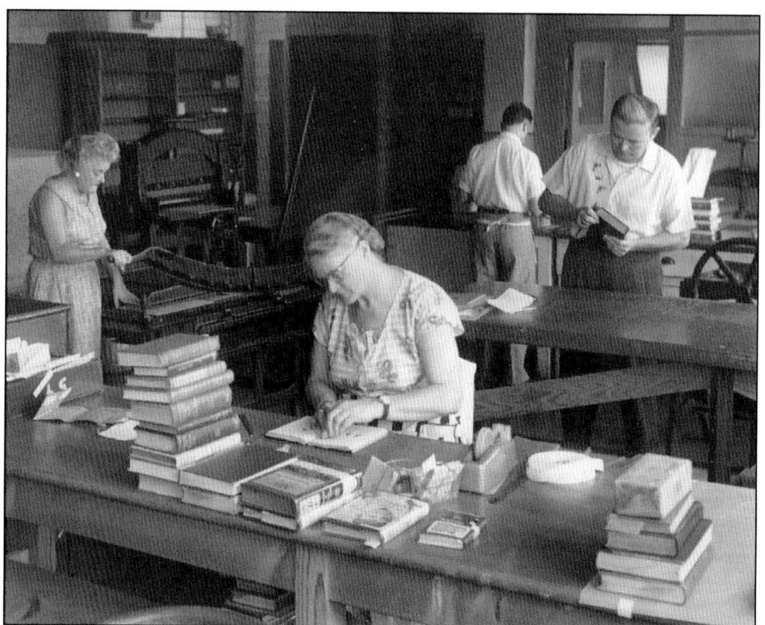

Wear and tear on the books were inevitable, and so a specially trained group of library workers performed general cleaning, removing pencil marks and other smudges, and repairing torn leaves, loose pages, or damaged labels. Known as the repair department, it was not considered a prestigious assignment, but it did perform an important function. (*Newark News.*)

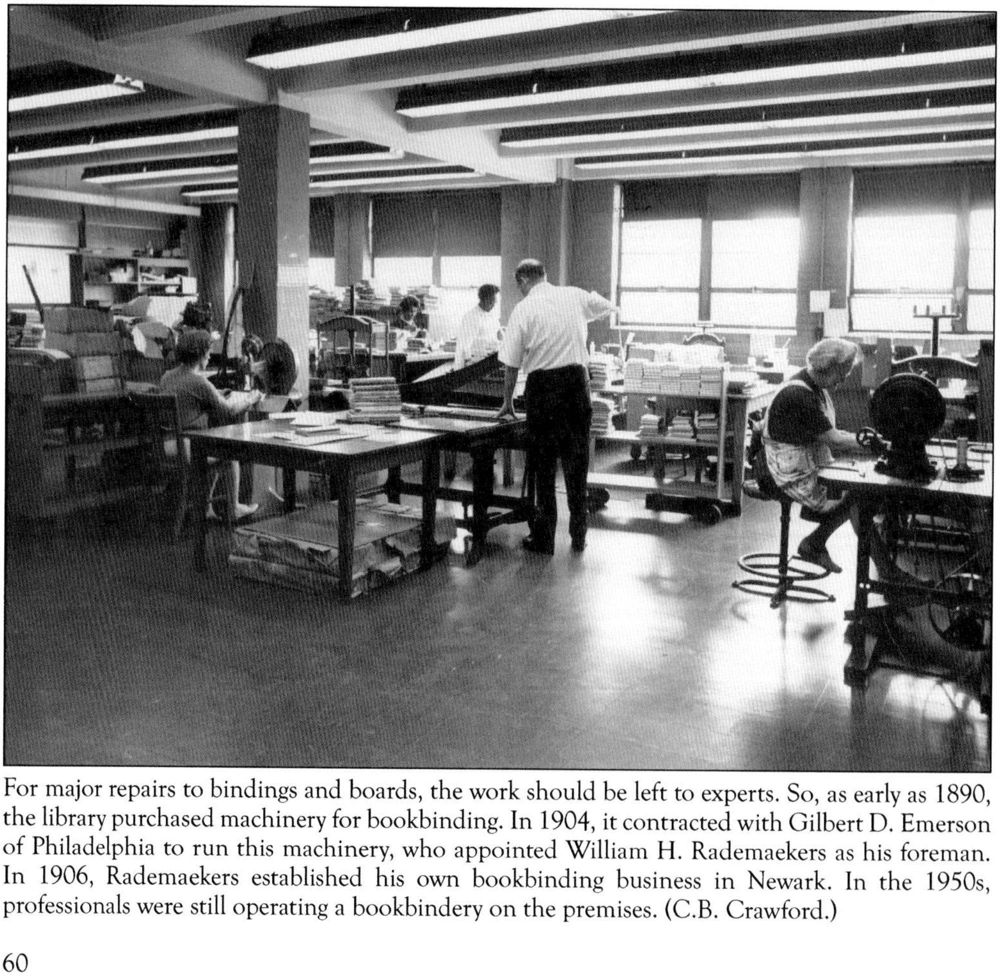

For major repairs to bindings and boards, the work should be left to experts. So, as early as 1890, the library purchased machinery for bookbinding. In 1904, it contracted with Gilbert D. Emerson of Philadelphia to run this machinery, who appointed William H. Rademaekers as his foreman. In 1906, Rademaekers established his own bookbinding business in Newark. In the 1950s, professionals were still operating a bookbindery on the premises. (C.B. Crawford.)

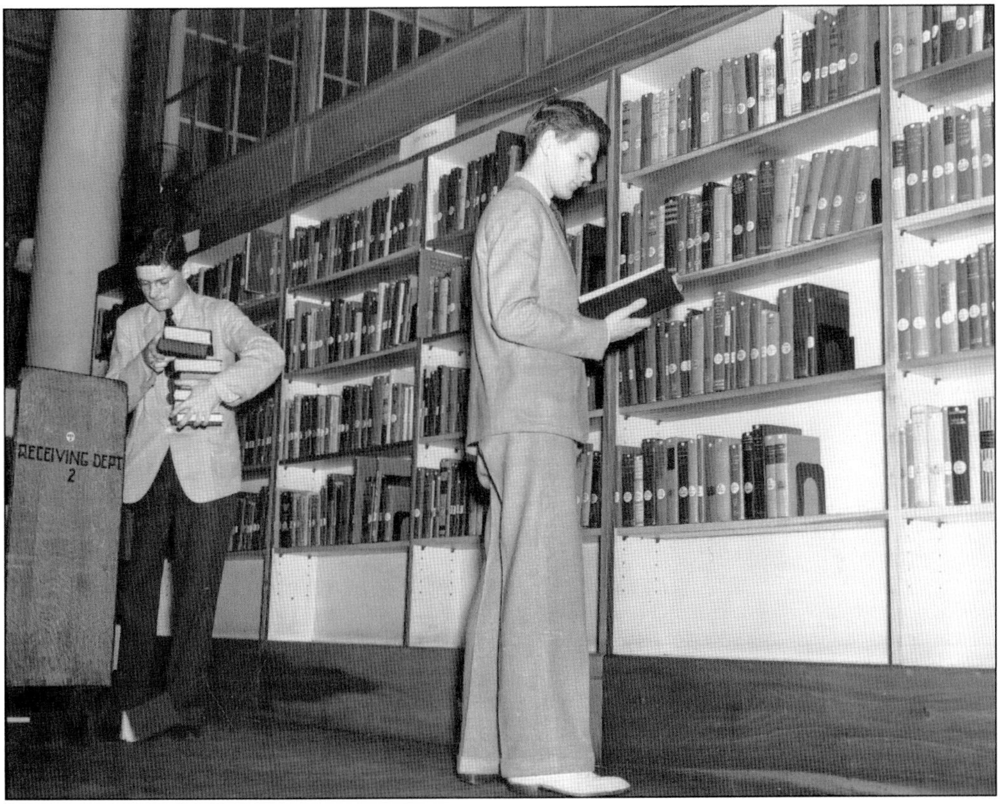

On the back of this photograph from 1938 (above) is the following caption: "A special shelf in the lending department is reserved for new books, and patrons seize upon them avidly." In addition, a special reading alcove (below) underneath the grand marble staircase was introduced in 1939 so patrons could peruse the books before checking them out. Even today, new books and books of special interest are highlighted in the main atrium of the library. (Above, *Newark Sunday Call*; below, Laura von Schnarendorf.)

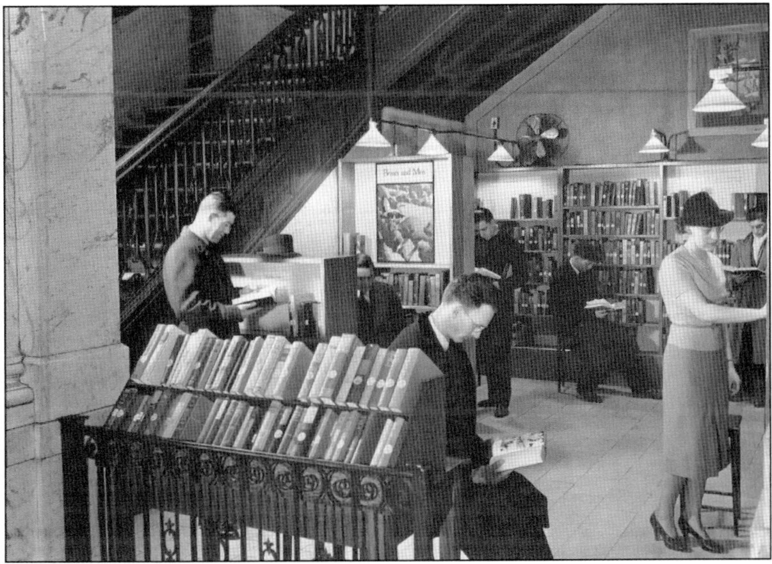

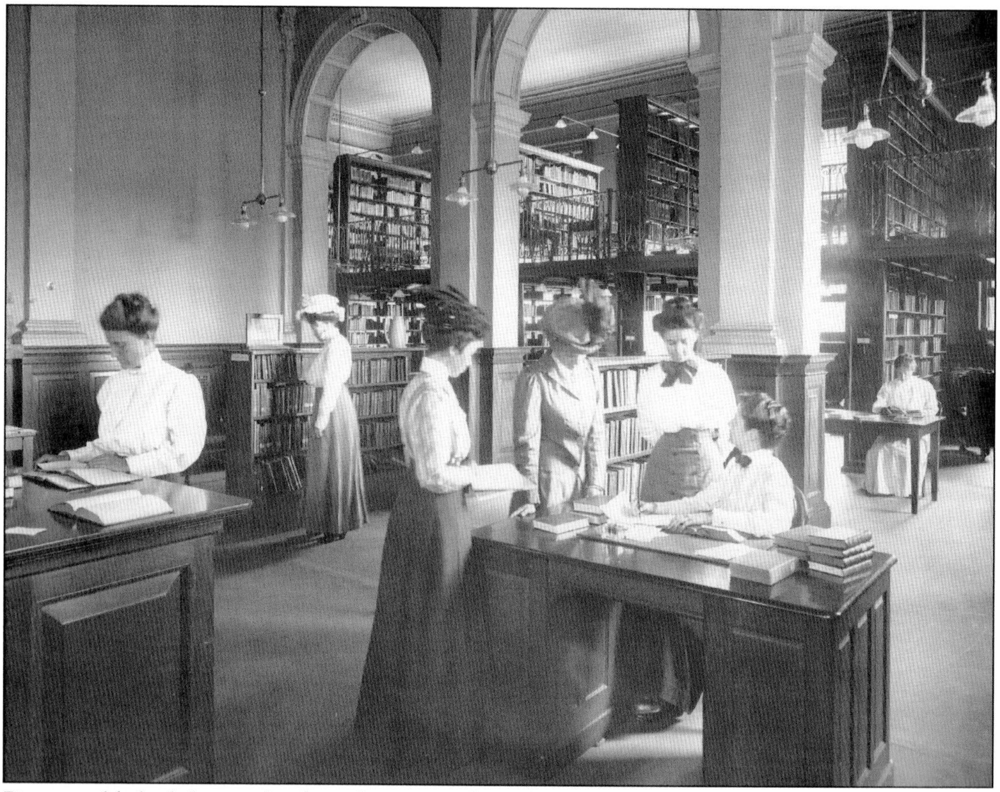

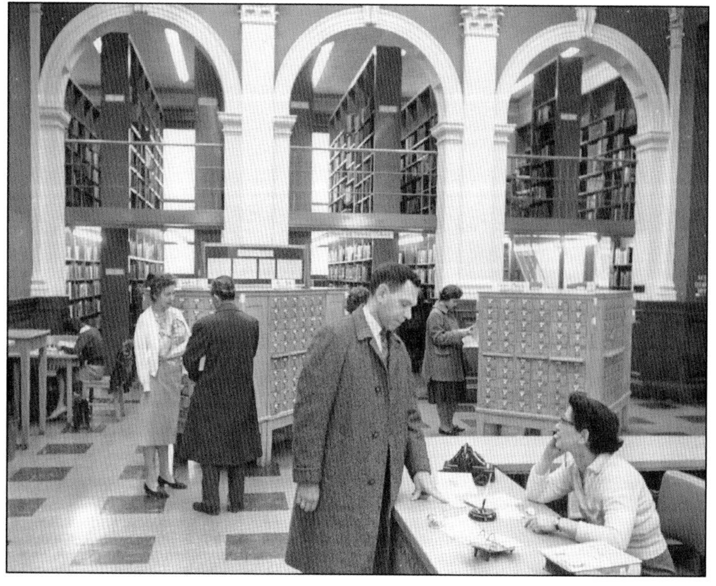

Dana established three rules for reference work in the early 1900s: first, "meet the inquirer more than half way," especially since he or she might feel intimidated in a library; second, "learn at once just exactly what the inquirer wants to know"; and three, "whenever possible show the inquirer how the answer is found so that he or she may next time in some measure help him- or her-self." (William F. Cone.)

Using dictionaries, encyclopedias, atlases, gazetteers, almanacs, indexes, and other reference sources, librarians answered questions such as: Is there a street in Newark called "Unnamed?" What was the salary of a congressman in 1844? How did Oliver Wendell Holmes define "a Harvard gentleman?" Where could one find quotations in a Scottish dialect suitable for a bar?

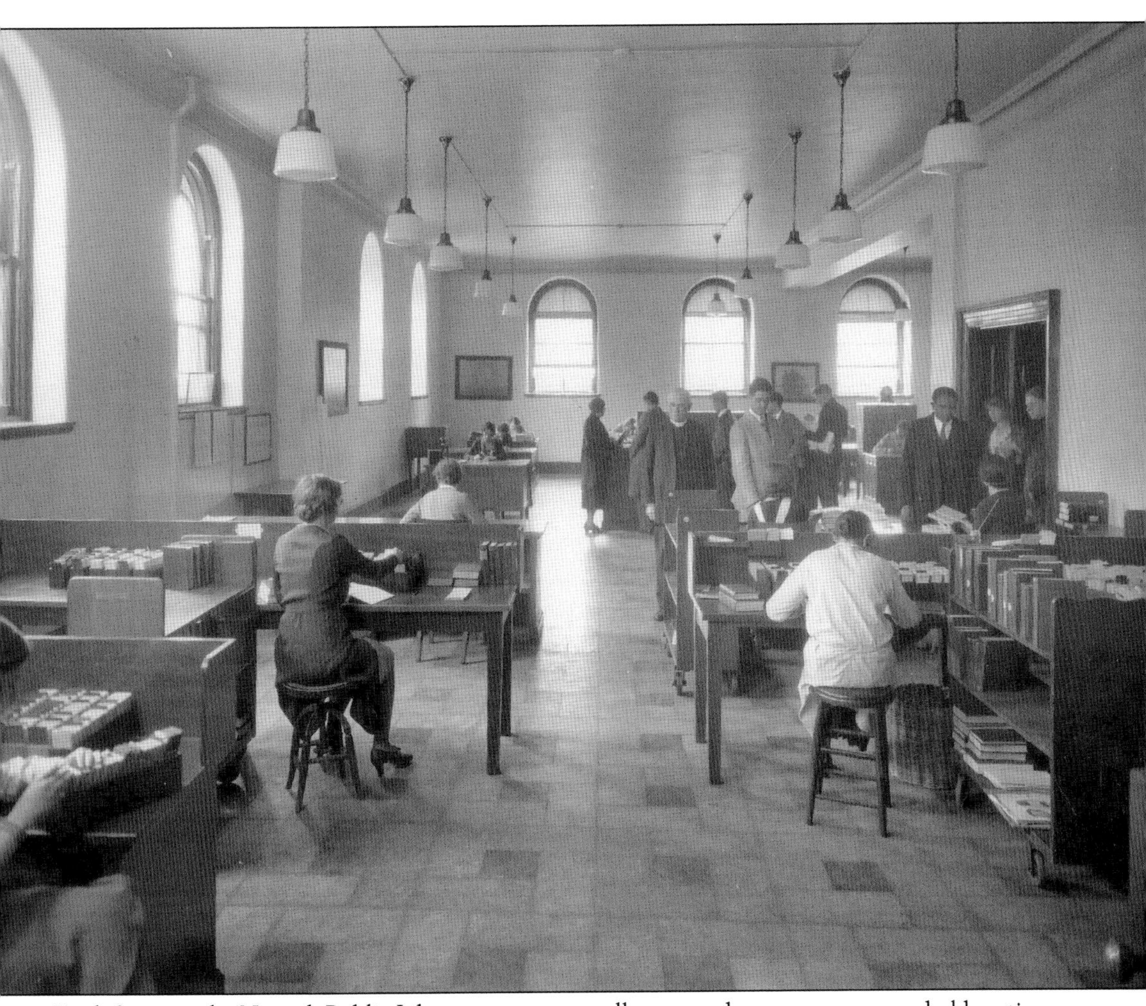

By definition, the Newark Public Library was open to all, men and women, young and old, native-born or immigrant, black or white, free of charge. All residents wishing to use the library had to fill out an application that contained very basic information: name, address, and occupation. If under 14 years of age, a parent had to cosign the form. This application process was to be quite simple so as not to "discommode" anyone. Patrons promised to take care of all books and to pay all fines, especially those levied for damages. In 1907, a total of 9,476 borrowers were registered; innumerable names and addresses were changed; some expired cards were renewed, others were removed; and many lost cards were replaced.

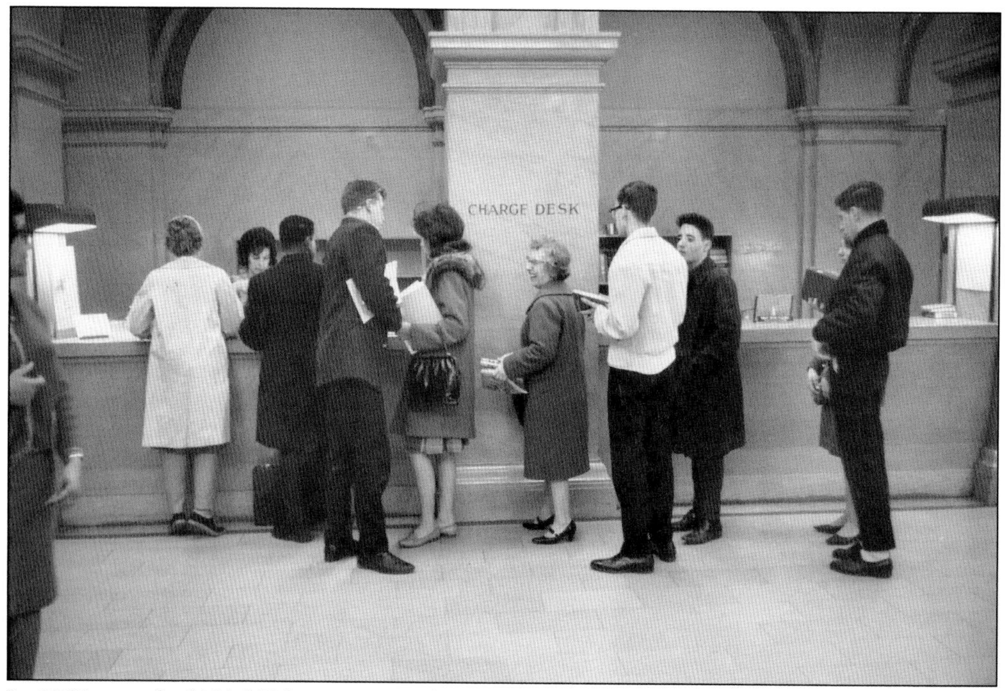

In 1957, a total of 101,389 borrowers took out 2,048,346 books (many books more than once by different patrons) from the main library, the eight neighborhood branches, the five sub-branches, and the ten stations. The most popular books were *Peyton Place* by Grace Metalious (fiction) and *Too Much, Too Soon* by Diana Barrymore (nonfiction), an autobiography covering her childhood of neglect and her cycle of abuse in adulthood. (Ann Zane.)

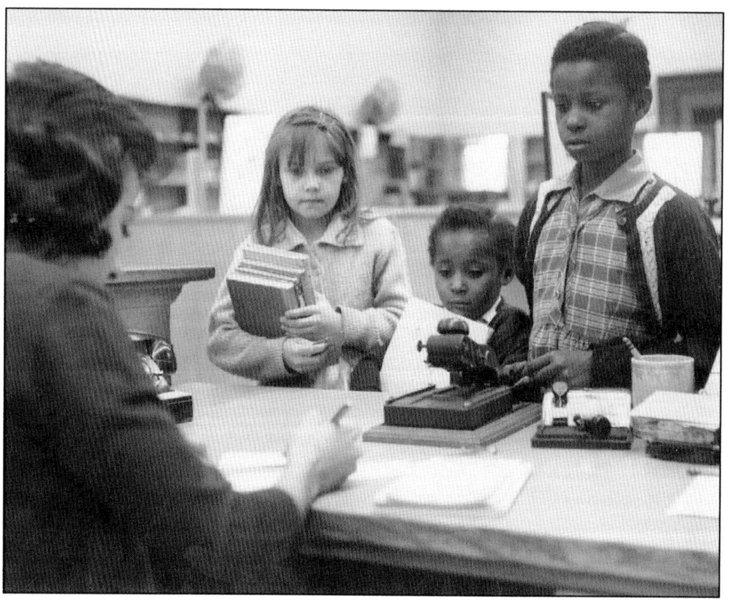

In this photograph, boys and girls wait their turn to check out books from the children's librarian. In 1957, the children's room extended its hours, since circulation had increased by 45 percent over the previous 15 years. Boys were reading books on science and current events (not cowboy and sports stories as in the 1940s), while girls were still reading stories about home, friendship, and love. (Ann Zane.)

The main reading room in the West
Park Street library, the original
building, was on the second floor. It
sat 150 readers, mostly men because
women preferred to sit apart in their
own room. It was fitted out with
wooden racks for newspapers and
magazines. "A generous fireplace
on the west end provided warmth
and cheer," as the celebratory
pamphlet, *The Free Public
Library of the City of Newark, New
Jersey (1889)*, expressed it.

In the new building, the entire
front of the second floor was set
aside for a monumental oak-paneled
reading room with an ornamental
22-foot-high ceiling. Wainscoting
and pilasters gave it an element of
grandeur, and two large limestone
fireplaces graced its two ends.
Tables and chairs accommodated
patrons, and bookcases held
reading materials.

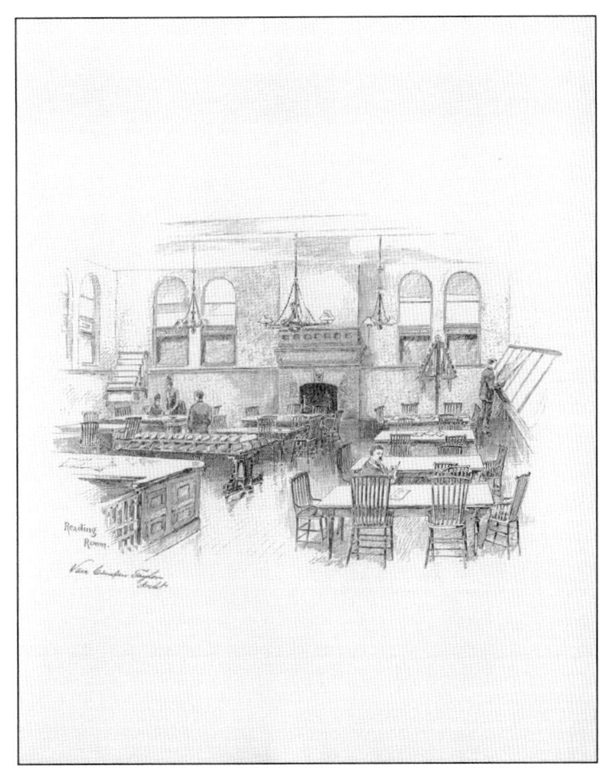

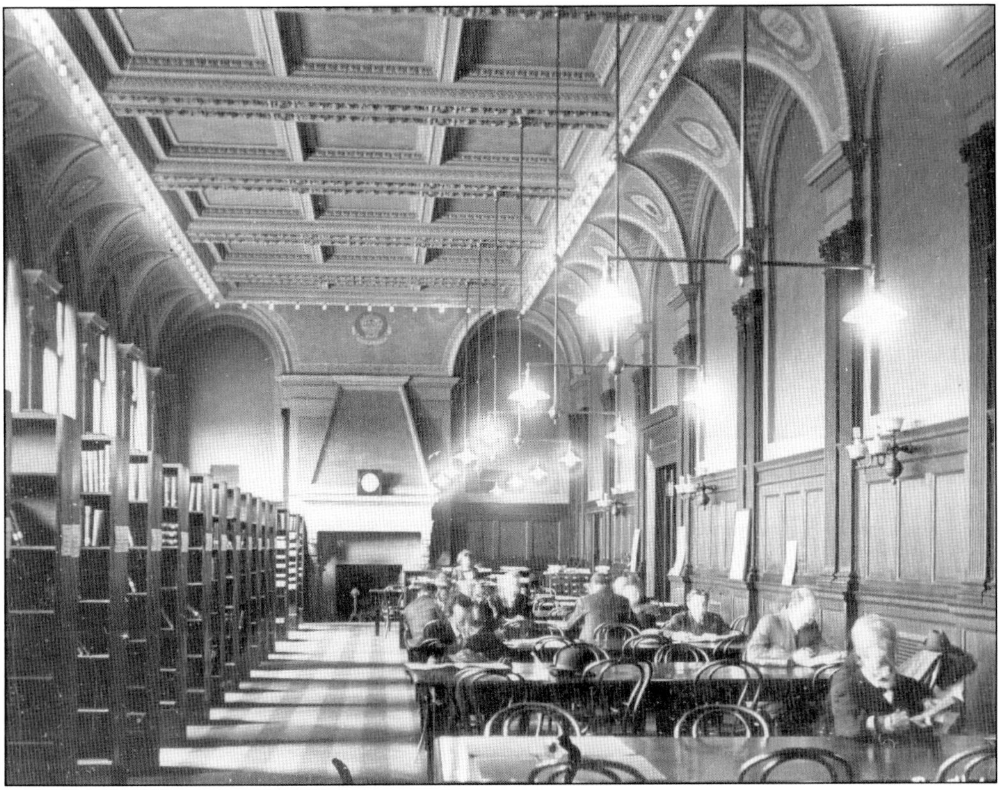

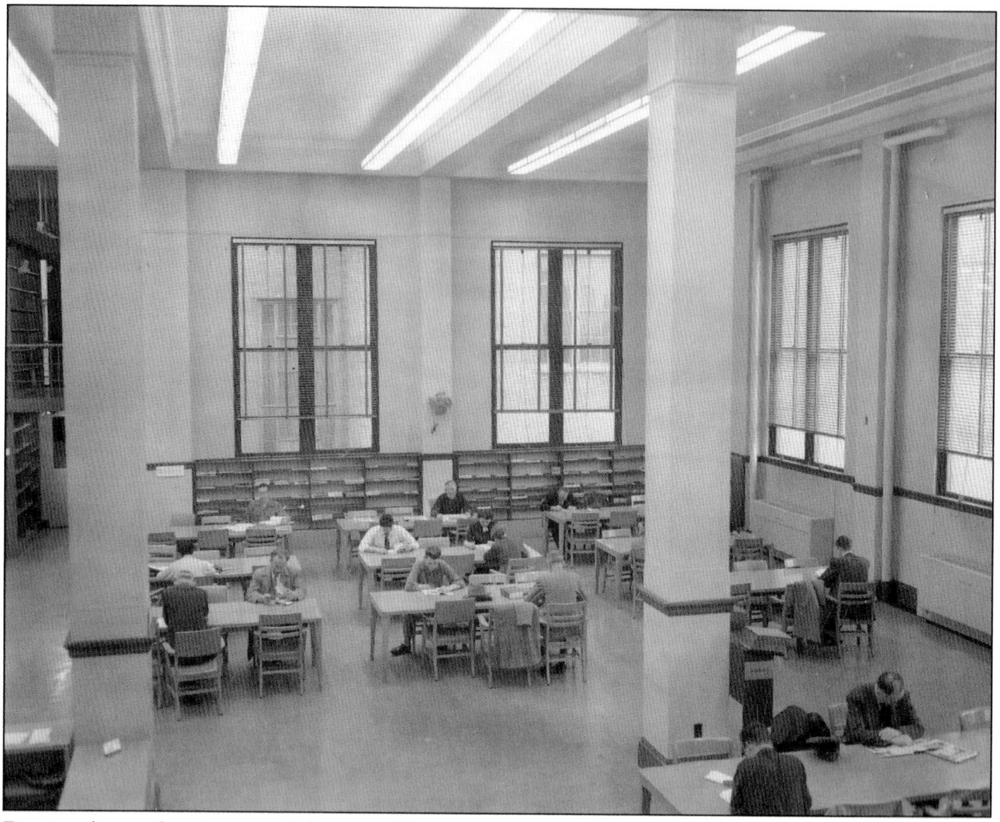

During the modernization of the main library in the 1950s, the reading rooms on the second floor in the back were renovated. One was reserved for the science and technology department, and the other one was devoted to general reference work (pictured). (*Newark News*.)

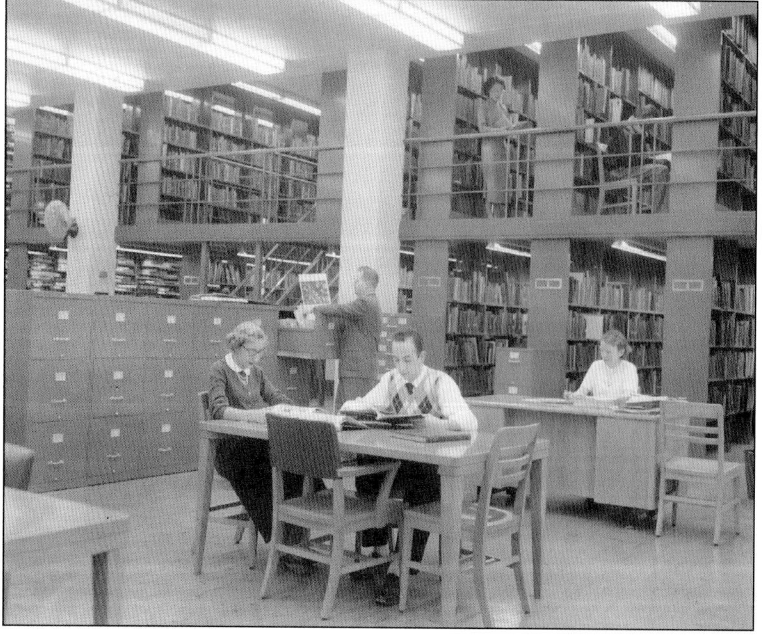

On the third floor, the art and music department was relocated with modern metal shelves for the oversized art books and new filing cabinets for the picture collection. Additional tables and chairs were set up for research, reading, and viewing. (*Newark News*.)

Two elegantly dressed women look over a book in one of the main reading rooms in the 1950s. Please note that smoking is no longer allowed in the library.

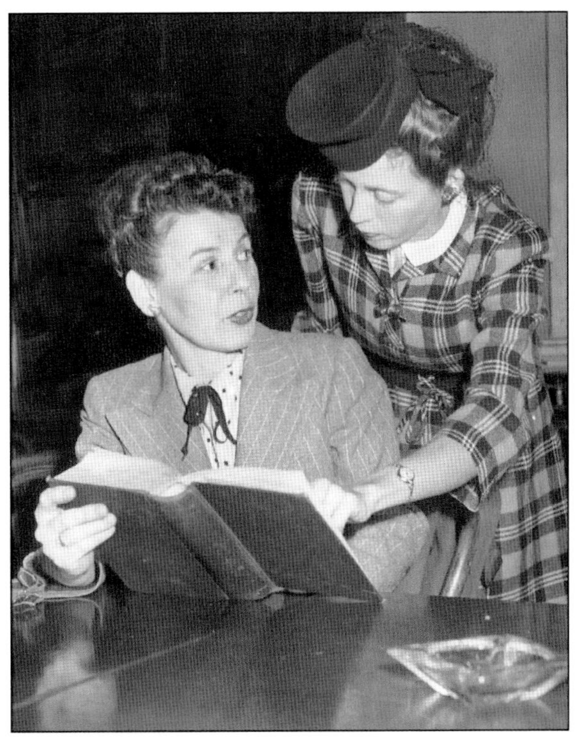

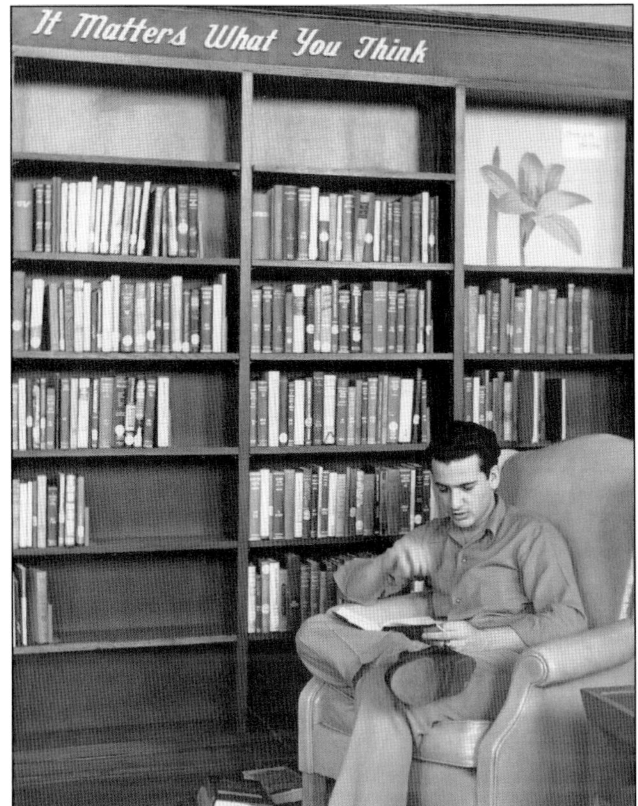

A young man enjoys a good book while relaxing in one of the easy chairs in the main library. A pile of other books lies on the floor beside him. "It matters what you think," proclaims the sign on the bookcase. (Ann Zane.)

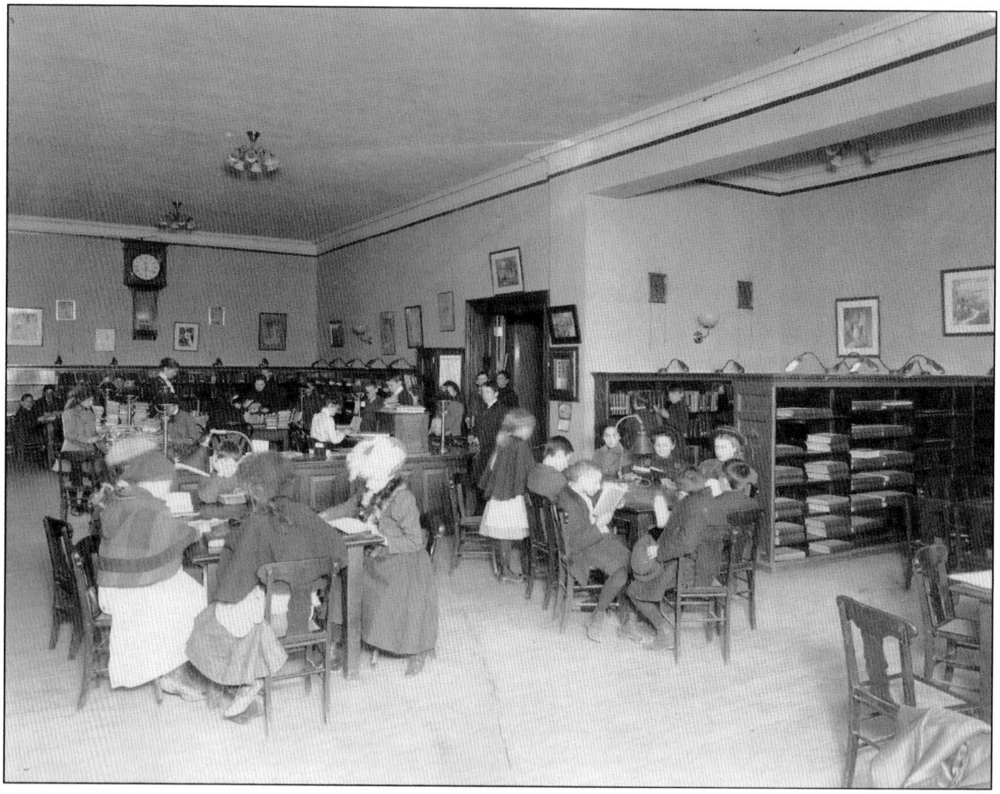

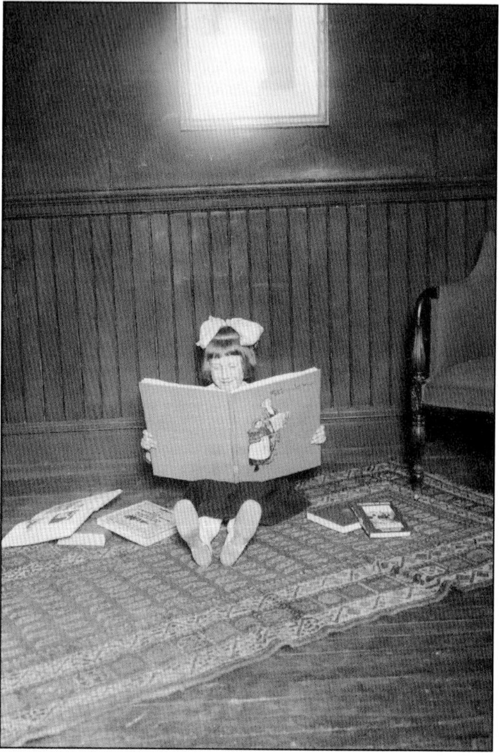

In 1898, when the library was still in the West Park Street building, Clara Whitehill Hunt, a librarian specially trained in children's work, set aside a special area for children, and she helped plan the children's room in the new structure that opened in 1901 (above). Later, in the 1920s, each city-owned branch had a separate room for children on the top floor. The Newark Public Library has had a long and sustained commitment to programs, such as story hours, reading clubs, and book talks as well as arts and crafts programs and other special events, all designed for children. Sometimes, the books were even bigger than the children (left).

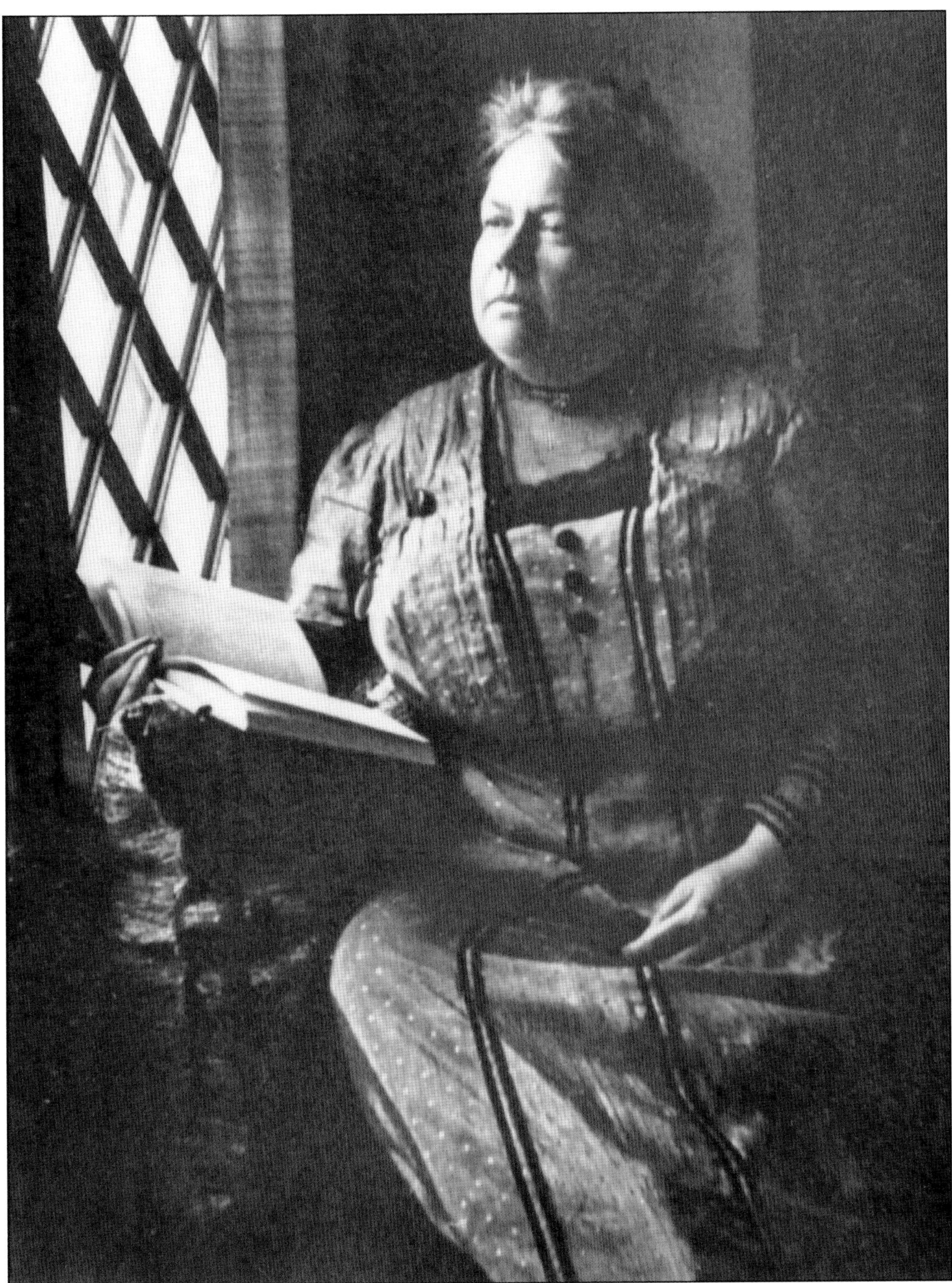

With over 20 years of experience as a teacher and a school administrator, Louise Connolly became the educational advisor for the Newark Public Library and the Newark Museum in 1912. Until her death in 1927, she became "an able helper" in stimulating the circulation of library books to teachers and students and in promoting lessons on library use. In 1926, she published *How to Use a Library*, which encouraged teachers and librarians to instruct their pupils and children "to help them help themselves." She oversaw the children's department and the school department for over a decade. She was also a firm believer in using the museum as a means of visual instruction.

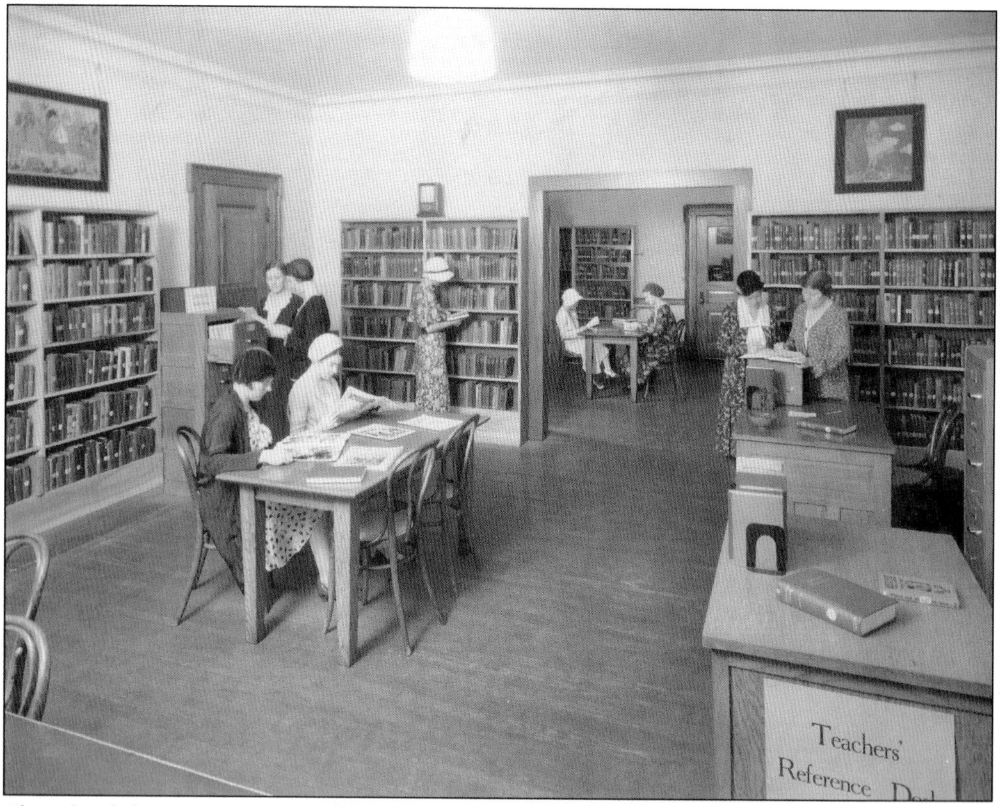

The school department was established in 1907 as a place for teachers to acquire the necessary skills in the knowledge and use of books that would make their jobs easier and more effective. Through their contacts with librarians, they would soon realize that children could be "more thoroughly and wisely trained for citizenship by training them more effectively in reading." And through their contacts with teachers, librarians could more effectively reach out to children.

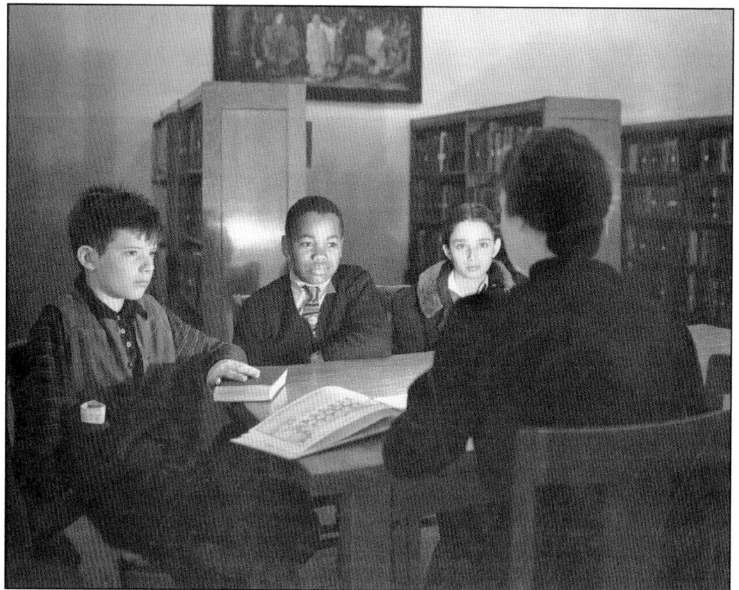

Frequently, teachers would bring their students to the library for lessons on how to use the library or for special programs. Sometimes the children would be encouraged to explore the library and its branches on their own, letting them discover for themselves what most interests them. (Laura von Schnarendorf.)

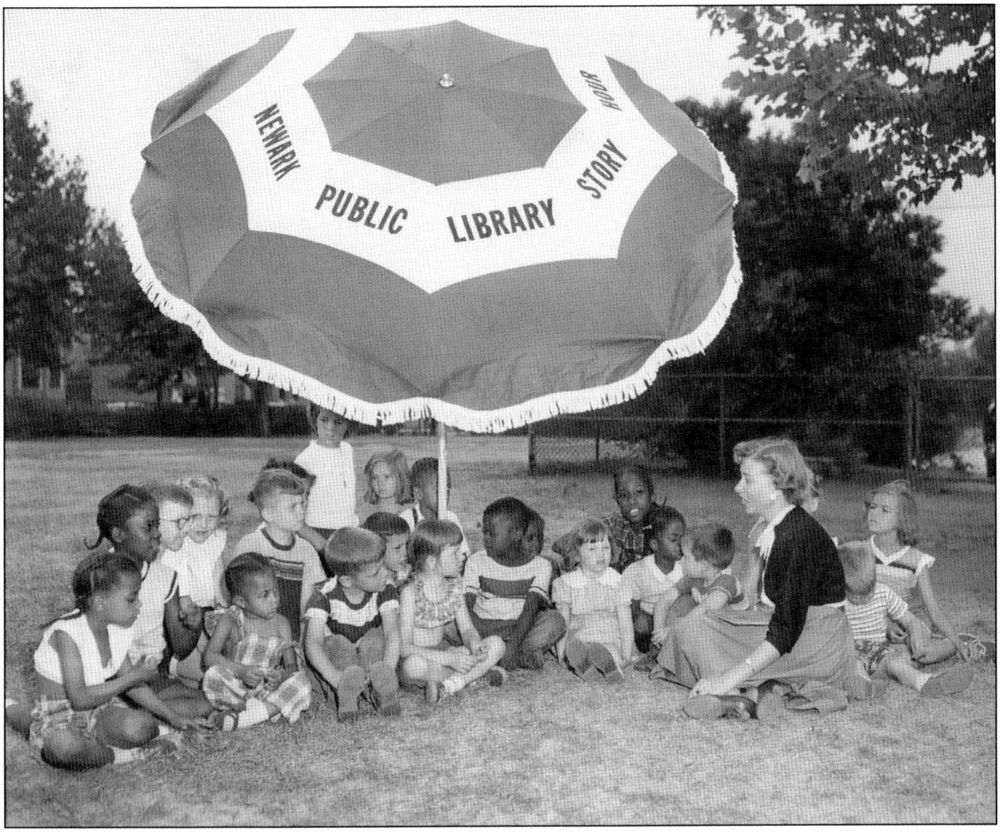

In 1962, a professional storyteller was added to the children's programs, and in 1970, a Spanish-speaking storyteller was hired. During the summers, story hours were held in parks or in branch library gardens (above). Additionally, the annual Summer Reading Challenge (below) reached children throughout the city and addressed literacy by encouraging children to read. Club Success, a homework assistance program, was initiated in 1994 and served Newark's children for several years. More recently, the library continues to offer fun and interesting programs, such as gaming, cooking, arts and crafts, and movies. (Above, *Newark Evening News*; below, the *Star-Ledger*.)

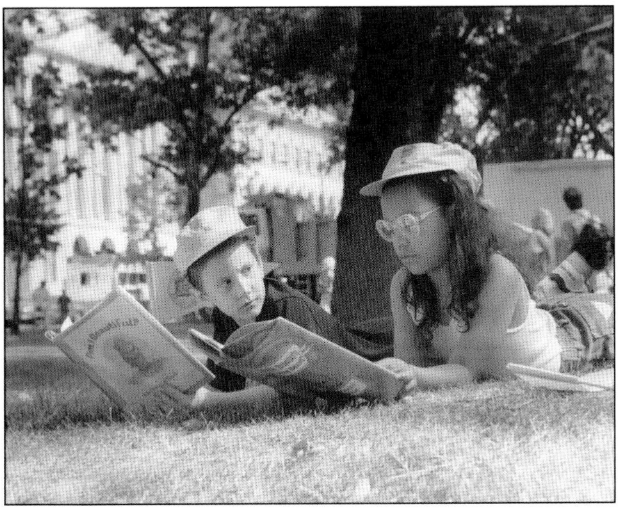

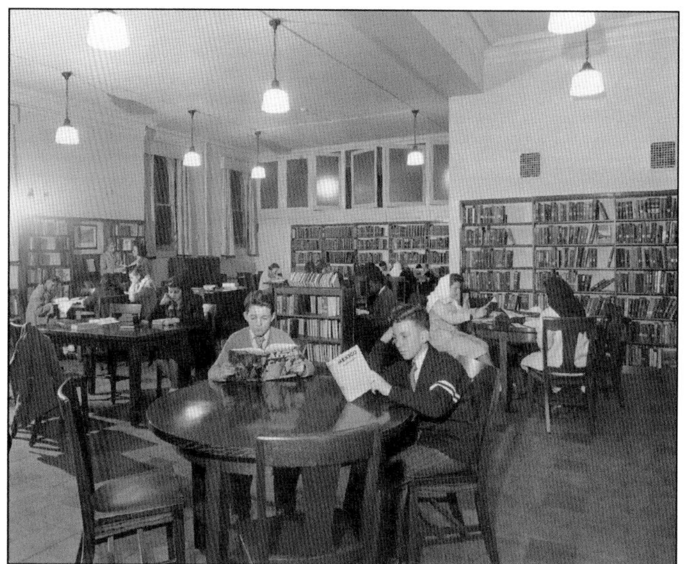

As early as 1903, the need for an intermediate department between children and adults was recognized. Therefore, a special shelf was established near the main desk in the delivery room for "Interesting Books for Young People." Despite the work that the Newark Public Library did in conjunction with the high schools throughout the city, a separate "Teen Corner" was not set up until 1944. (Handy & Boesser.)

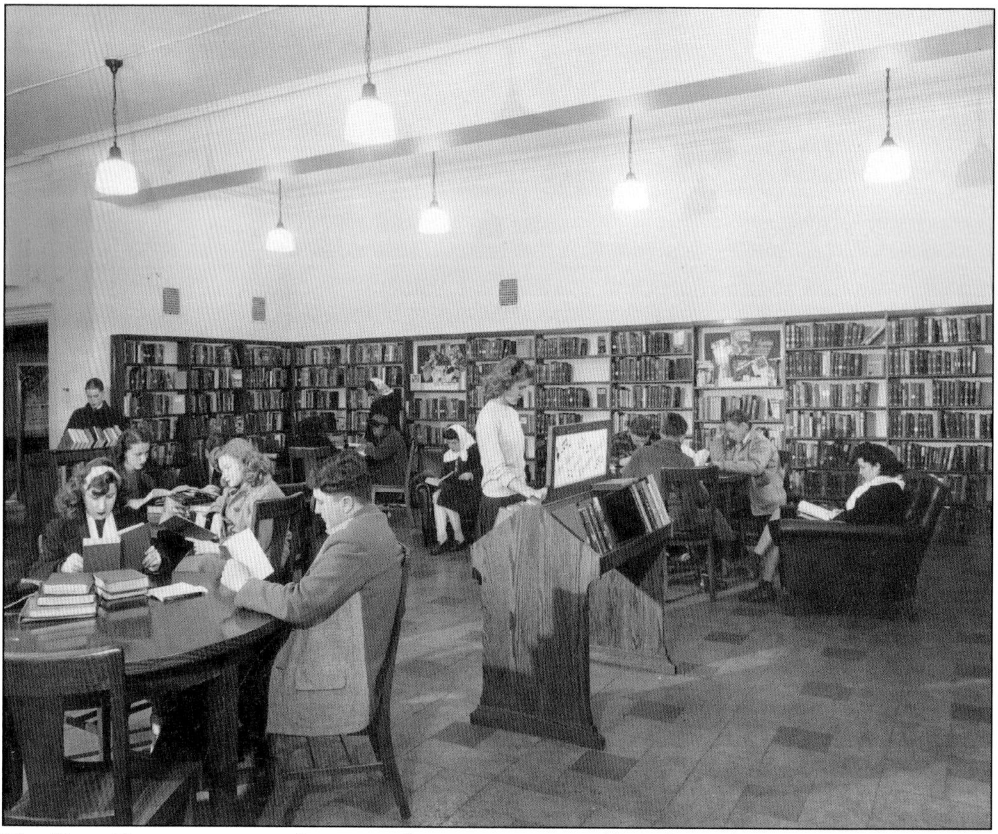

The Teen Corner was a study room where teenagers could find standard reference works and over 6,500 volumes on inventions, chemistry, and pet-raising (for young men) and love stories and etiquette books (for young women). More than that, though, it was a place for them to meet. During its first year, 300 youngsters jammed into the room to listen to Barringer High School's swing band, the Blue Jackets. (Handy & Boesser.)

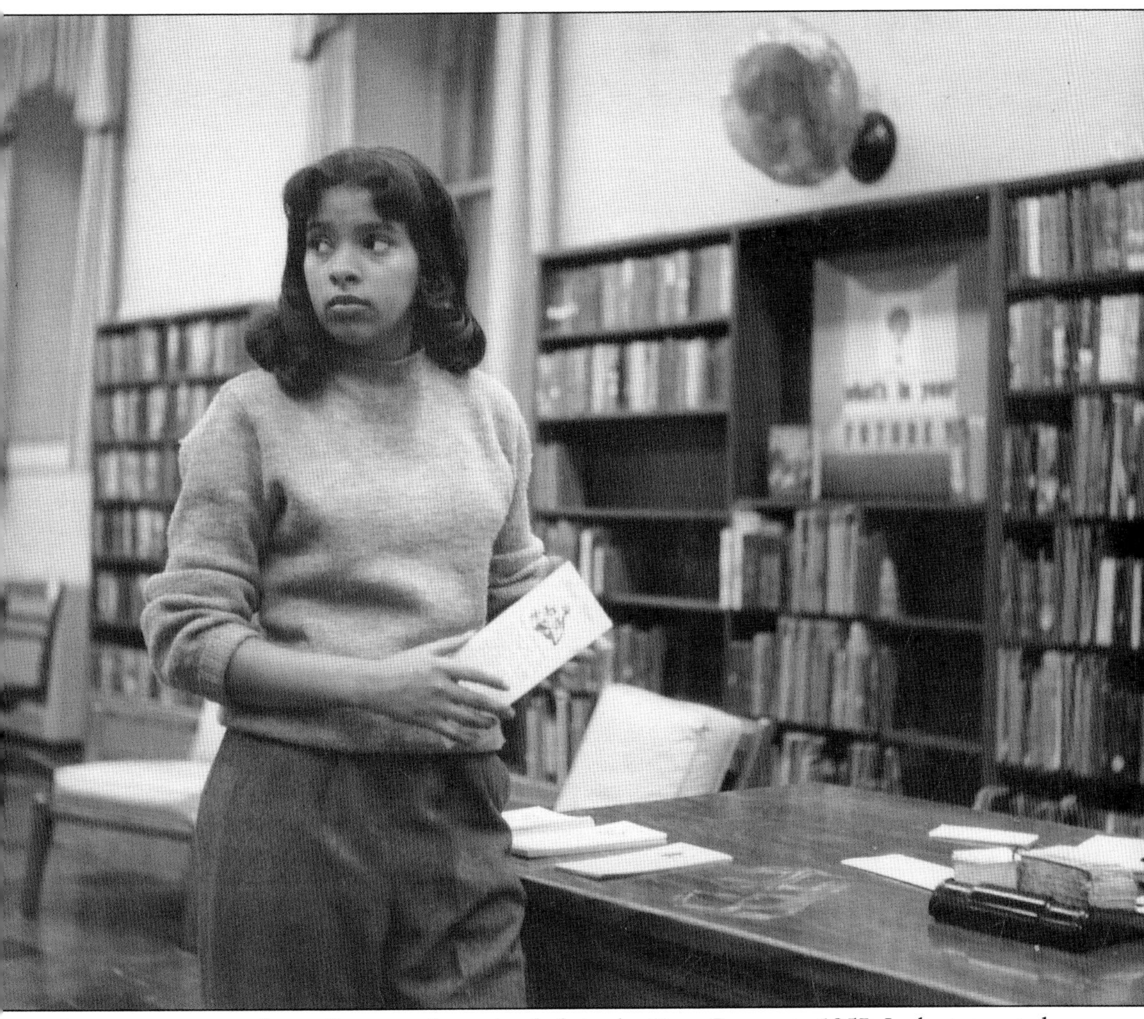

A young woman picks up literature from the desk in the Teen Corner in 1957. Is she interested in possible careers or educational opportunities? Maybe she has a question about bestsellers. In the 1950s, adult fiction was becoming more popular among this segment of the population than teenage stories. In the 1990s, graphic novels were of interest to young adults, so the library added them to its collections at the main library and at its branches. (Ann Zane.)

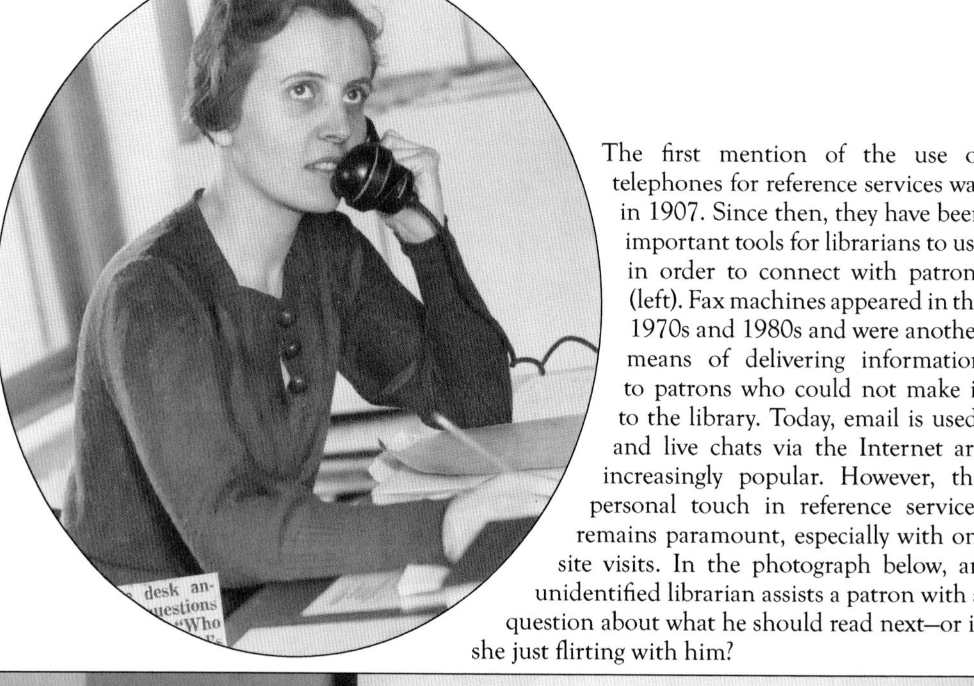

The first mention of the use of telephones for reference services was in 1907. Since then, they have been important tools for librarians to use in order to connect with patrons (left). Fax machines appeared in the 1970s and 1980s and were another means of delivering information to patrons who could not make it to the library. Today, email is used, and live chats via the Internet are increasingly popular. However, the personal touch in reference services remains paramount, especially with on-site visits. In the photograph below, an unidentified librarian assists a patron with a question about what he should read next—or is she just flirting with him?

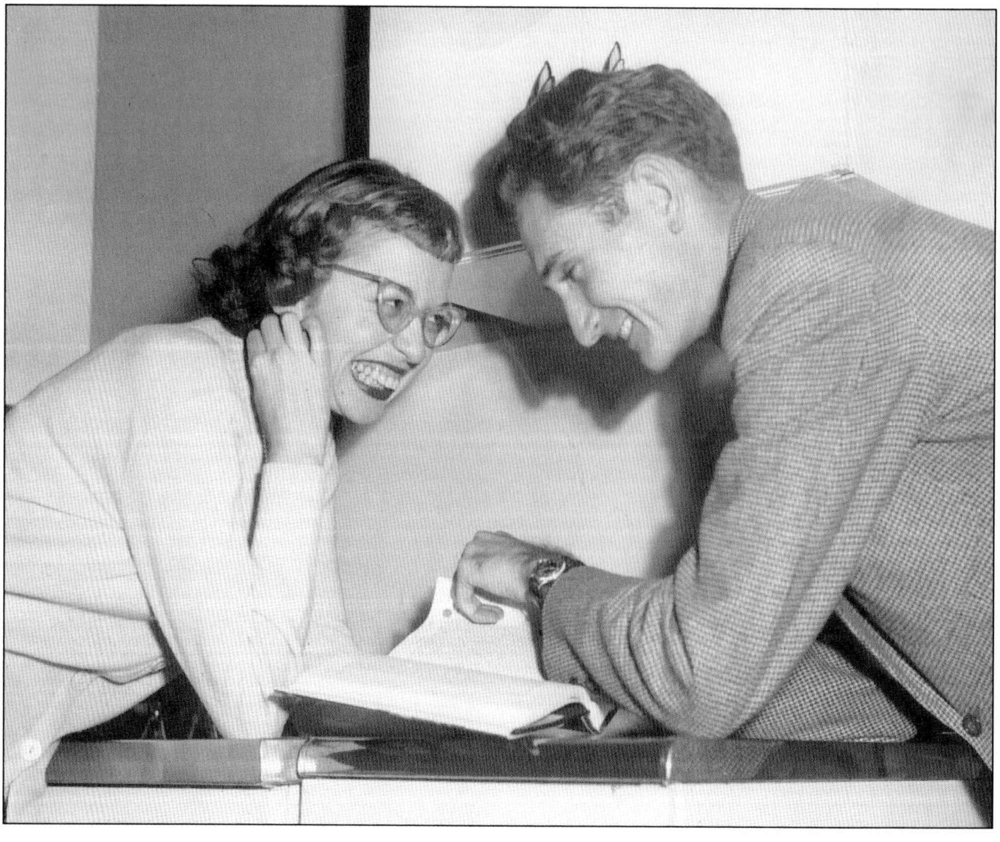

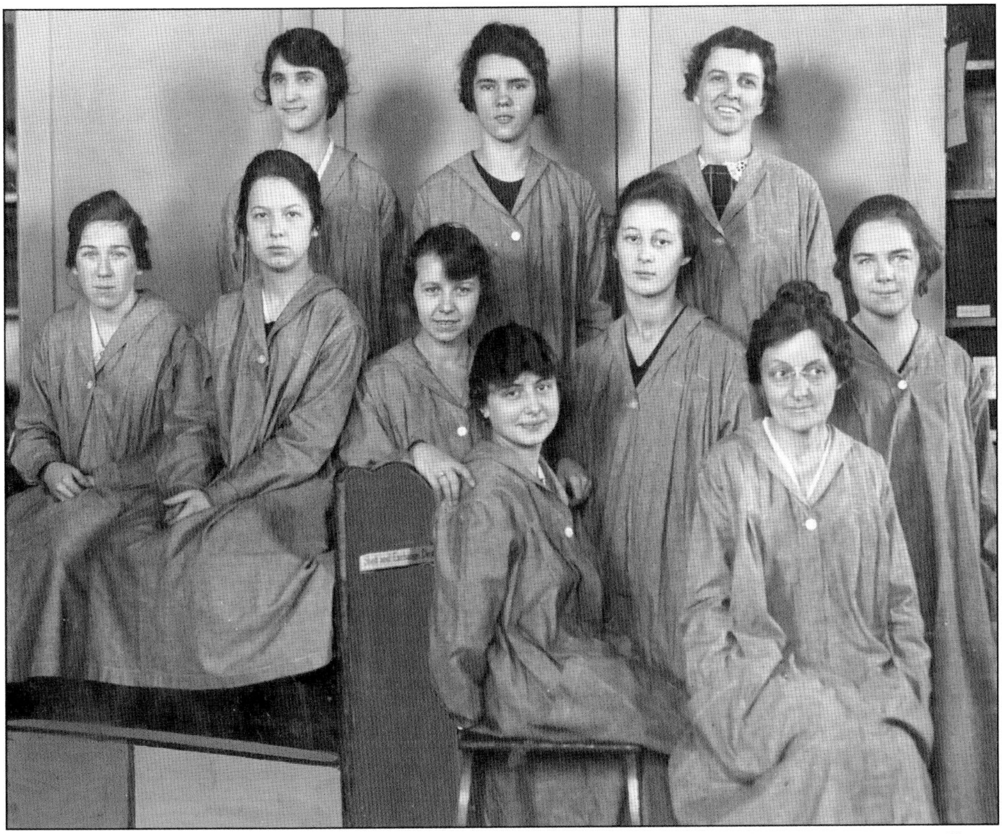

The library has always made spaces available to groups to discuss historical topics or current affairs, civic issues or social concerns, or the arts and humanities. In the above photograph, a group of Brownies meet at Newark Public Library in 1919 for a day of arts and crafts. Below are members of the Committee to Abolish Discrimination listening to a librarian describe information resources at one of its meetings in 1947. Some of these groups were independent, and some of them were sponsored by the library. (Above, Newark Public Library; below, George Van.)

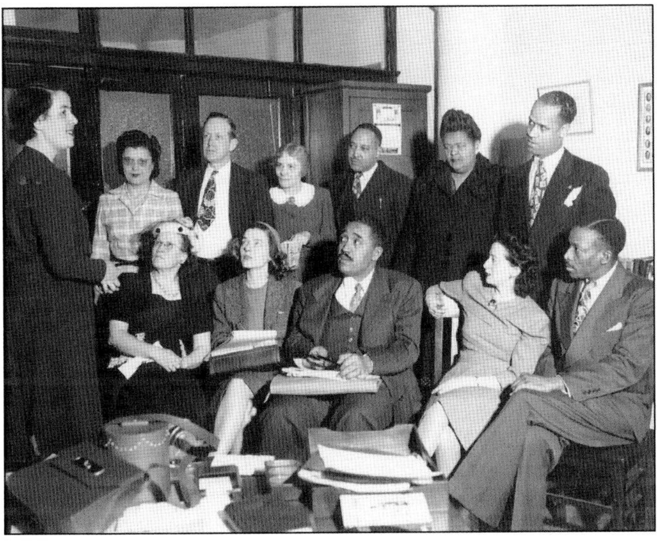

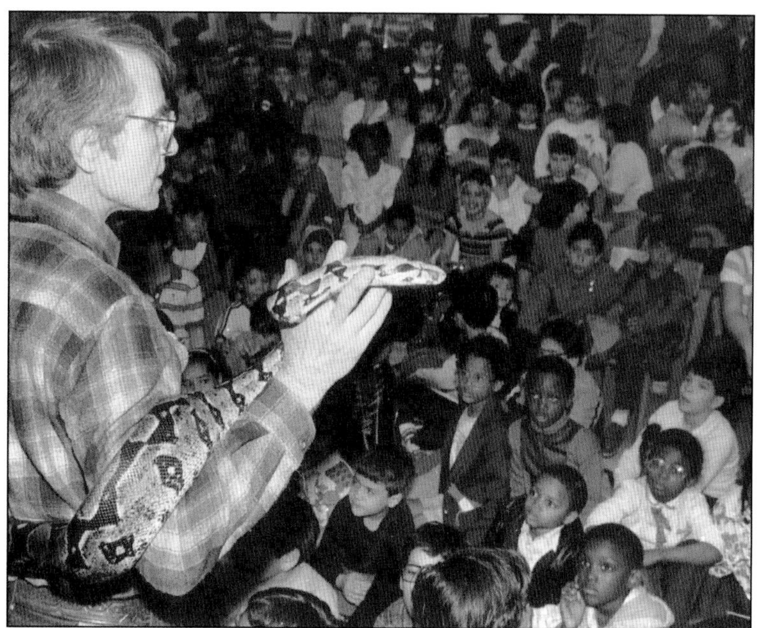

Public programming has been an important part of the library's services, frequently partnering with neighboring institutions to introduce children and their parents, and others, to the wider world. In this photograph from 1986, Vince Sharp from the Turtle Back Zoo shows off a boa constrictor to an audience at the North End Branch. (The *Star-Ledger*.)

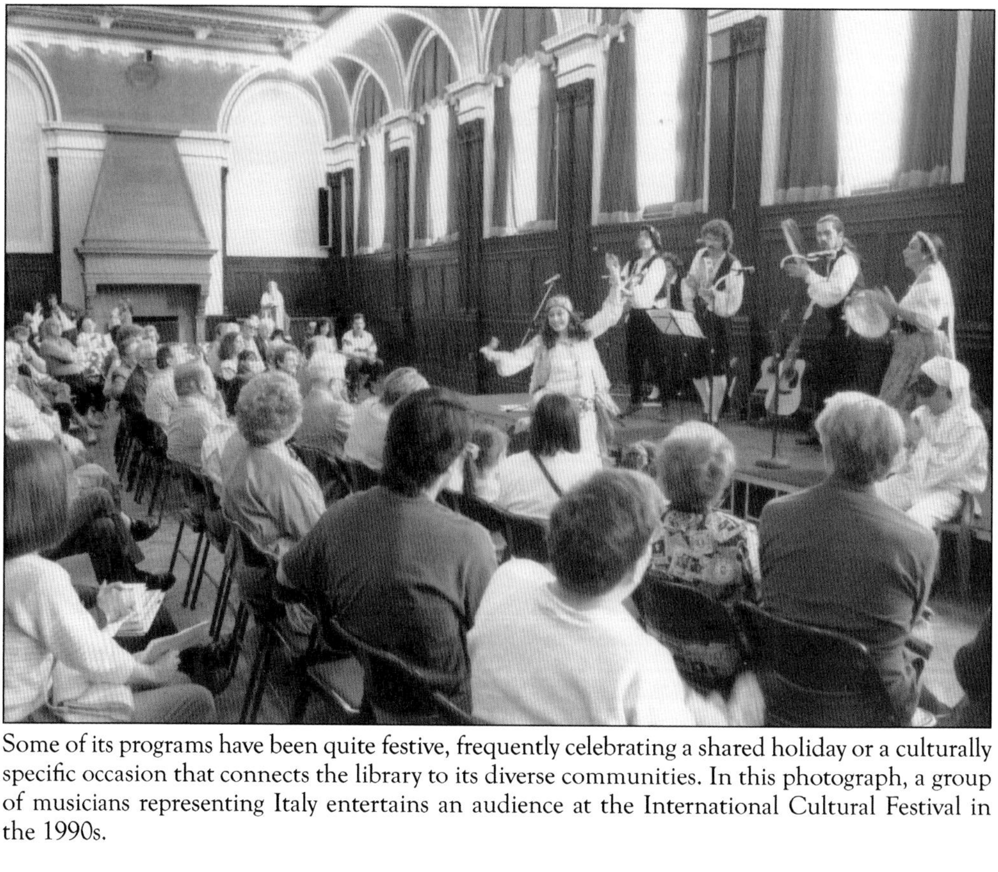

Some of its programs have been quite festive, frequently celebrating a shared holiday or a culturally specific occasion that connects the library to its diverse communities. In this photograph, a group of musicians representing Italy entertains an audience at the International Cultural Festival in the 1990s.

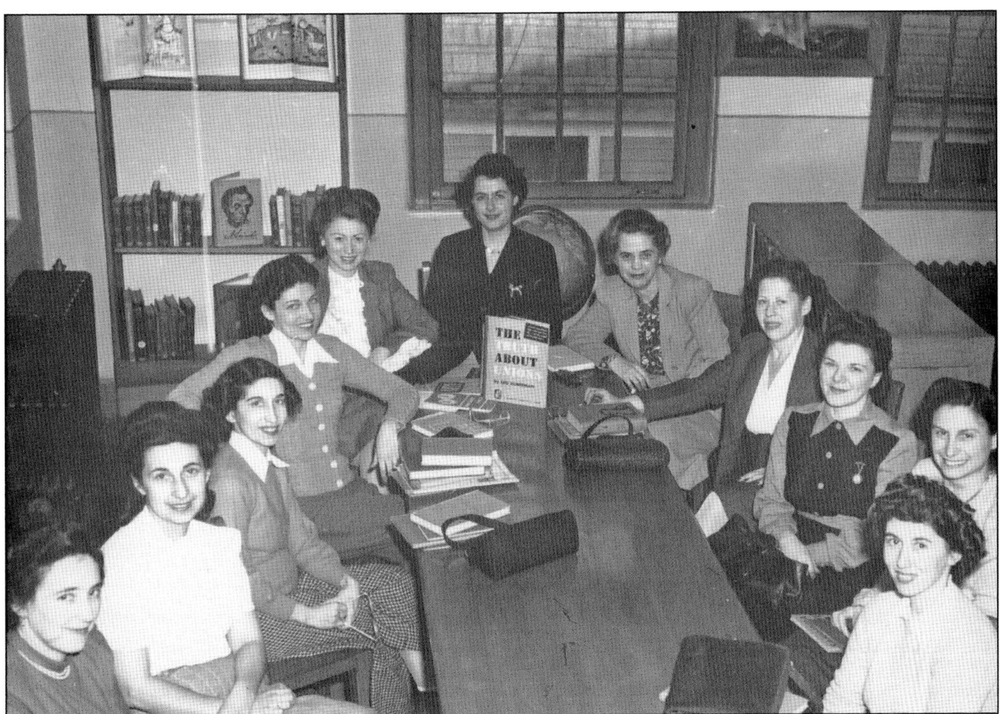

In the postwar era, the library worked with unions to put together a collection of books dealing with labor and industrial relations. In the photograph above, a group of women get together to discuss the role of unions in a democratic society. (Henningsen's Studio.)

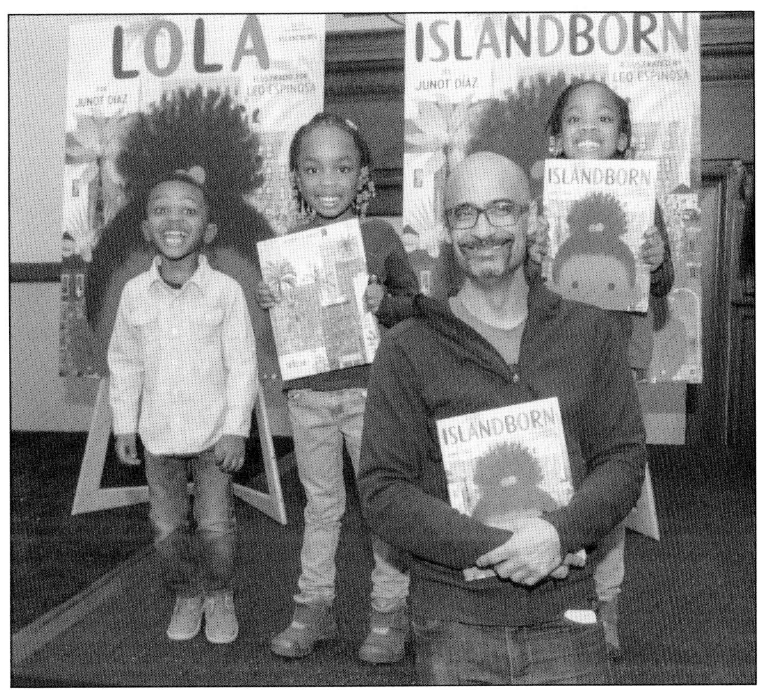

After speaking about his children's book *Islandborn* (English edition) or *Lola* (Spanish edition) in 2018, Junot Diaz smiles at the camera with three very happy readers. Illustrated by Leo Espinoza, the book is the story of a young Dominican American girl living in the Bronx, trying to discover her island roots.

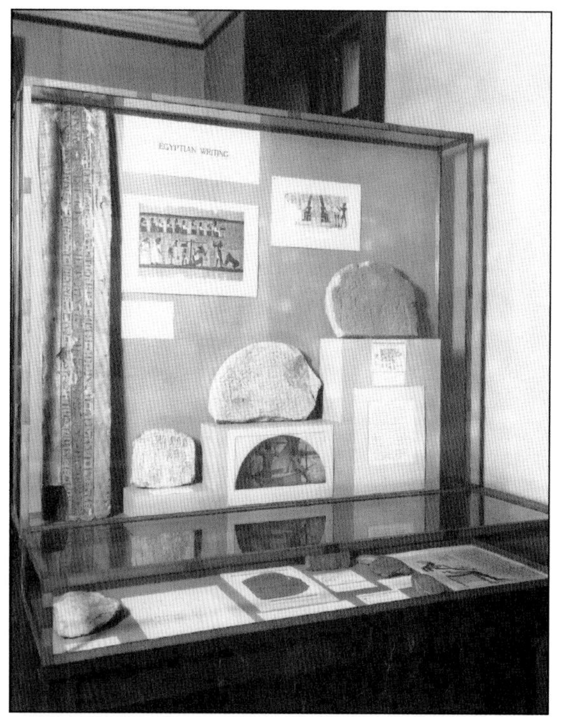

As soon as the new building on Washington Street opened in 1901, the Newark Public Library began to host exhibitions on numerous topics several times a year. Many of them highlighted books and objects from the library's own collections; others included loans from various institutions and organizations. *The Origins of Writing* exhibition of 1930 showcased Egyptian scarabs, Babylonian tablets, Greek papyri, Latin manuscripts, and two bound copies of the Koran in Arabic.

In a lavish display of patriotism, the library mounted an exhibition of war posters in 1942. Newark was a major point of disembarkation for the troops trained in New Jersey. In addition, the men, women, and children who remained on the home front were eager for information on the war and its progress across the Pacific and in Europe.

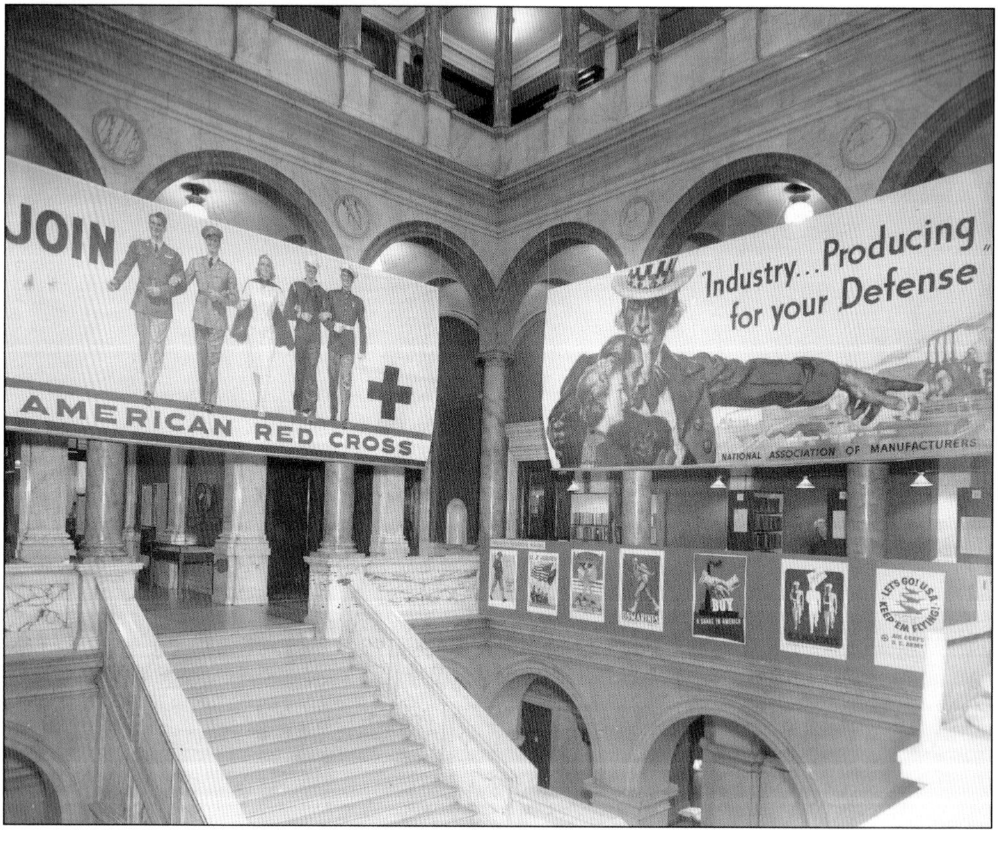

Four

COLLECTIONS

On the facade of the new building are engraved the words: philosophy, religion, sociology, philology, science, fine arts, and history, the seven major areas of nonfiction. Curiously enough, literature is missing, and yet novels, short stories, plays, and poems were all very popular. At the time, though, fiction in public libraries was a controversial topic. In 1892, it was recorded that 80 percent of the books borrowed were fiction. "Novels are of such character," the librarian reported, "that no permanent injury can come from reading them." Between 1904 and 1939, the library published a guide to fiction (in eight editions) entitled *A Thousand of the Best Novels*.

The first collection in the Newark Public Library included both fiction and nonfiction books selected from the Newark Library Association's collection. From this modest selection of 7,000, the collection grew dramatically, and special subject areas were developed. The Business Branch, specializing in city directories, trade directories, investment guides, information on labor relations, and other topics, opened in 1904; it closed in 1997. Government documents and information on patents and trademarks were added in 1906. The New Jersey Collection was founded in 1929; it received its own room in 1951, and in 2006, it was renamed the Charles F. Cummings New Jersey Information Center.

Collecting art books and music scores was important from the very beginning. Eventually, a picture collection was established. This "institute of visual instruction" was an amazing assemblage of prints and photographs on all kinds of topics. Today, the special collections division includes etchings from old masters, prints from modern artists, woodcuts from Japan, and other printed materials from other countries, cultures, and traditions.

The branches, the topic of the next chapter, catered to the various ethnic groups within the city—and their various religious makeup. As the demography of the city changed, so too did the outreach focus of the Newark Public Library. In 1989, the library established the Sala Hispanoamericana (later called the New Jersey Hispanic Research and Information Center) and the African American Room (later renamed the James Brown African American Room). The latest additions to these special collections are the Philip Roth Personal Library in 2021 and the LGBTQ Resource Center in 2019.

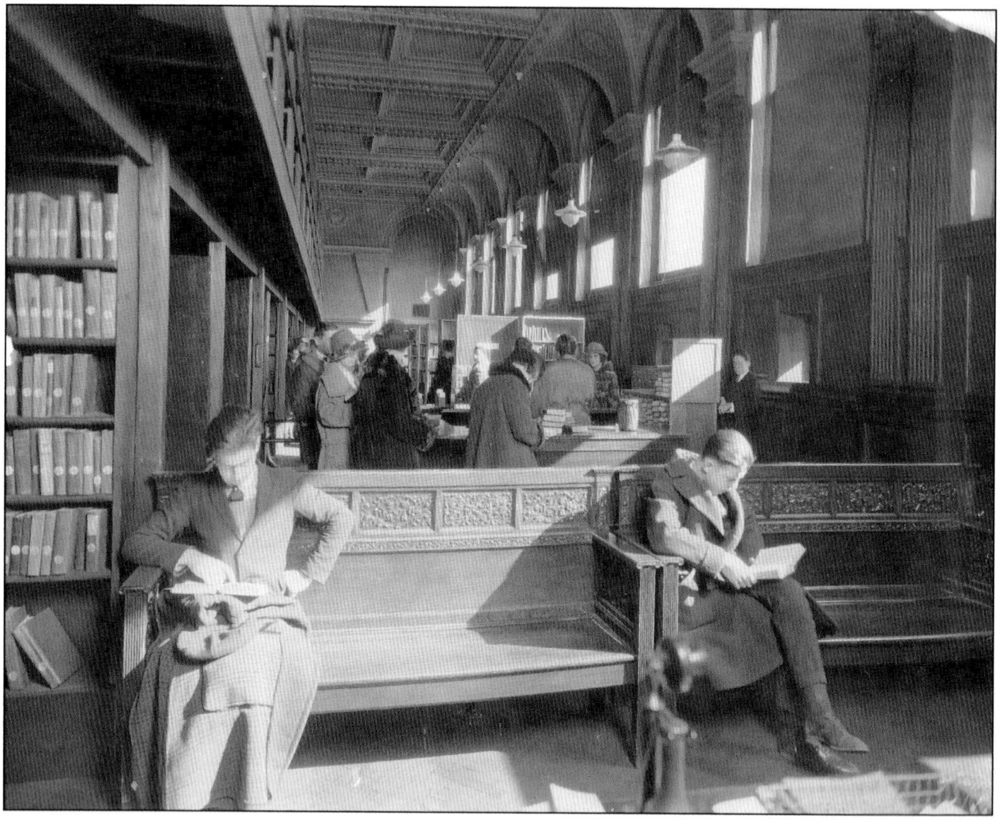

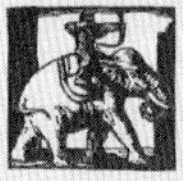

RUDYARD KIPLING

POET AND STORY TELLER

Rudyard Kipling was born in Bombay, India, of English parentage 70 years ago, December 30, 1865. He was educated in England at United Services College, Westward Ho!, North Devon. He returned to India to be assistant editor on the Civil and Military Gazette at Lahore, until 1889. In 1886 his first book, Departmental Ditties, was published. Among his best loved works are The Light That Failed, Barrack-Room Ballads, Jungle Book, Just So Stories and Kim.

All we have of freedom - all we use
or know -
This our fathers bought for us, long
and long ago.

From The Old Issue, composed on the outbreak of the Boer War

NEWARK PUBLIC LIBRARY

On the back of the above photograph is written just one word: "Fiction." In the first edition of his list of *A Thousand of the Best Novels* in 1904, in which he included old books frequently used and new books of critical acclaim, John Cotton Dana stated, "Novels must be praised. They belong, with the dramas and the poems, among the good things which make our heritage, which unite men [and women] by community of thought and feeling, and which make it a joy to have the art of reading." In 1890, the two "best" novels checked out by patrons were *Black Beauty* by Anna Sewell and *The Sign of the Four* by Sir Arthur Conan Doyle. By the mid-century (1960), the two novels were *The Constant Image* by Marica Davenport and *The Leopard* by Giuseppe di Lampedusa. Kipling's works (left) made the list several times.

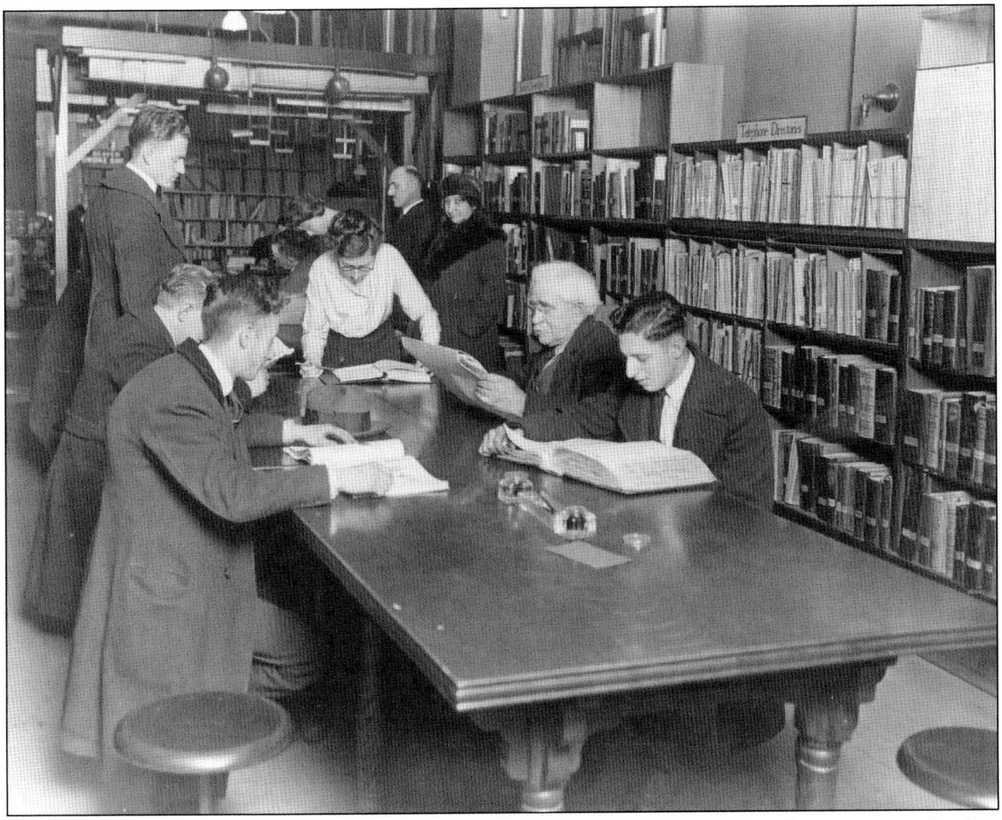

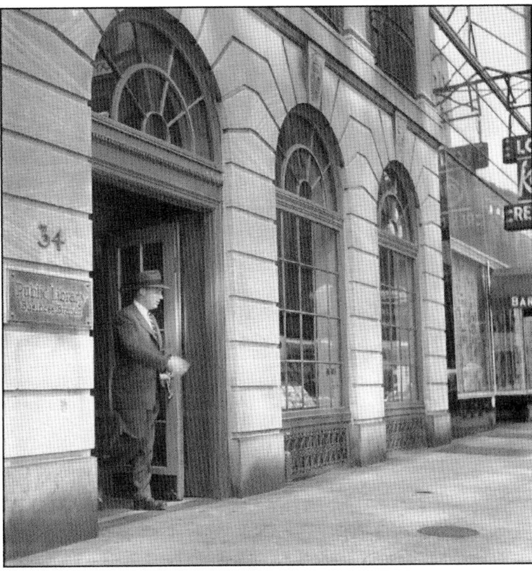

A collection of city and trade directories; investment, financial, and tax information; and other books, pamphlets, and magazines on accounting, marketing, personnel management, real estate, and related topics formed the nucleus of a collection devoted to business issues. Located originally on Academy Street in downtown Newark in 1904, it became known as the Business Branch in 1908 and the Business Information Center in 1990. It was the first of its kind in the country. (Ewing Galloway.)

The Business Branch's own three-story building opened on Commerce Street in 1927, still close to the intersection of Broad and Market Streets. It served businessmen, professionals, clerks, workers, men, and women at the beginning, middle, or end of their careers. It closed in 1997, and its contents were transferred to the main library. (Ann Zane.)

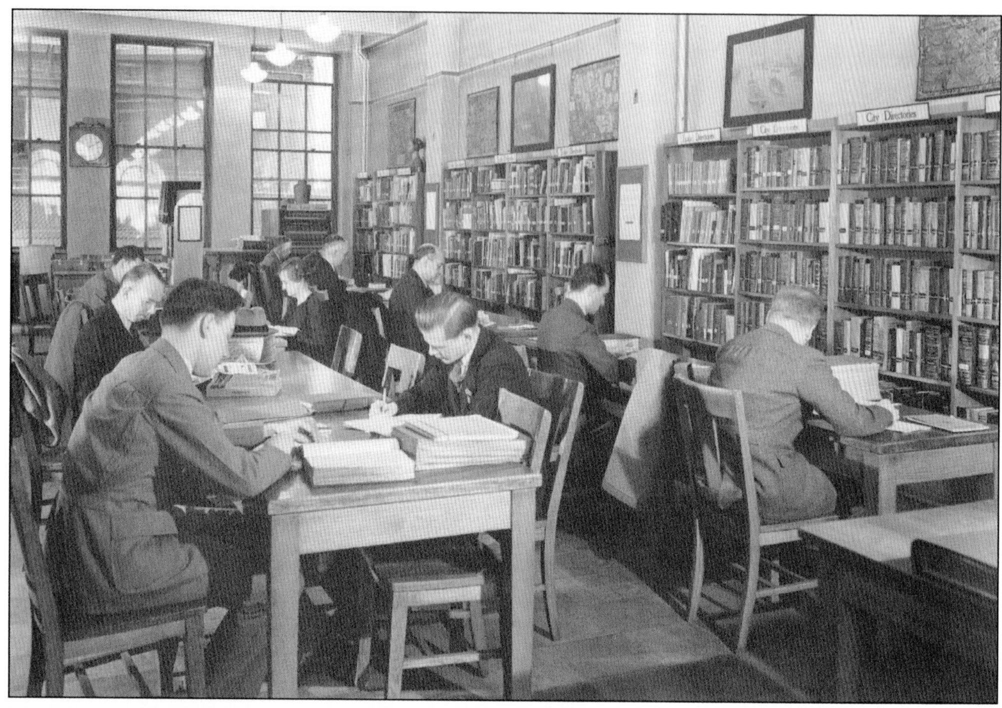

In 1954, the library noted that "bright young men often map their careers by studying business trends," "lawyers depend on the extensive collection to trace heirs," and even "Prudential girls" use the library to seek lost beneficiaries. (Laura von Schnarendorf.)

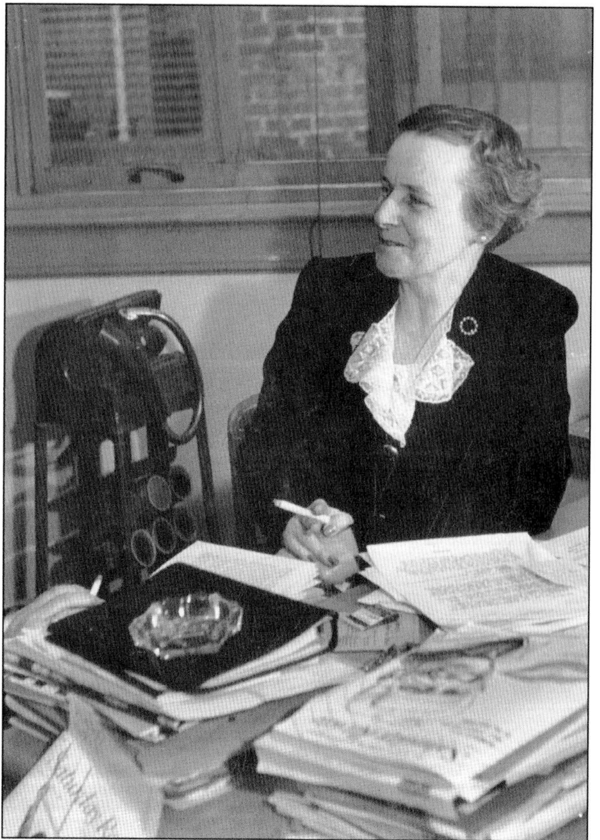

Recruited at a women's suffrage rally in 1915, Marion Manley quickly demonstrated "executive ability," and from 1925 to 1954, she served as the chief librarian at the Business Branch. "What I have tried to do," she summed up her career at her retirement, "is to make the business library part of the working community, tied to the economic life of the country." (Ann Zane.)

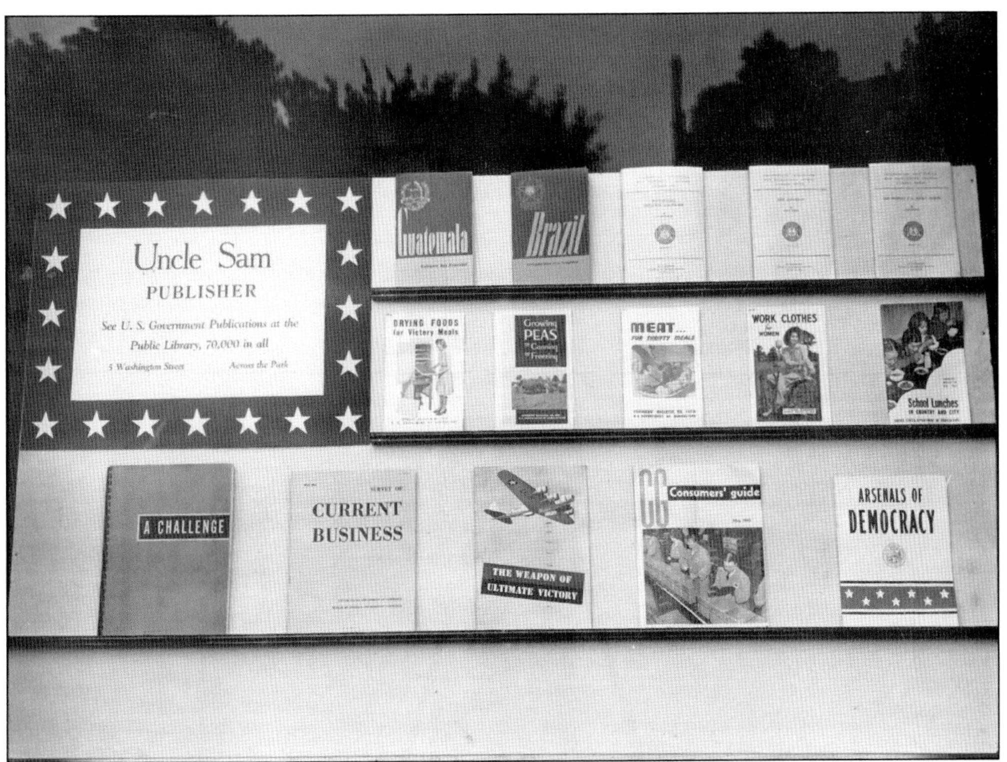

The library became a federal depository for US government documents in 1906 and for New Jersey government documents in 1963. Its responsibility was to accept and preserve statistical data, legislative and executive reports, and other information produced by the US government so that all American citizens could have free and open access to materials relating to their democratic institutions. (Handy & Boesser.)

In the same year, 1906, the library also became a center for patents and trademarks. Expert librarians have been providing information, assistance, and instructions in this area ever since, but they do not offer legal interpretation or advice.

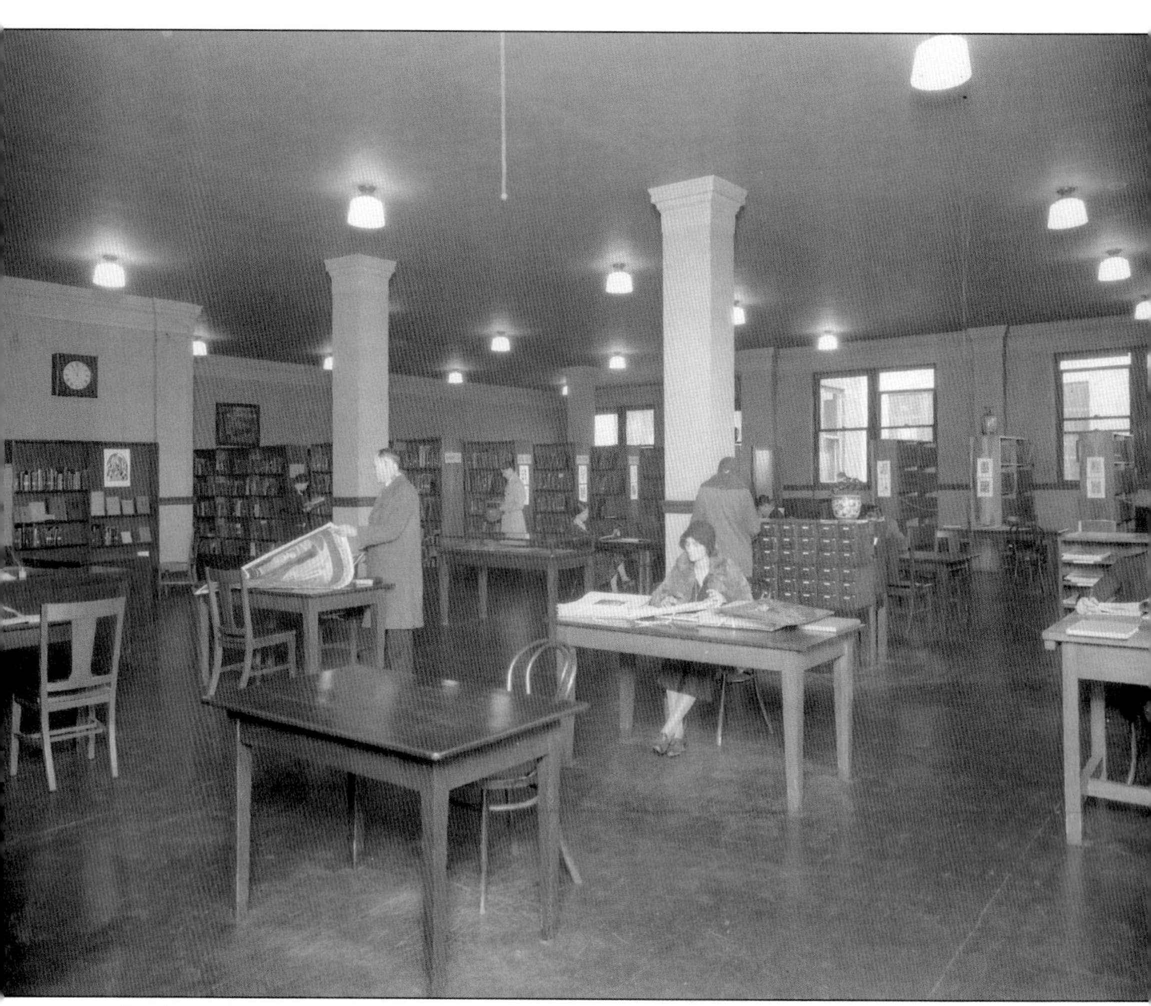

The first exhibition of art books was held in 1893 in the West Park building when Frank Hill was the librarian. It was recorded that over 2,000 people attended this exhibition. His successor, John Cotton Dana, believed that some people learned through books and others learned through objects, so he created a separate art department in 1907. Books on artists and artistic movements as well as manuals on paints, colors, and techniques were all included. Later, musical scores and books on music and musicians were incorporated. By 1928, the art and music department included over 13,000 items. It became the state center for art research in 1972 and for music research in 1978.

In 1906, Spaulding Frazer, a lawyer and composer, raised $525 for the purchase of over 600 musical scores. The Newark Madrigal Society then contributed 126 sheets of music. By 1909, the library had 1,462 bound volumes of operas and operettas, classical music and popular music, studies on musical movements, and biographies of composers and musicians.

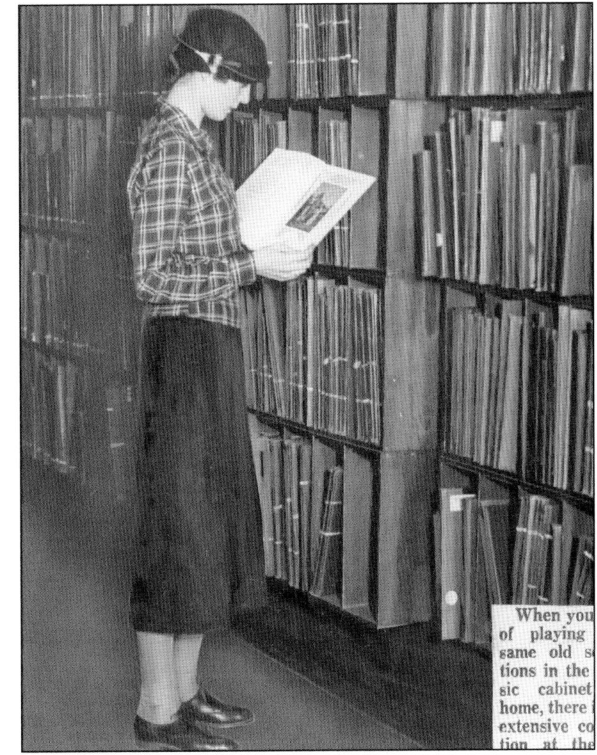

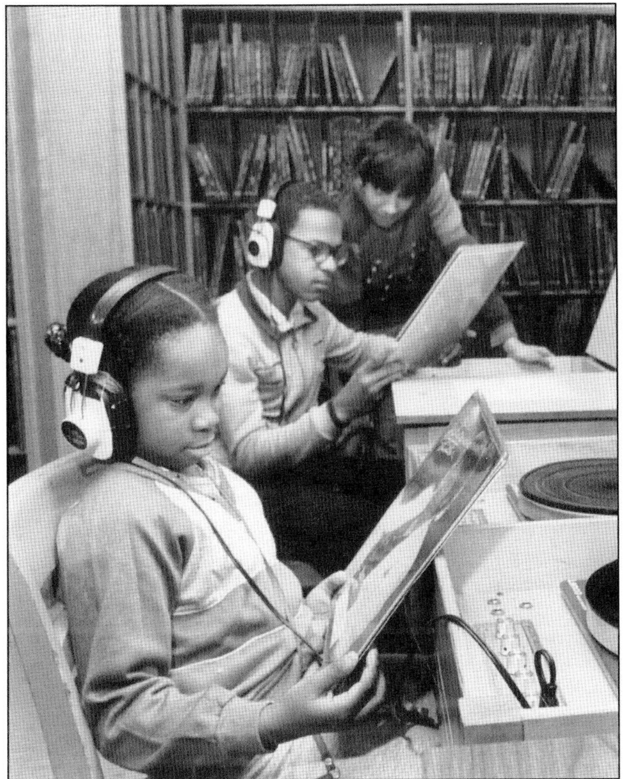

In 1940, the Griffith Foundation, the leading seller of musical instruments in Newark, donated hundreds of 78 rpm records. By the 1960s, 33⅓ rpm records were replacing them; by the 1970s, cassette tapes were replacing the records; and by the 1990s, CDs were replacing the tapes. No matter the format, though, patrons were able to check them out or to hear them in soundproof booths. (The *Star-Ledger*.)

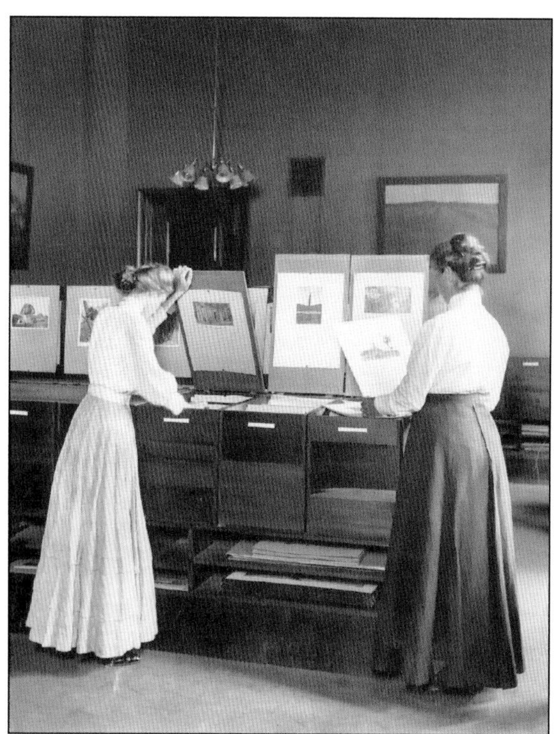

The picture collection began in 1908 with 270 large, mounted pictures from books, periodicals, and other published sources that could be checked out by patrons for wall decorations or by teachers for educational purposes. By 1943, there were over 200,000 pictures covering topics as diverse as plants and animals; glass, paper, and silk; automobiles and weather vanes; portraits from A to Z; and costumes subdivided by country. (William F. Cone.)

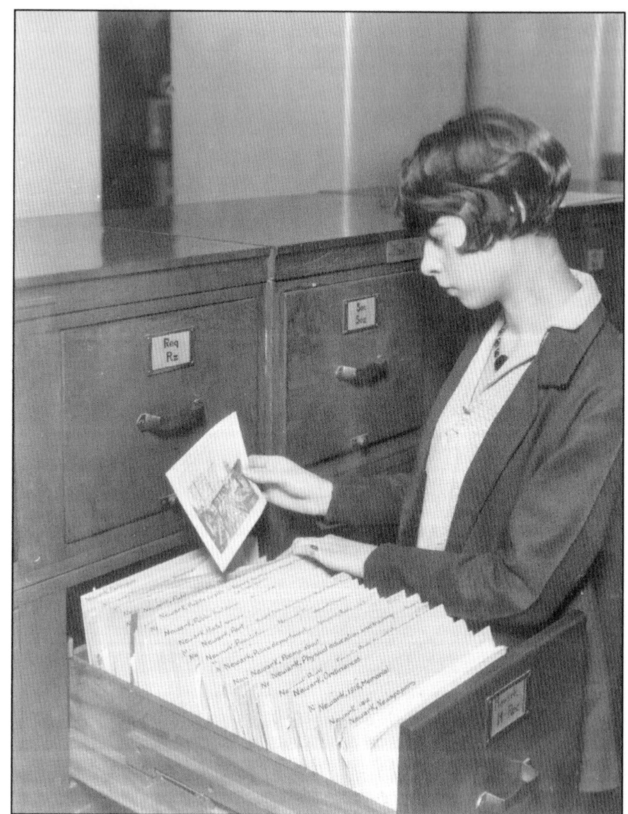

Reproductions of paintings and photographs of sculptures, both arranged by artists, complemented the art books, and so did images of historic and modern buildings, all designed as aids in the study of architecture.

Julia Sabine started in the art and music department in 1927. Eventually, she became the supervising librarian. She retired in 1971. She was an expert in rare books, fine prints, and art librarianship, which she taught at Rutgers University's Library School. A colleague once wrote of her, "Her often-quiet manner was combined with an unbroken thirst for knowledge and scholarship" (Commercial Photographic Company.)

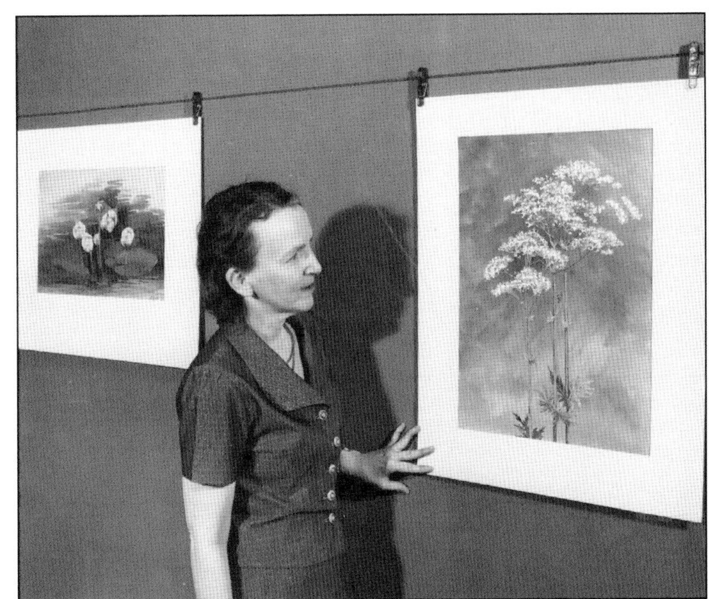

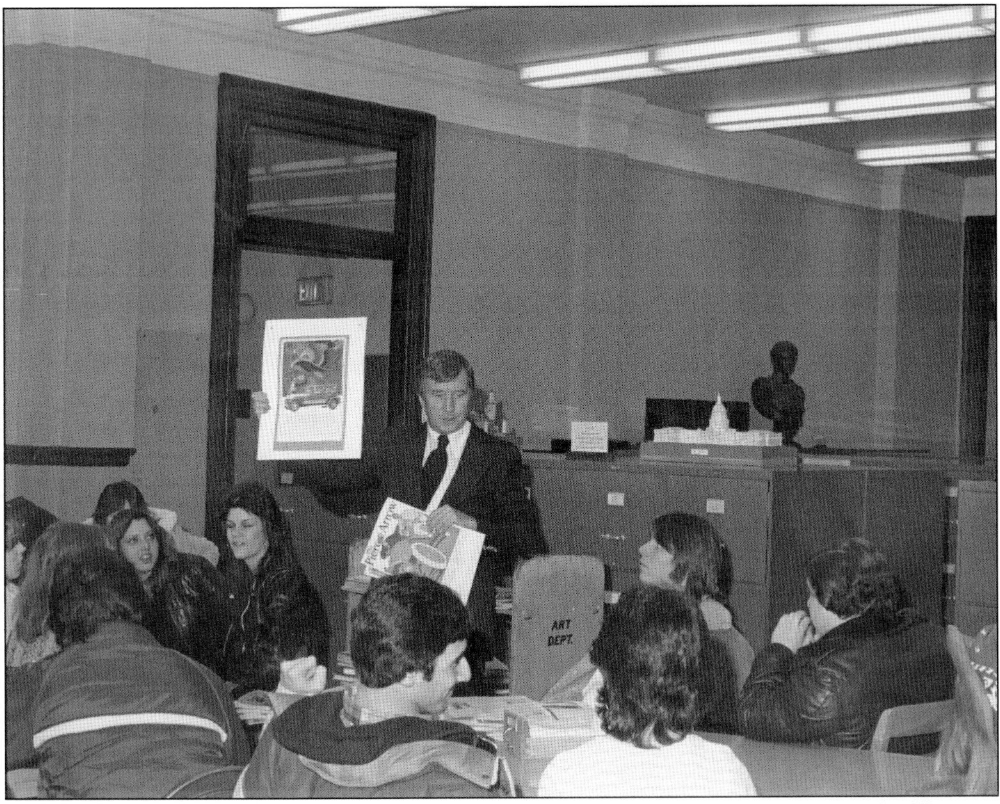

Over the six decades that he worked for the Newark Public Library, William J. "Bill" Dane advanced from clerk to librarian to supervisor. At the end of his career, he was calling himself the "keeper of prints." Always curious and inquisitive, Dane increased the size and quality of the special collections. In 1997, the print collection was renamed the William J. Dane Fine Prints Collection. (Peter Silvia.)

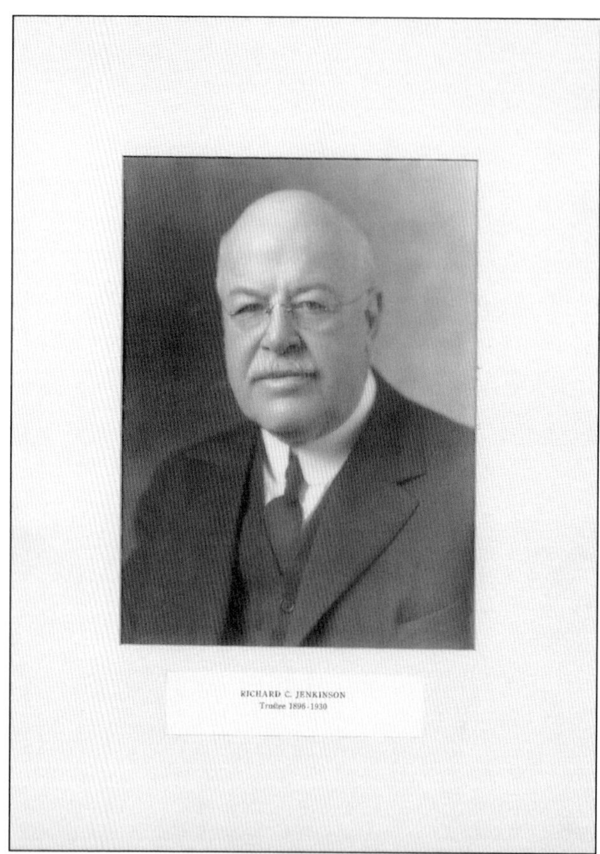

In 1925, Richard C. Jenkinson, a longtime trustee of the Newark Public Library, donated his collection of rare books exemplifying the history of the printed book and written communication as well as the arts of typography and fine printing to the library. The purpose was to show the best in type, ink, and paper that men and women of talent have used to produce books throughout the centuries.

In this image, a library assistant shows off the title page for *A Dictionary of the English Language* by Samuel Johnson (1785), one of the many treasures in the rare book collection of the Newark Public Library. Other treasures include Sumerian cuneiform tablets, Egyptian papyrus, scrolls from Ethiopia, Islamic manuscripts, medieval codices, and Asian woodcut books. (Photograph by John A. Gibson Jr.; courtesy of the *Star-Ledger*.)

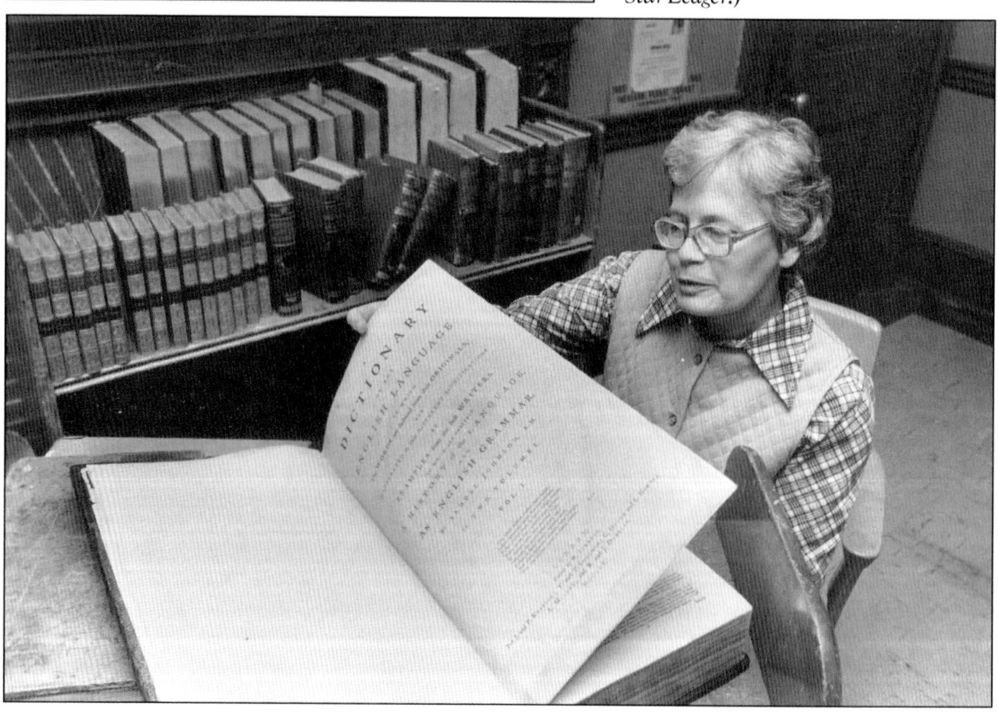

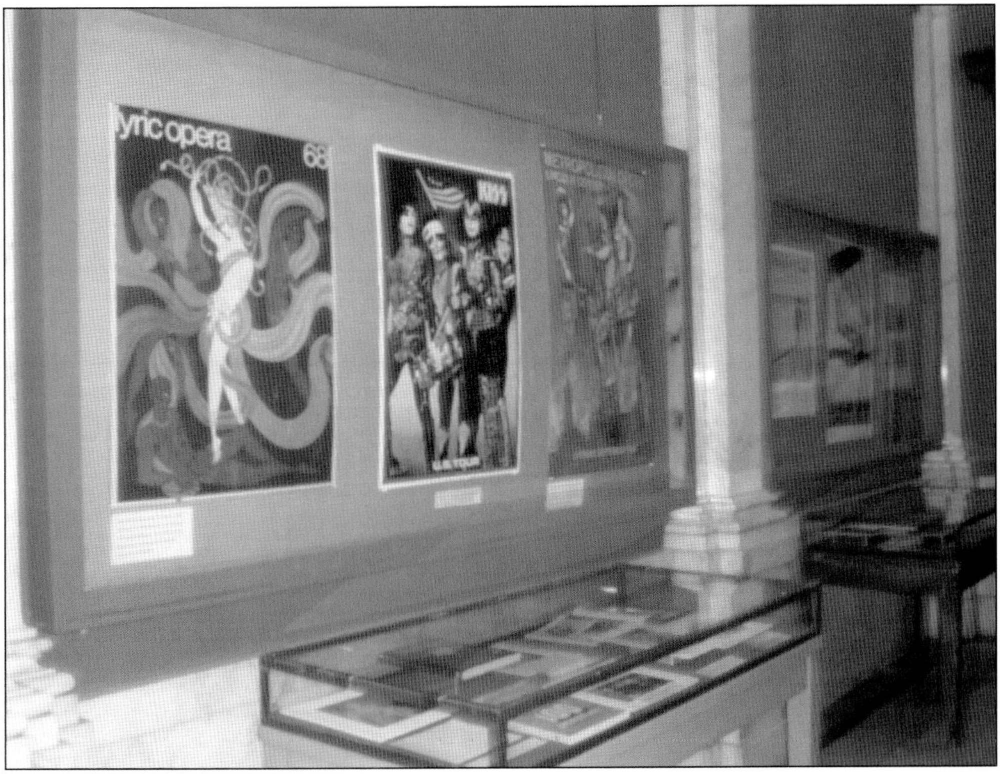

Today, the special collections division preserves and provides access to thousands of rare books, artists' books, fine prints, and other works on paper in order to enhance, inspire, and encourage the study of the visual arts. It includes 25,000 fine prints, 5,000 posters, and 1,000 autographs, plus artists' books, pop-up books, and rare books. Greeting cards and postcards, broadsides, and advertisements as well as photographs, drawings, and other examples of the graphic arts were also collected. Above is the display of musical posters on the wall and related books in the case. Below are three examples of shopping bags, which were collected as "everyday objects of good design," in Dana's words.

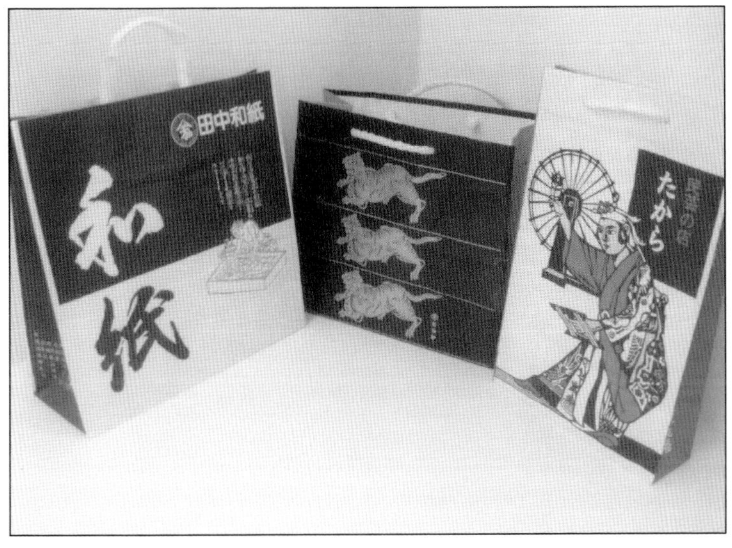

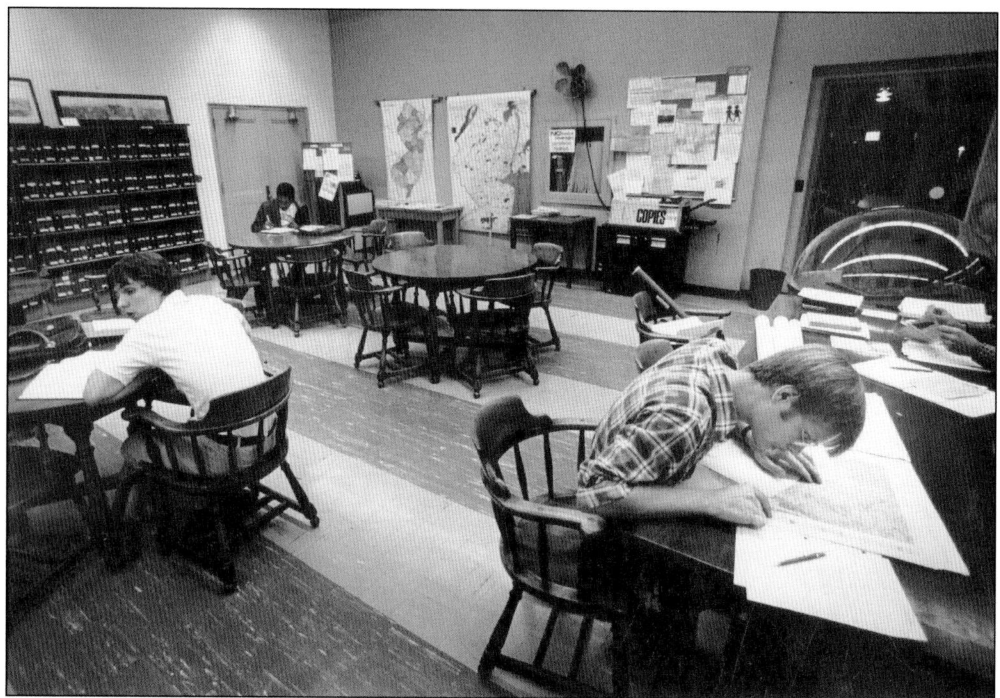

Materials relating to New Jersey have been collected since the library's founding in 1889, but not until 1929 was the material organized in a distinct collection that encompassed books, pamphlets, periodicals, directories, manuscript material, government documents, maps, and photographs. In 1951, it became a separate department. This is a photograph of the room with researchers dating from 1982. (Photograph by John A. Gibson Jr.; courtesy of *the Star-Ledger*.)

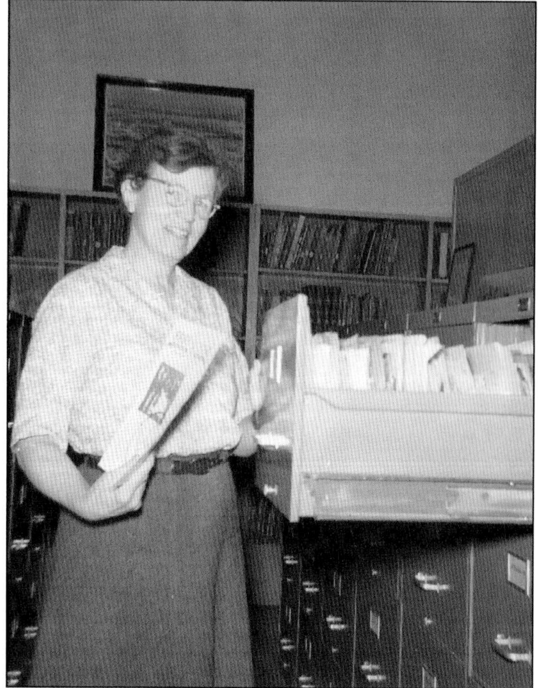

Several individuals have managed the New Jersey Collection, including Miriam Studley (pictured) and Charles F. Cummings, both of whom wrote extensively about Newark's history in local newspapers. Studley's articles were entitled "When Newark was Younger," and were published in the *Newark Evening News* from April 1949 to May 1950. (Civil Air Patrol Essex Squadron.)

From 1963 to 2005, Charles F. Cummings worked in the New Jersey Room as a librarian and a historian. Over the years, his knowledge of the city's history led to his appointment as the city historian, and throughout his tenure, he enthusiastically shared his knowledge through exhibitions, lectures, classes, and a long-running series of articles known as "Knowing Newark" for the local newspaper, the *Star-Ledger*. (The *Star-Ledger*.)

In 2006, the collection of current and historic materials relating to Newark, Essex County, and New Jersey was renamed the Charles F. Cummings New Jersey Information Center. It continues to provide library users with research-level books, pamphlets, newspapers, documents, manuscripts, archives, and photographs. This is a photograph of the current staff (from left to right, Tom Ankner, Greg Guderian, Beth Zak-Cohen, and Vanessa Castaldo) while the room was undergoing renovations in 2023.

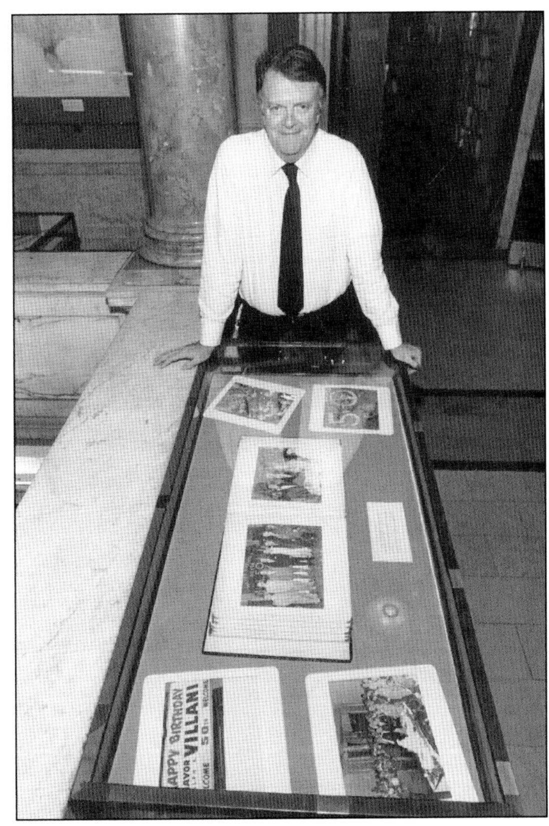

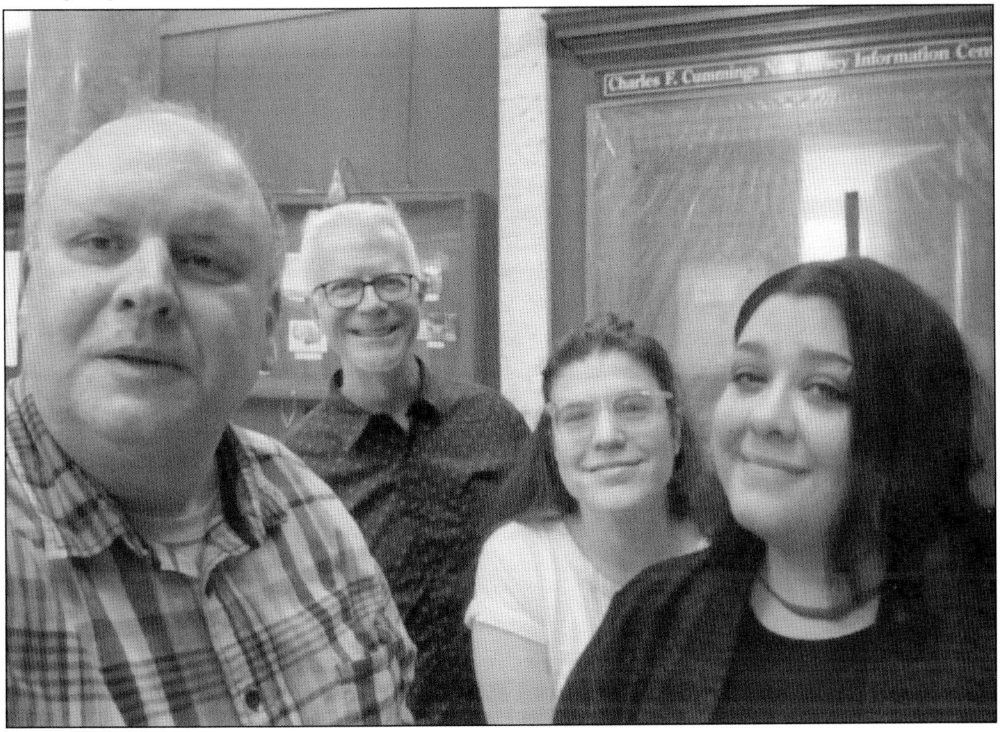

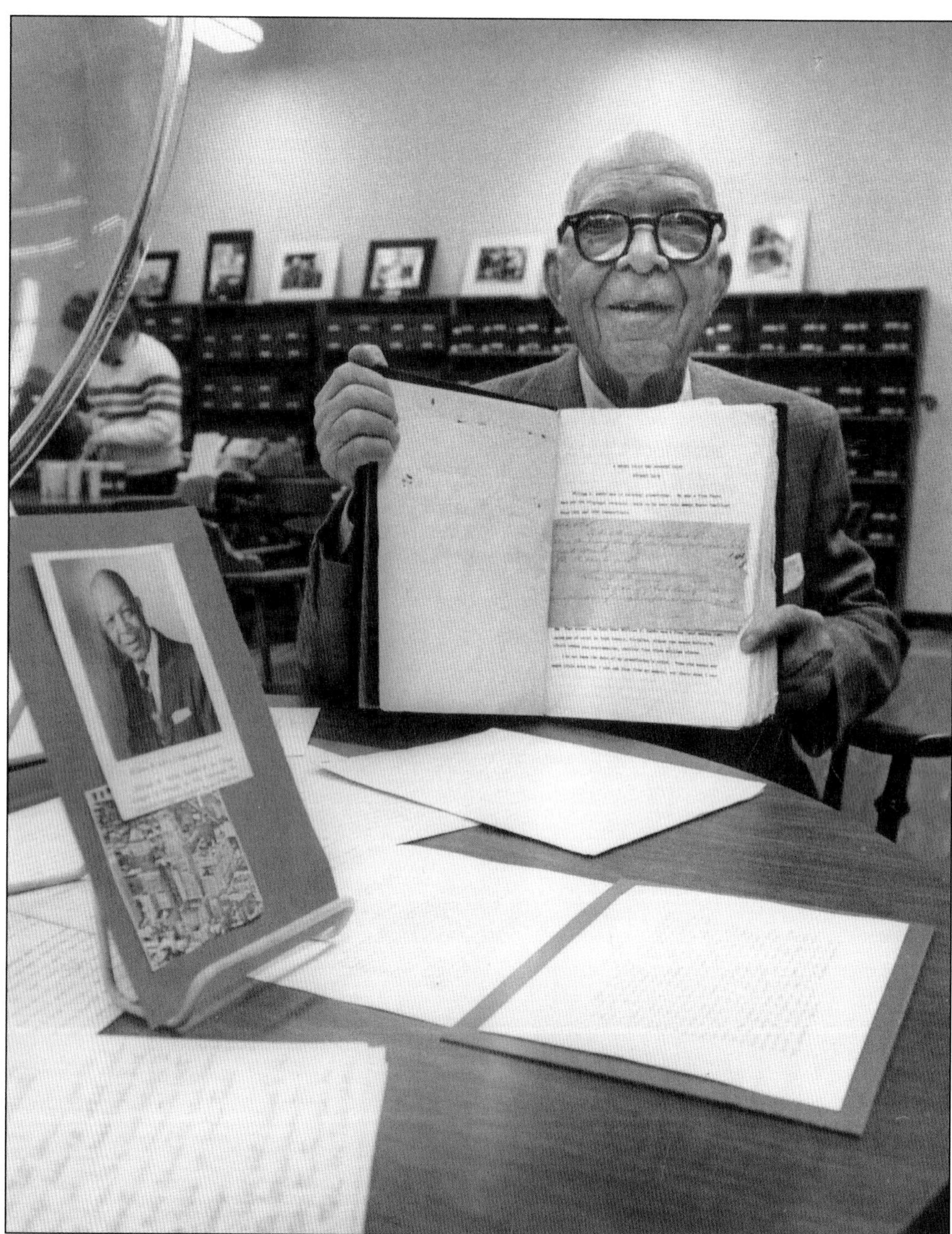

William M. Ashby was "a passionate writer" and "a voracious reader," according to his friend Walt Chambers. The first black social worker in Newark, Ashby was a civil rights activist involved in the Urban League and other organizations. His autobiography, *Tales without Hate*, chronicled his journey from poverty in Virginia to education at Lincoln University in Pennsylvania, from waiting on tables to leading social justice campaigns in Newark. He was an avid user of the library, especially the New Jersey Room, which he visited regularly to prepare his speeches and his essays on all topics, including one on the singing group Peter, Paul and Mary. In this photograph, he is surrounded by some of the treasures in his own papers, which he donated to the New Jersey Room in 1980.

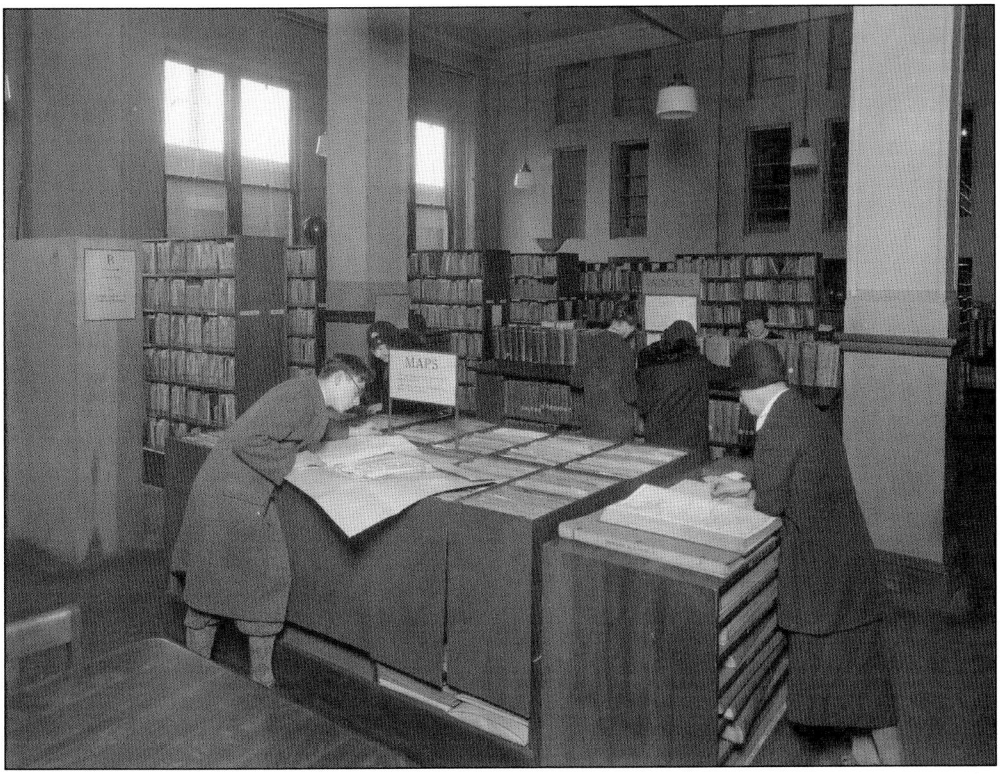

Maps were a popular source of visual information that patrons found very useful. In 1927, the chief of the Map Division of the Library of Congress noted that the Newark Public Library's map collection was unlike "any public library anywhere in America" because of "its advanced method of keeping and serving maps."

Because of their ephemeral nature, college catalogs were not formally cataloged but shelved alphabetically according to the name of the issuing institution in the education department. Like the pamphlet collection, which was another group of brochures, leaflets, and booklets on current, popular topics that became quickly out-of-date, these catalogs had to be weeded and replaced on a regular basis.

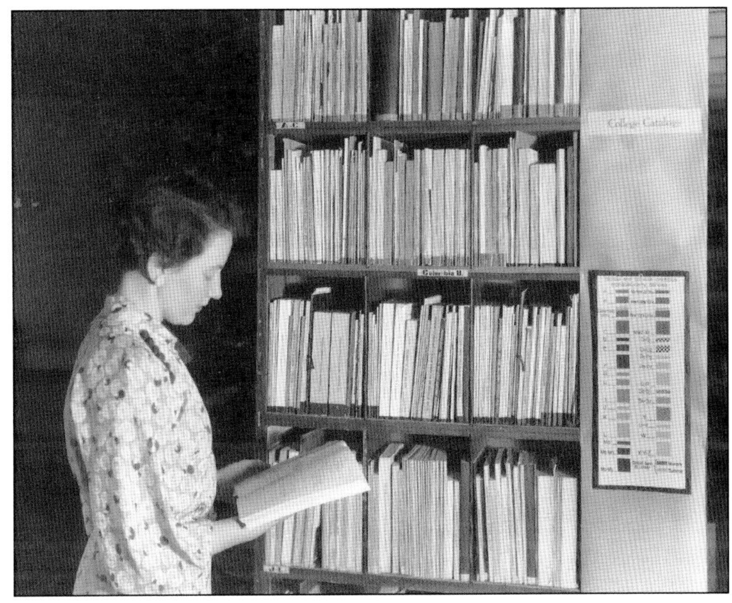

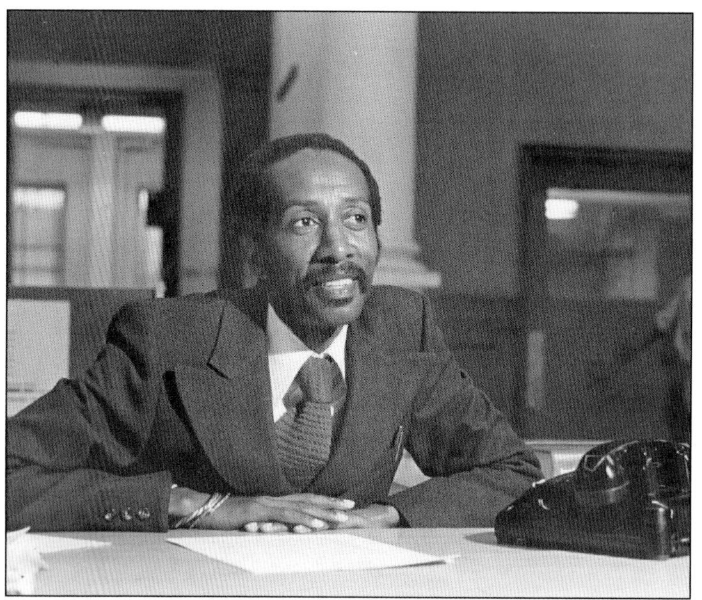

James Brown was a librarian at the Newark Public Library for 29 years. He was instrumental in expanding the library's resources on the African American experience in the 1960s, 1970s, and 1980s. He was particularly committed to urging young men and women to pursue their education and to use the public library as a resource for their own personal and professional development.

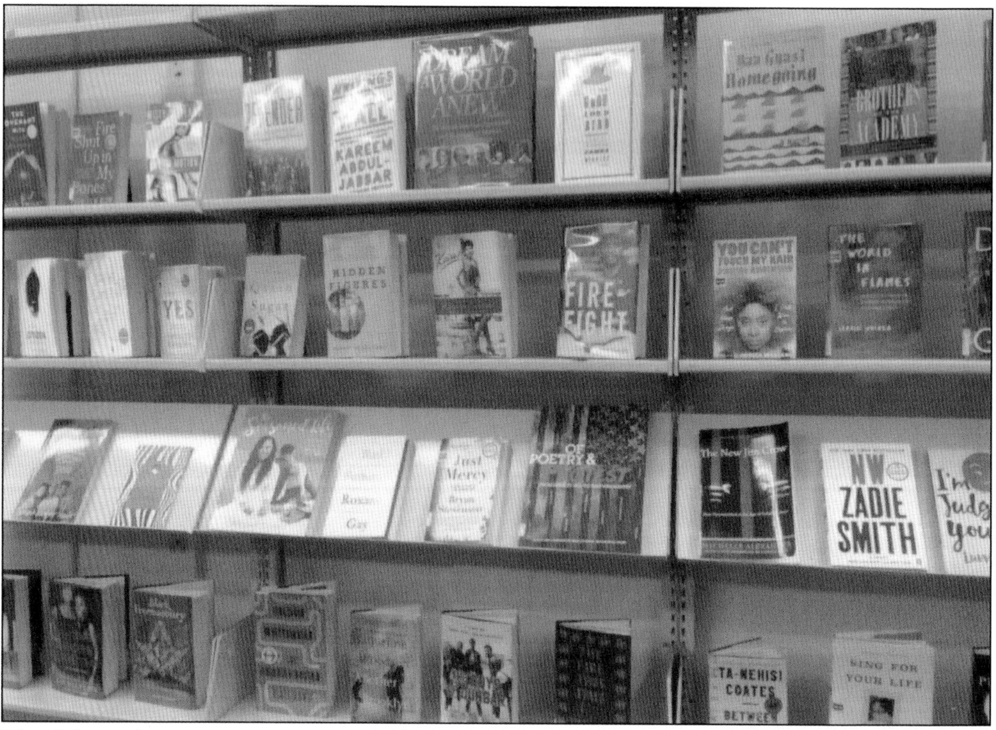

The African American Room was established in 1989 and named after librarian James Brown in 1991. It has a collection that is principally used for providing cross-disciplinary access to materials about African American life, history, and culture. Titles of current issues, classics from the 19th and 20th centuries, contemporary literature, and standard reference sources are all available, along with services, like reader's advisory, exhibitions, and programs.

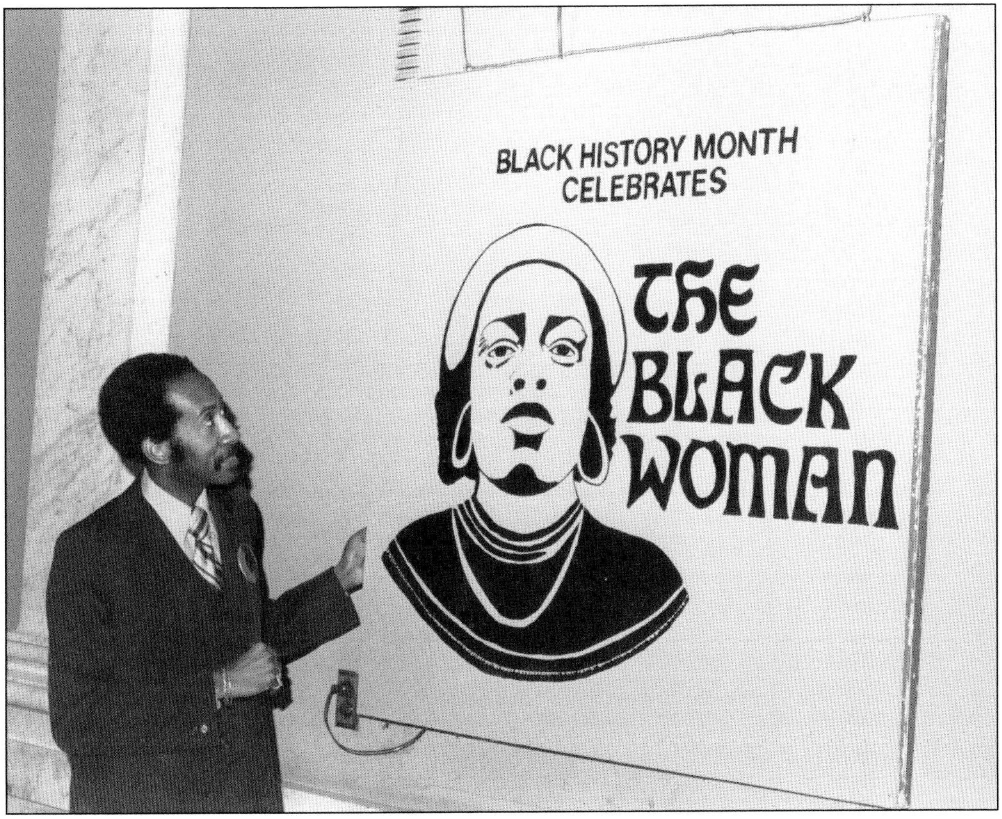

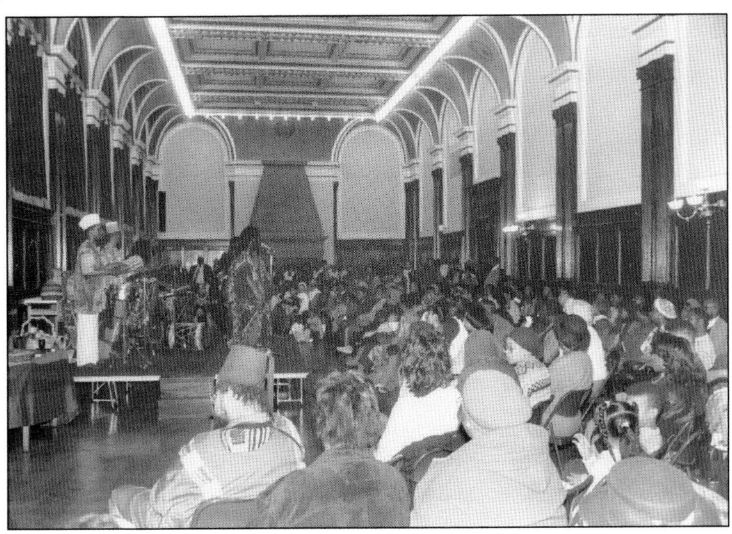

During the 1950s and 1960s, Newark changed from a city of immigrants, mostly from southern, central, and eastern Europe, to one of African Americans, Hispanic Americans, and others. During its entire history, the Newark Public Library has always tried to meet the needs of the city's diverse communities. In 1982, as part of the annual Black History Month, an exhibition, *The Black Woman*, was installed (above). It was accompanied by lectures, films, book signings, and musical presentations. In 1991, a Kwanzaa celebration was marked by music and dance in Centennial Hall (below).

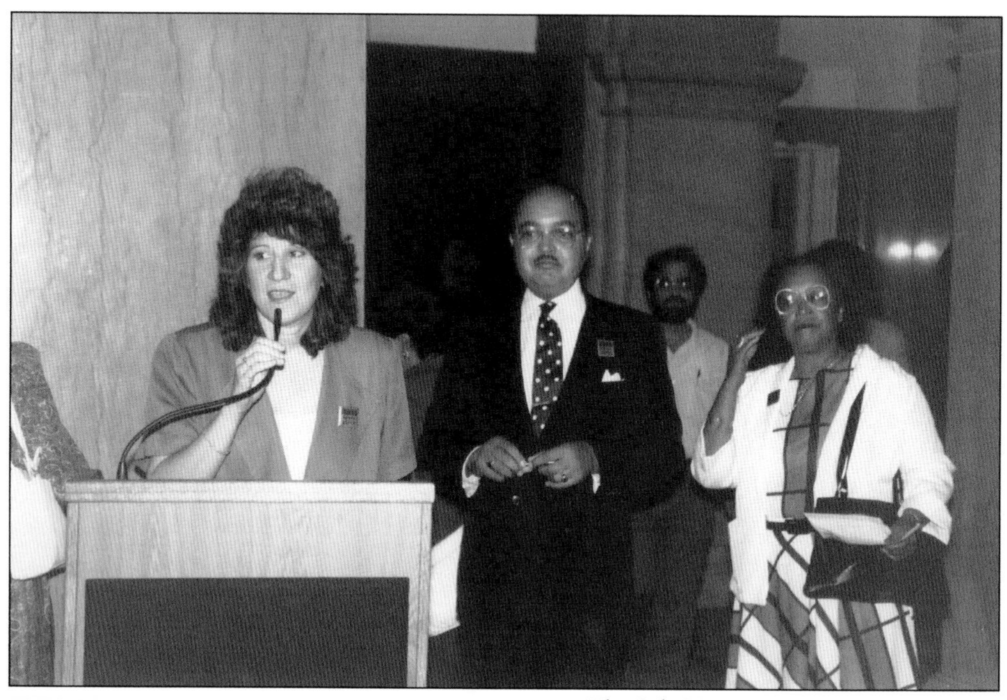

The Sala Hispanoamericana was established in 1989 as the largest Spanish-language resource in the state with a special emphasis on Central and South America and the Caribbean. Since its inception, it has served as a valuable educational, informational, and cultural resource for immigrants and residents interested in Latin American cultures. In this photograph, librarian Ingrid Betancourt addresses the crowd at the opening, while others look on.

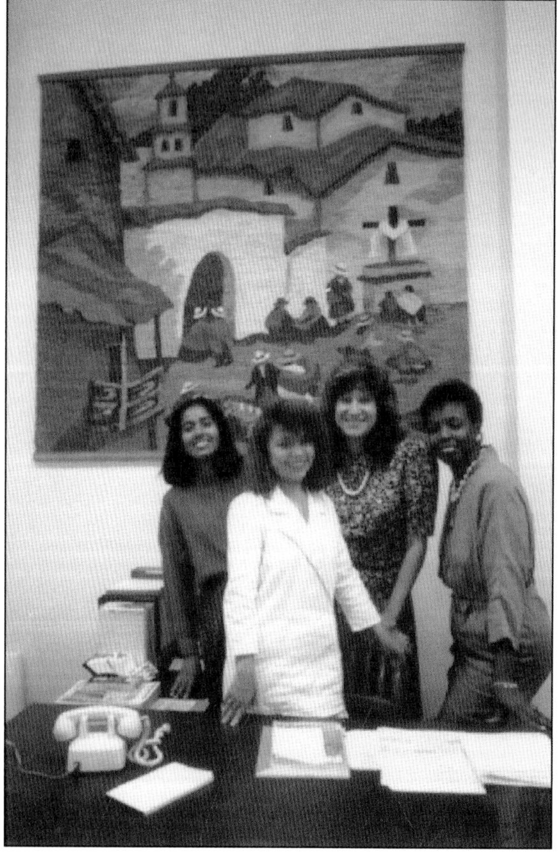

The collection grew from almost 5,000 books in 1979 to over 30,000 today. In addition to its collection of popular literature, the Hispanic Reference Collection allows students and scholars to conduct in-depth research in both Spanish and English. In 2002, these two components were renamed the New Jersey Hispanic Research and Information Center (NJHRIC) with a statewide mission.

The Puerto Rican Community Archives officially began in 2006 with a four-year plan to seek out potential archival materials to document the study of that island's contributions to the State of New Jersey. Today, it contains 55 collections of personal and professional papers as well as records from community and cultural organizations. The archivist has called this photograph a "shelfie."

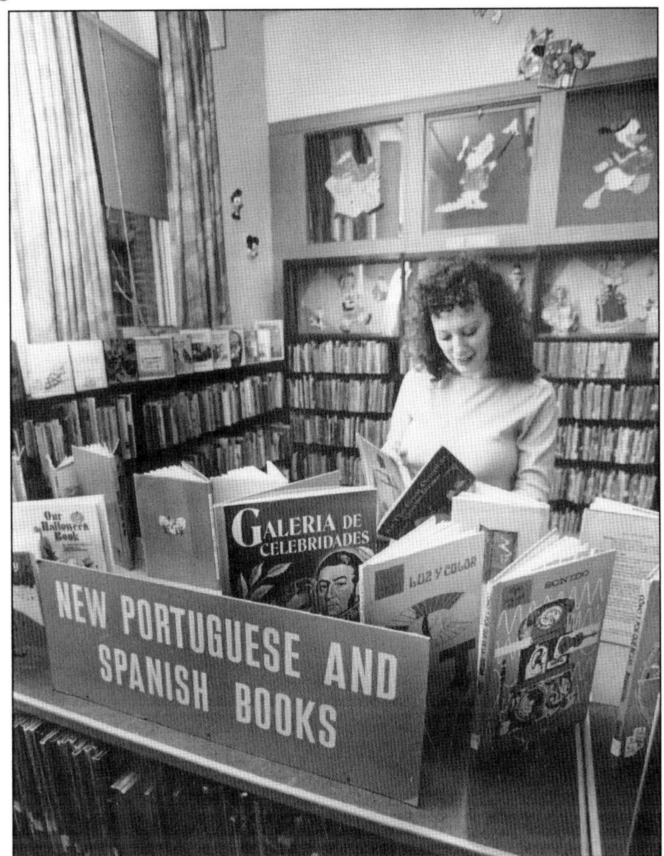

In 1898, the library added 43 books in Polish for the Polish American community that had grown up around St. Casimir's Roman Catholic Church in the Ironbound. Books in German, Lithuanian, and Italian were added at the same time. By the 1970s, when this photograph was taken, the library was acquiring Spanish and Portuguese books for communities in the Ironbound and elsewhere.

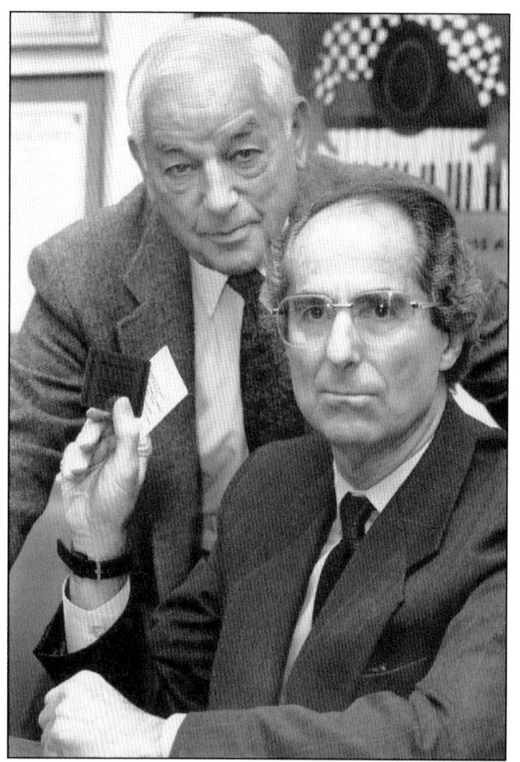

The renowned American author Philip Roth (seated) grew up in the Weequahic neighborhood of Newark where he was an enthusiastic borrower of books from the local branch. As he grew into adulthood, he continued to support the library, especially its New Jersey Information Center. In 1991, he gave the first John Cotton Dana Distinguished Lecture. The historian John T. Cunningham (standing) introduced him.

Upon his death in 2018, Roth's personal library of over 7,000 volumes was bequeathed to the Newark Public Library. It is made up of books of fiction, drama, poetry, and literary criticism as well as history, biography, sociology, and psychology—books that he collected over his life as he studied his times and critiqued his society. It also includes manuscripts, notes, correspondence, and other objects that document his literary career.

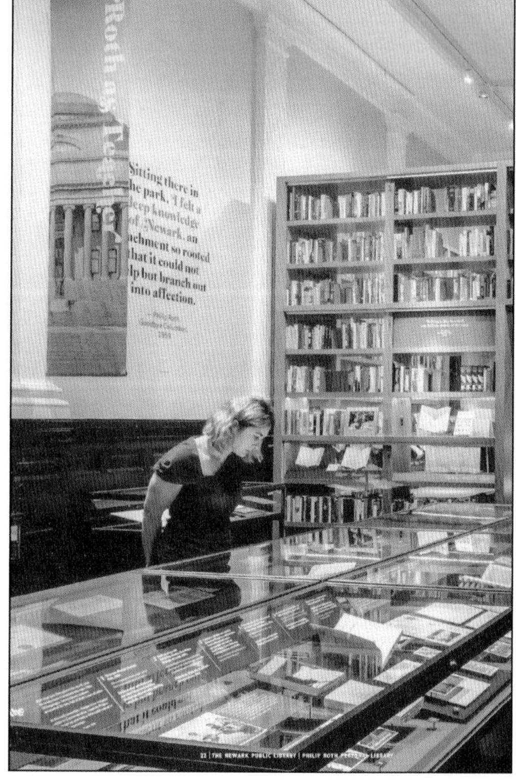

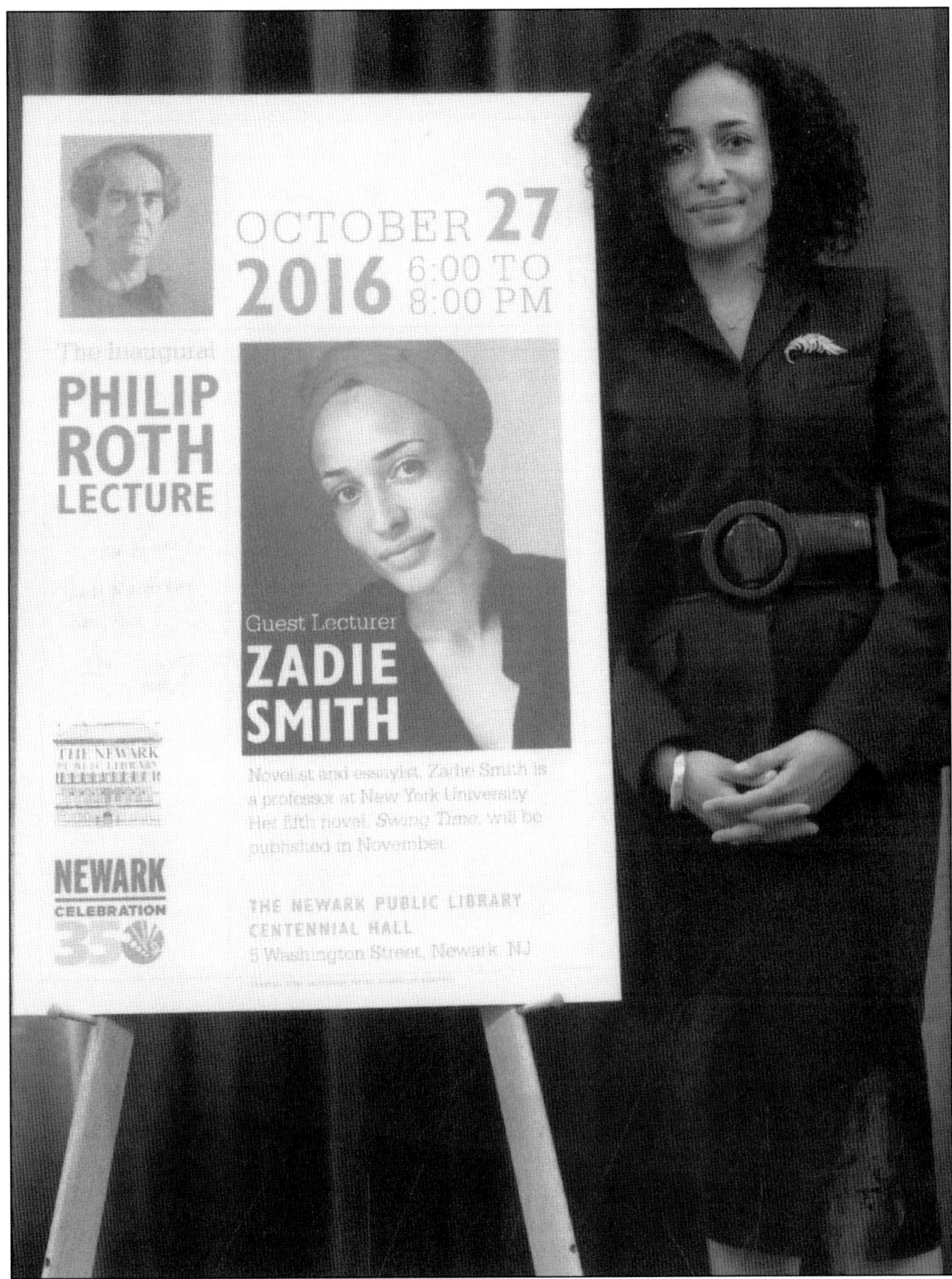

Roth also endowed a lecture series. The African-Jamaican-English novelist, Zadie Smith, was the inaugural lecturer in 2016, and she compared Roth's transgressive freedom, which he made inseparable from his challenging characters, to her own freedom as an author in "telling a true lie." In her novels (*White Teeth*, *The Autograph Man*, *On Beauty*, *NW*, and *Swing Time*), she has tried to craft stories in such a way that gives the reader a sense of immediacy. Other speakers have included Robert Caro, the biographer of Lyndon B. Johnson and others; Salman Rushdie, the author of *The Satanic Verses*; the poet Tracy K. Smith; and the historian Sean Wilentz.

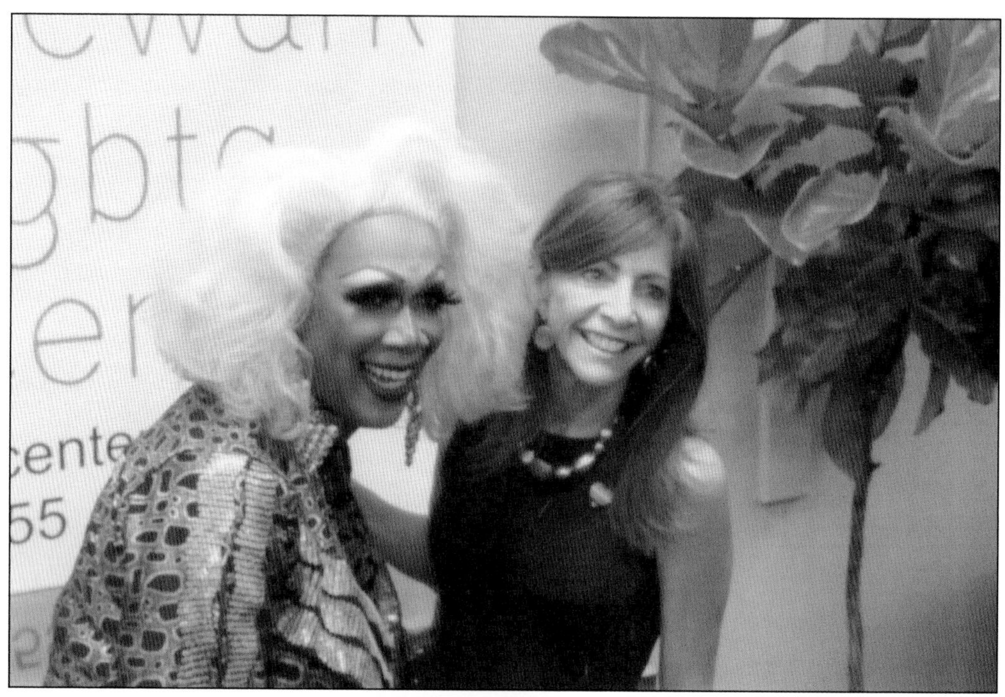

In 2019, the Newark Public Library set aside space within its main library for the LGBTQ Resource Center. As an open, safe, inclusive, and welcoming place where individuals are comfortable to be themselves, the library hired a librarian to maintain and expand the collection and to acquire circulating and reference materials appropriate to this diverse community. It also operates as a liaison to other nonprofit organizations in and around Newark, which offer social services to lesbian, gay, bisexual, transgender, and queer individuals. Above, Harmonica Sunbeam, one of the leading promotors of the Drag Queen Story Hour, smiles at the camera with the then first lady of New Jersey, Tammy Murphy, at the opening of the center. To the left is the cover of *Queer Newark*, a collection of stories of resistance, love, and community, put together by activists, academics, and other members of the community.

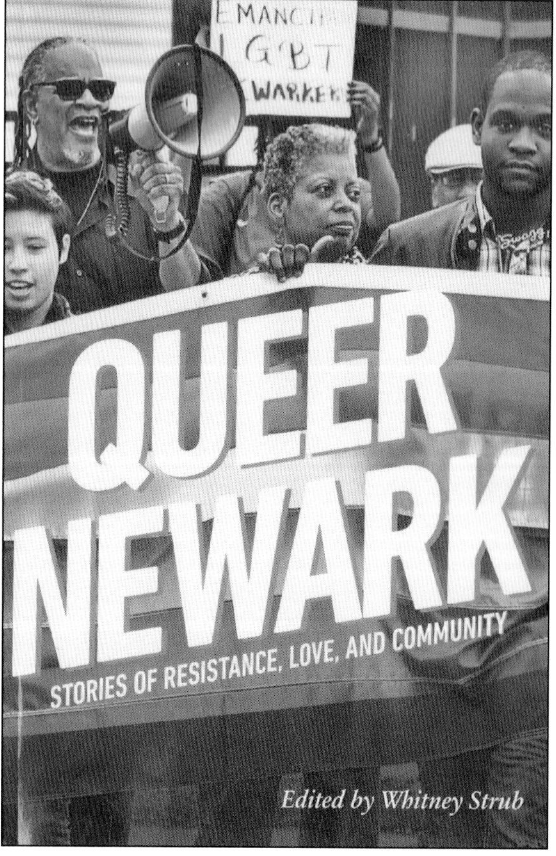

Five

BRANCHES

As early as 1891, librarian Frank Hill wanted to make sure that the people of Newark had access to library materials in the easiest way possible, so he established nine delivery stations throughout the city. The experiment lasted less than a year, but in 1894, he tried again. By 1898, he had initiated a delivery system to several schools and several firehouses.

Plans for the establishment of a branch at the new high school near Branch Brook Park (now Barringer High School) materialized in 1900. In 1915, four other branch libraries in elementary schools were administered jointly by the Newark Public Library and the Newark Board of Education. The first formal branch library, known as Branch 1, opened in 1904 in rented space on Academy Street. It included city directories and other business information that appealed to the businessmen and office workers of downtown Newark. Over the next decade, it moved four times, and with each move, it became more and more specialized. By 1908, it was known as the Business Branch, the first of its kind in the nation.

Branch 2 opened in quarters provided by the Clark Thread Company, and its employees checked out fiction and nonfiction in great quantities. Branches 3, 4, and 5 in the Roseville, Springfield, and Ironbound neighborhoods, all opened in 1907, all in rented spaces. All of them contained a modest but general collection of best-selling fiction and nonfiction. Two additional branches opened in 1909 and 1914 in the Clinton and West Side Park sections of the city. Unfortunately, the pressures of World War I put an end to these branches.

In the 1920s, the City of Newark agreed with the board of trustees that the Newark Public Library needed city-built, city-owned branches, and so, between 1923 and 1930, seven buildings were constructed in the Springfield, Van Buren, Roseville, Clinton, Vailsburg, Weequahic, and North End neighborhoods.

By the 1930s, the Newark Public Library also had 33 extension libraries in department stores, hospitals, churches, factories, offices, and schools. It even had libraries in a jail, an orphan asylum, and a convalescent home. During the summers, the library shipped small traveling bookcases, containing 40 books each, to eight summer camps and four school playgrounds.

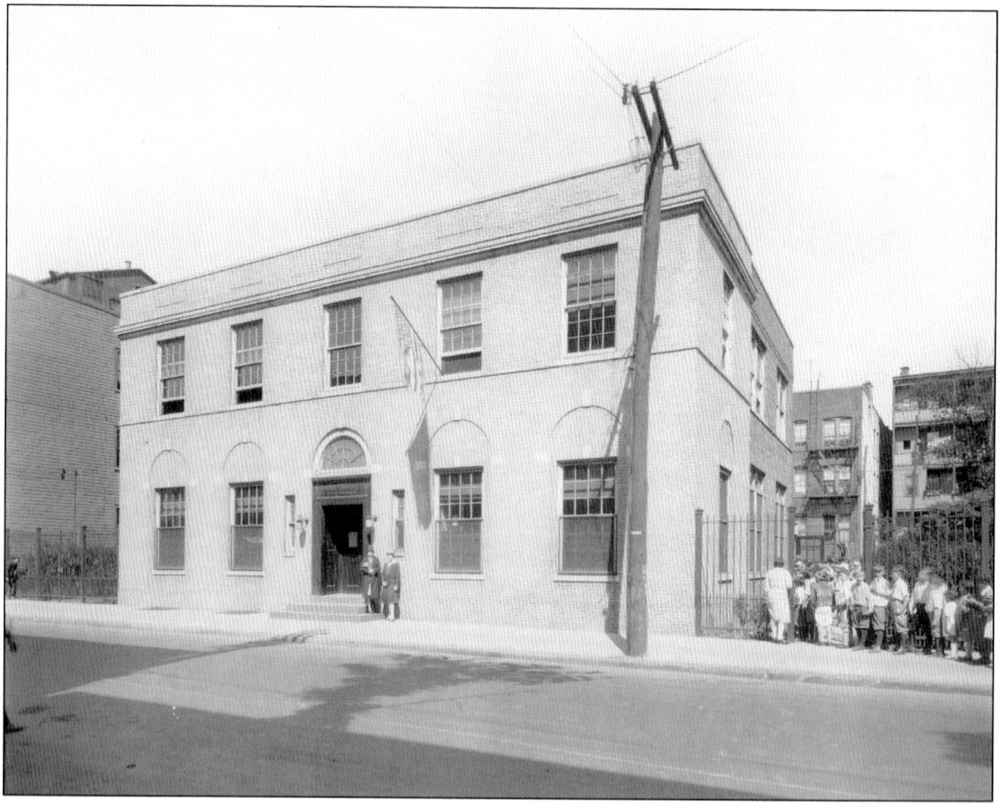

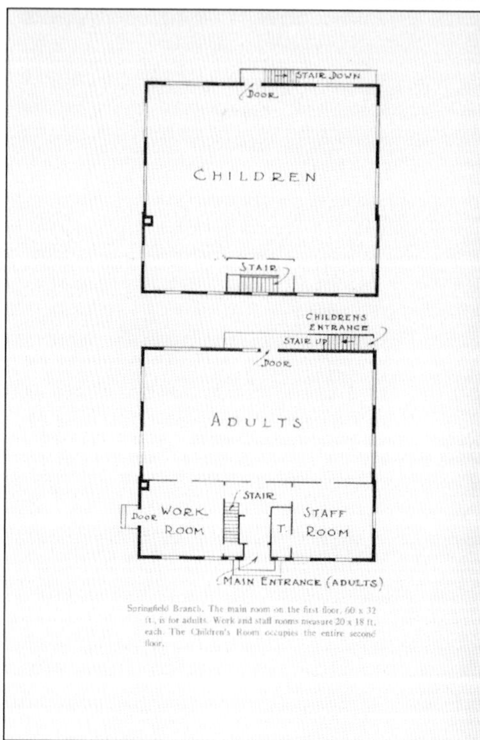

Springfield Branch. The main room on the first floor, 60 x 32 ft., is for adults. Work and staff rooms measure 20 x 18 ft. each. The Children's Room occupies the entire second floor.

The Springfield Branch was the first city-built, city-owned branch to open in March 1923. It was a modest, two-story building of cream brick in a modified Colonial style. It cost the city $68,000 for the land and the construction. The book collection of 22,000 volumes in fiction and nonfiction was extra. It was staffed by six full-time assistants and one janitor.

The floor plan became the blueprint for all the neighborhood branches with only modest modifications. The first floor contained a work room and a staff room as well as a large, spacious reading room for adults. The second floor was entirely set aside for children, who could use a discreet staircase in the front or a separate staircase in the back.

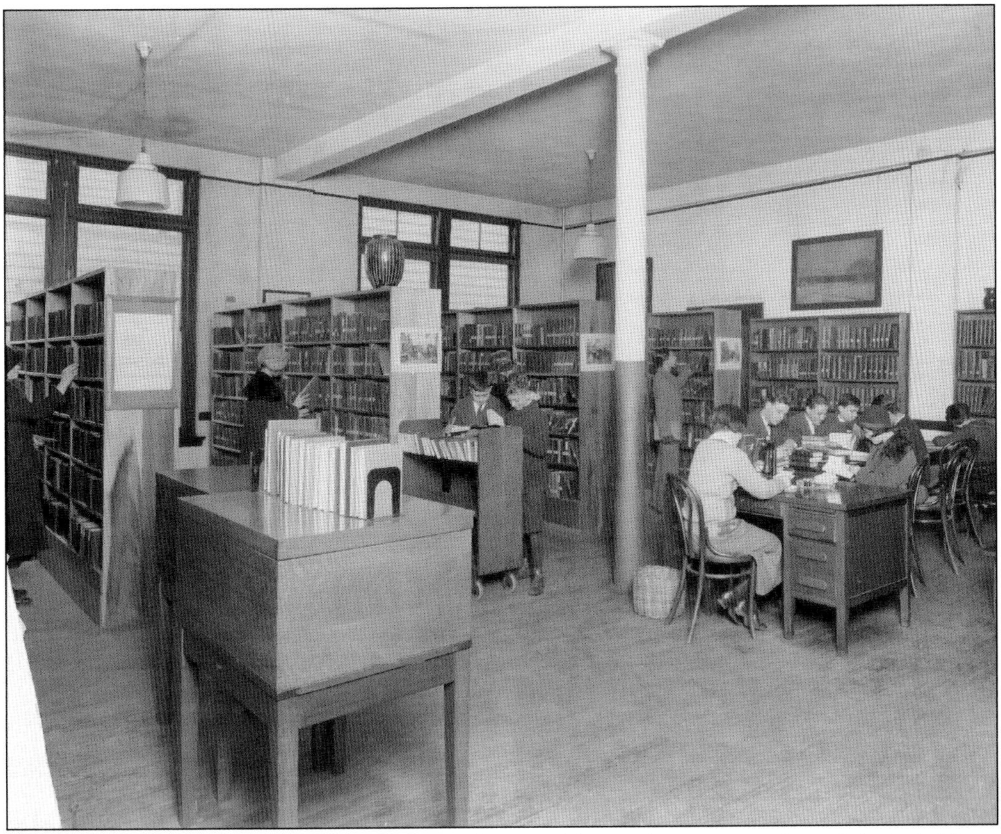

The neighborhood consisted of a dense population of foreign-born nationals and their children; consequently, they heavily used foreign language materials in Polish, Yiddish, German, and other European languages. A large and increasing community of African Americans complemented this diverse section of the city. Together, they borrowed 63,000 books in 1928.

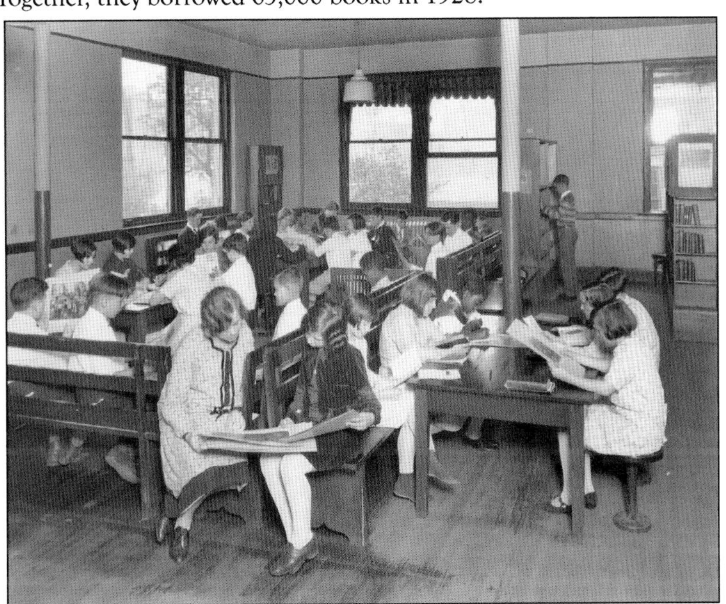

Students from 16 elementary schools, 2 junior high schools, and 6 parochial schools used the upstairs room. Sometimes, they came with their teachers, or they came with their parents, and sometimes, they came by themselves after school or on weekends. In 1928, they checked out 123,000 books.

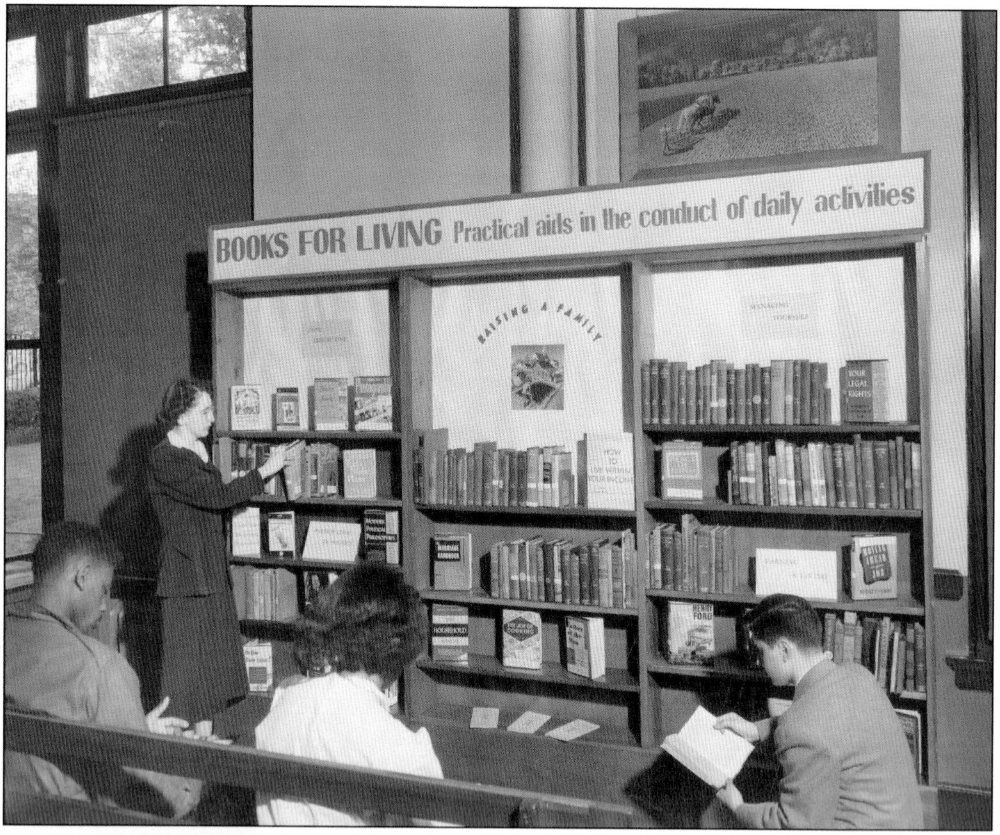

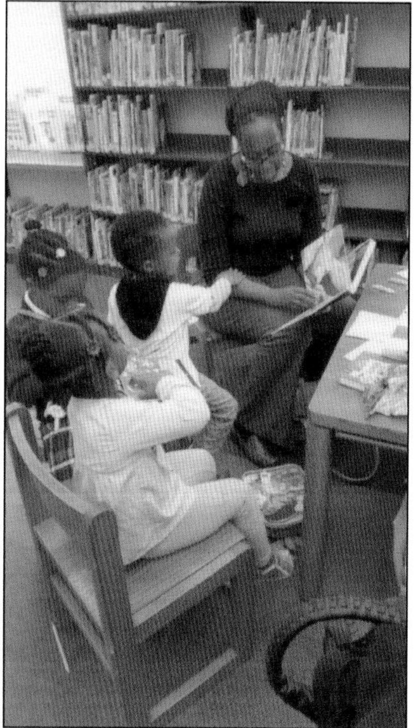

Special displays of books on special topics rotated around the branch libraries. This display of "books for living" from 1949 contained practical advice on earning a living, raising a family, participating in politics, and using leisure time. The titles included *How to Live within Your Income*, *The Marriage Handbook*, *Modern Political Philosophies*, *The Joy of Cooking*, and *This is Photography*. A friendly librarian discusses some of these titles with a few neighbors. (Commercial Photographic Company.)

The Springfield Branch is still located in a neighborhood with 17 schools (elementary, secondary, private, and charter). One of them is Science Park High School. Students still use its diverse collection of nonfiction books for classroom assignments and its fiction collection for entertainment. It still serves as a learning center for those who are just beginning to read.

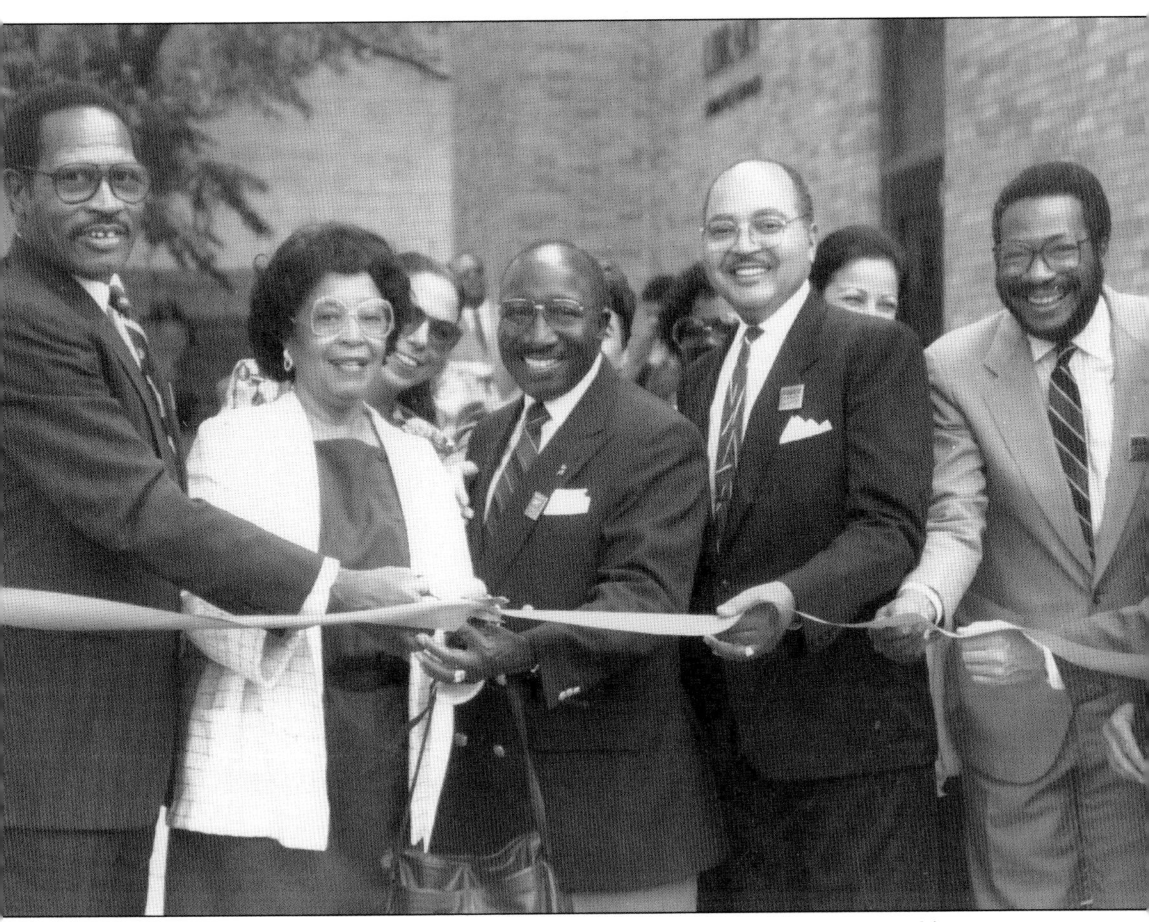

In 1989, the Springfield Branch reopened after extensive renovations. At its ribbon-cutting ceremony, Mayor Sharpe James is joined by Josephine Janifer (president of the board of trustees), George Branch (councilman for the Central Ward), Alex Boyd (library director), and Clement Alexander Price (library trustee and professor at Rutgers University). This renovation, like other renovations of the branches in the 1980s and 1990s, created auditorium space for meetings, performances, and other activities; upgraded climate control; and provided convenient access for the handicapped.

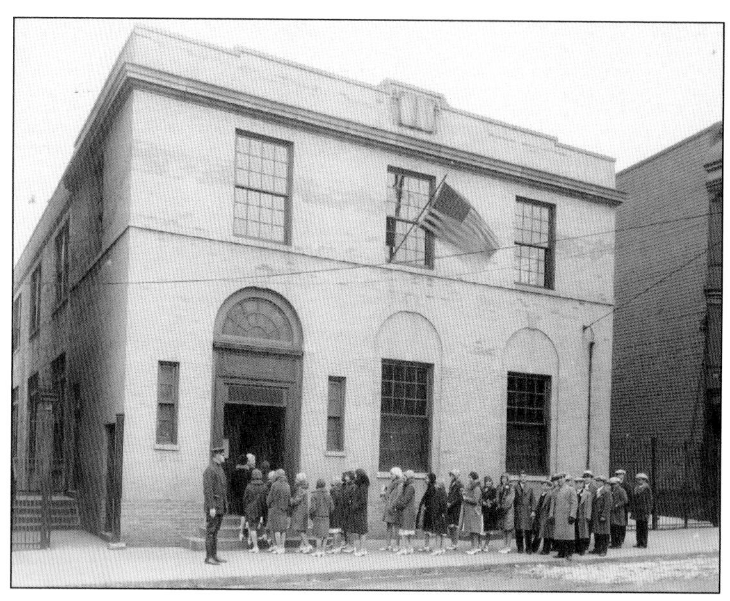

The Van Buren Branch opened in September 1923 in the Ironbound section of the city. This neighborhood was industrial with factories producing tanned hides, leather goods, celluloid products, and other industrial materials. The workers were Italian, Polish, Lithuanian, Czech, Hungarian, and German. Small groups of Spanish and Portuguese speakers were beginning to establish themselves in this neighborhood.

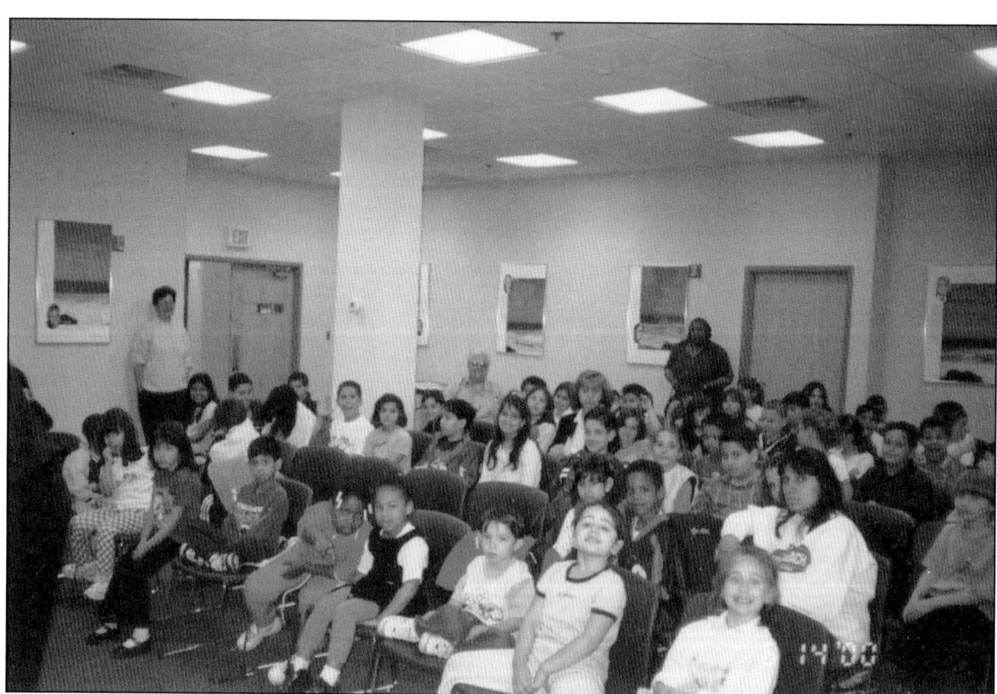

The Van Buren Branch was renovated and expanded in 1997 with a large meeting room that seats 50 visitors. It now serves a village of immigrants and their families from Portugal, Brazil, and other countries in Latin America. It contains a large collection of Portuguese and Spanish language materials, and it houses the Ironbound Environmental Justice History and Resource Center.

In the 1920s and
1930s, the adult
users of the Van
Buren Branch
read newspapers
and magazines on
current affairs for
the most part, but
when they turned
to books, they
chose fiction over
nonfiction by more
than two to one.
Their children were
even more avid
users of this branch
than their parents.

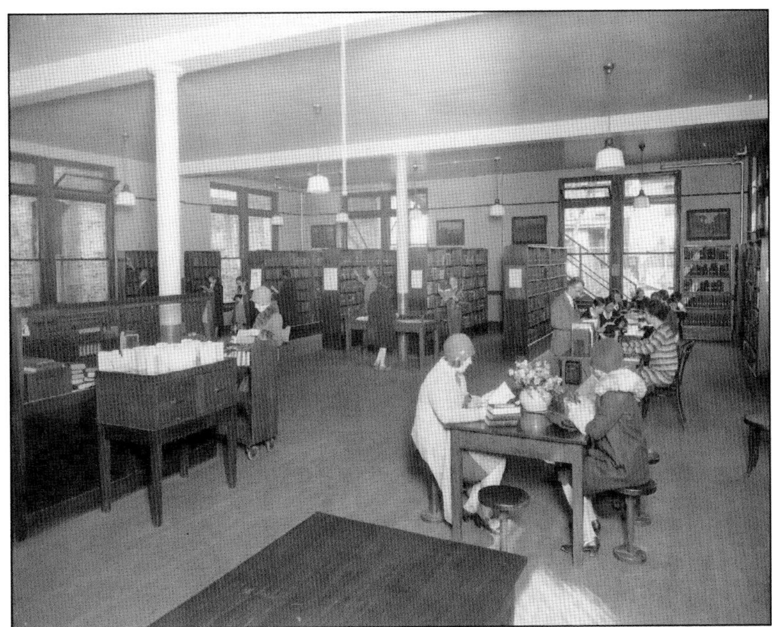

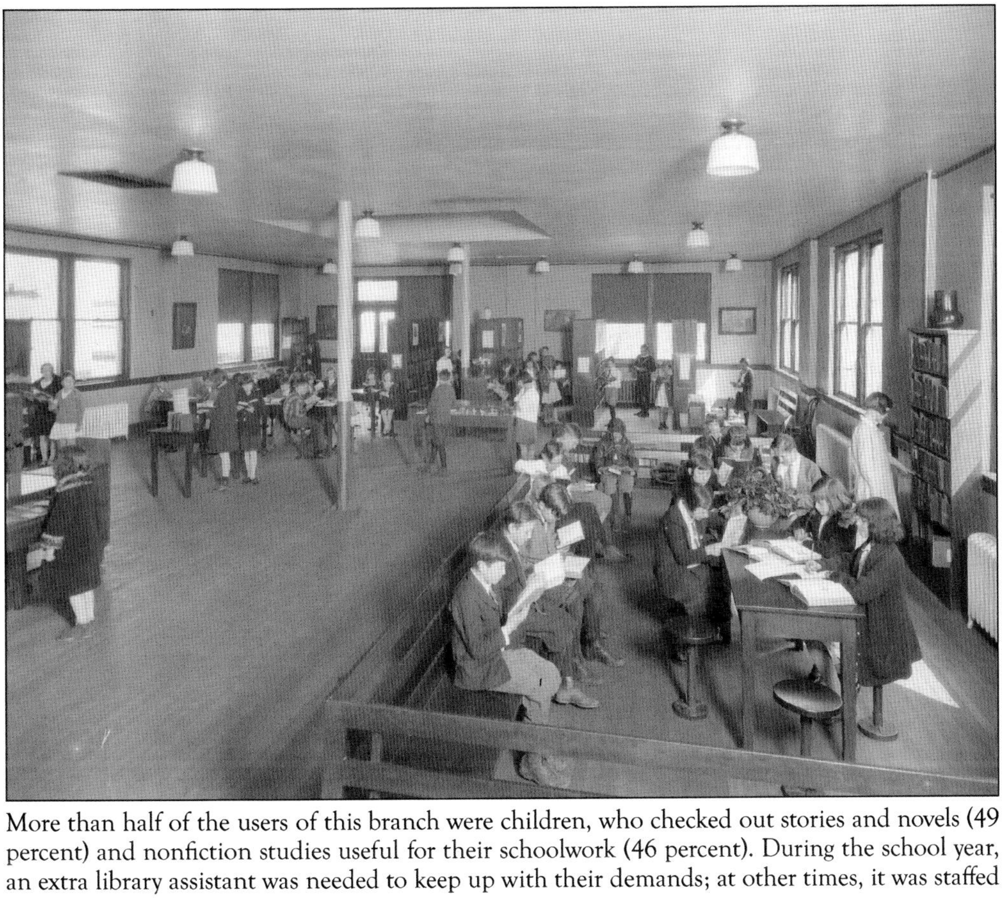

More than half of the users of this branch were children, who checked out stories and novels (49
percent) and nonfiction studies useful for their schoolwork (46 percent). During the school year,
an extra library assistant was needed to keep up with their demands; at other times, it was staffed
by five assistants.

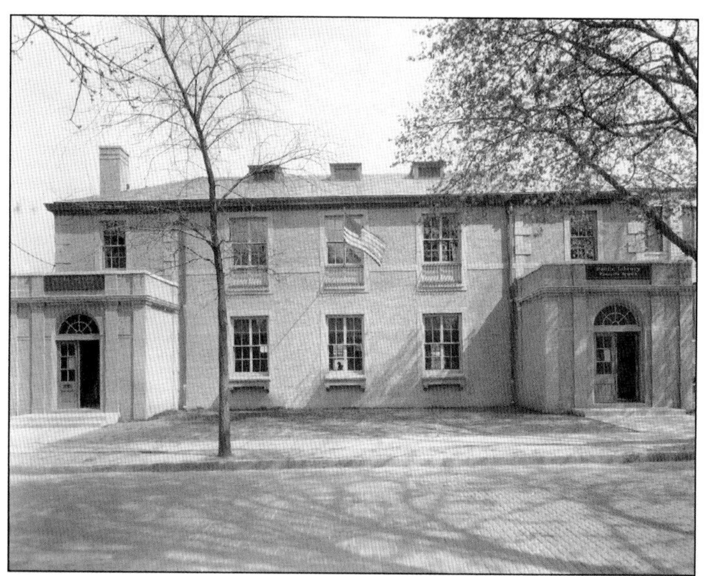

Opening in October 1924, the Roseville Branch was a brick building with two very distinct entrances. The one on the left was for children, and the one on the right was for adults. Primarily a residential neighborhood with single-family homes, the construction of apartment buildings was beginning to reshape the area. Small factories and stores appeared here and there. In 2009, because of changes to the neighborhood, this branch closed.

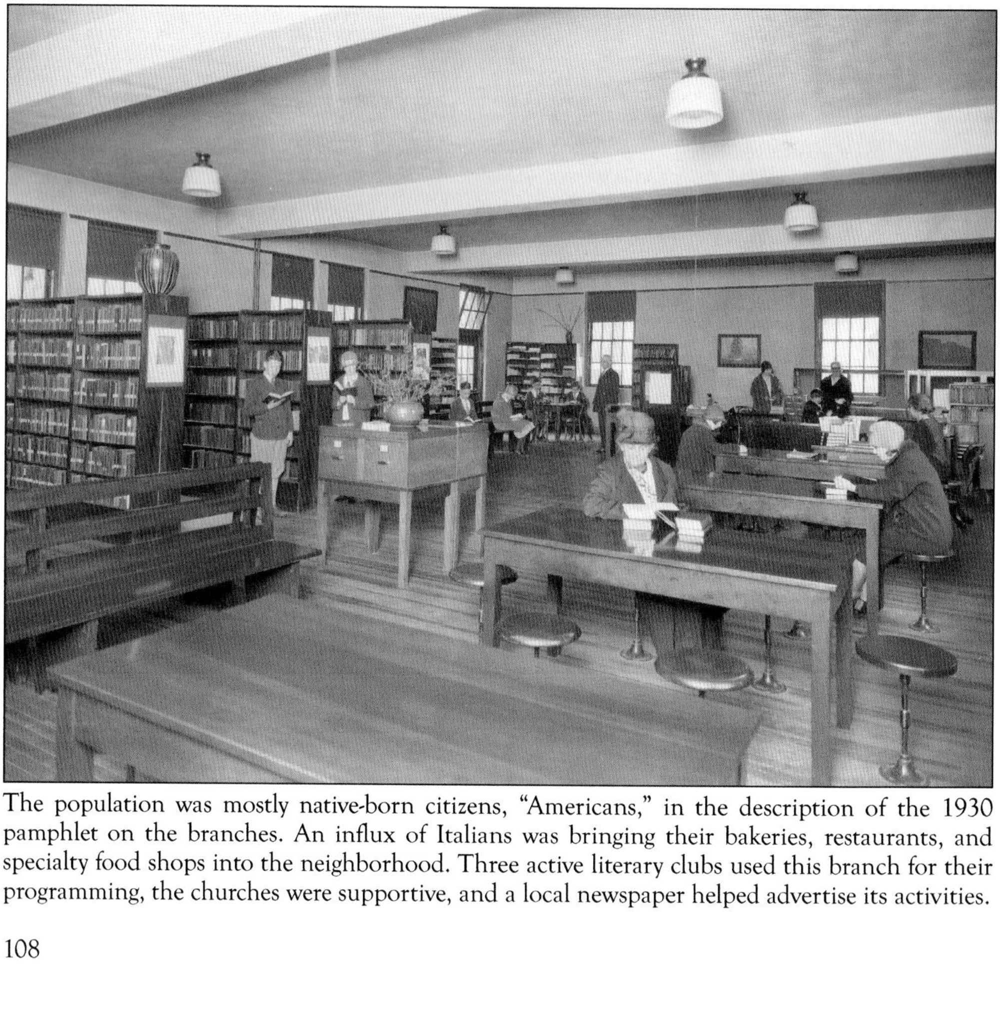

The population was mostly native-born citizens, "Americans," in the description of the 1930 pamphlet on the branches. An influx of Italians was bringing their bakeries, restaurants, and specialty food shops into the neighborhood. Three active literary clubs used this branch for their programming, the churches were supportive, and a local newspaper helped advertise its activities.

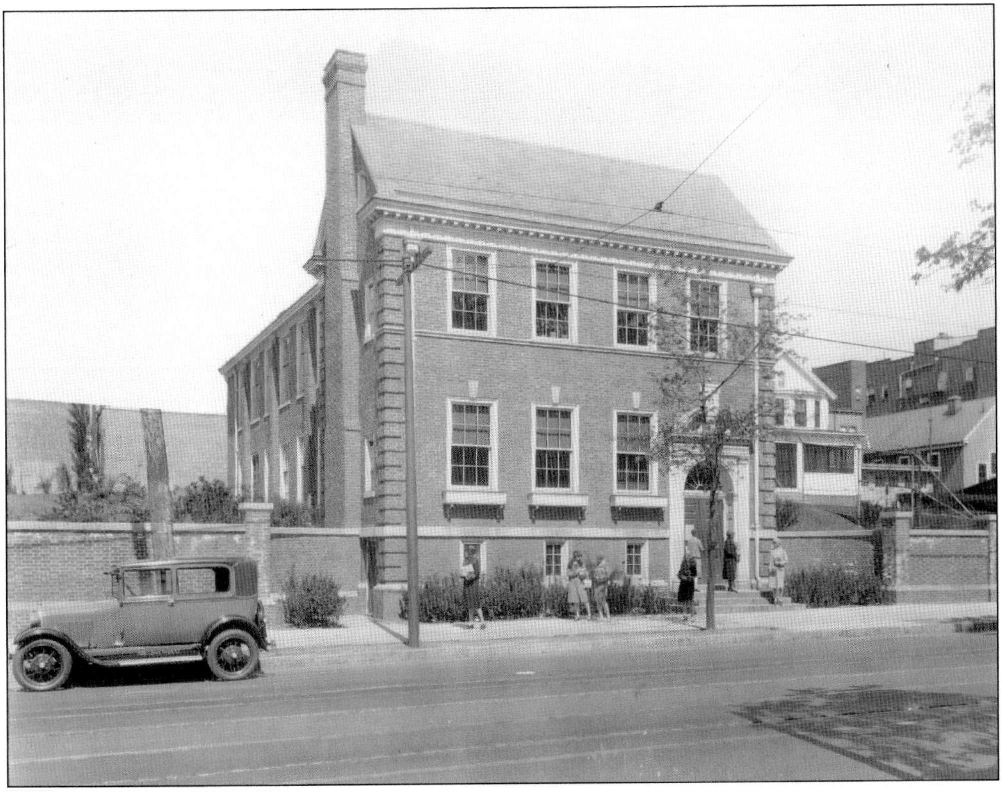

This redbrick building with white trim opened in December 1925 as the Clinton Branch. Its interior was finished in oak with tables and chairs also of oak; the bookshelves were of pine. With 18,000 volumes, it was staffed by six full-time library assistants and one janitor.

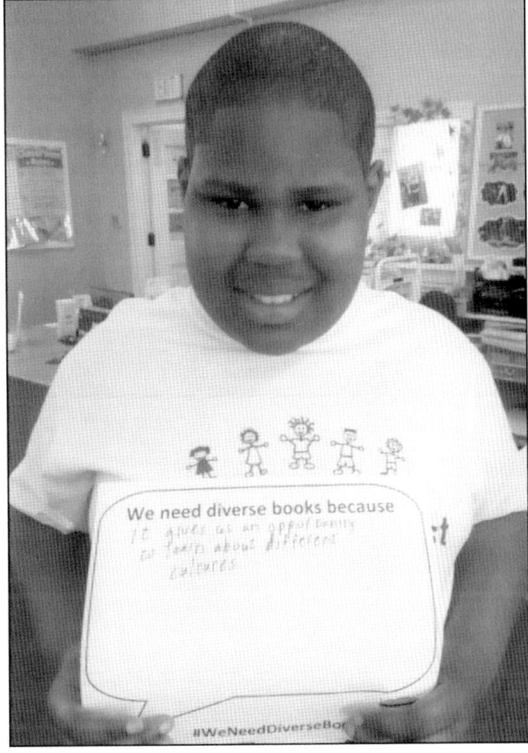

Like much of the city, this neighborhood has changed demographically over the last century. It is now far more diverse than it was, and its branch library has a collection that is far more diverse than it was. Unfortunately, because of structural problems, this branch closed in 2021.

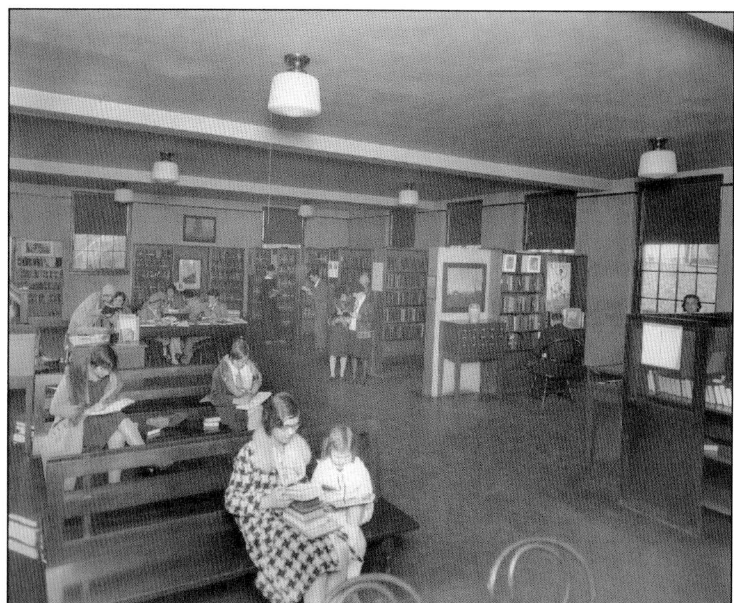

The Clinton neighborhood was a residential one with two thriving business centers. Its population was largely Jewish (both German and Russian) with two synagogues and two Hebrew schools. There were other churches and schools as well. The adults read fiction (77 percent), nonfiction (16 percent), and periodicals (5 percent).

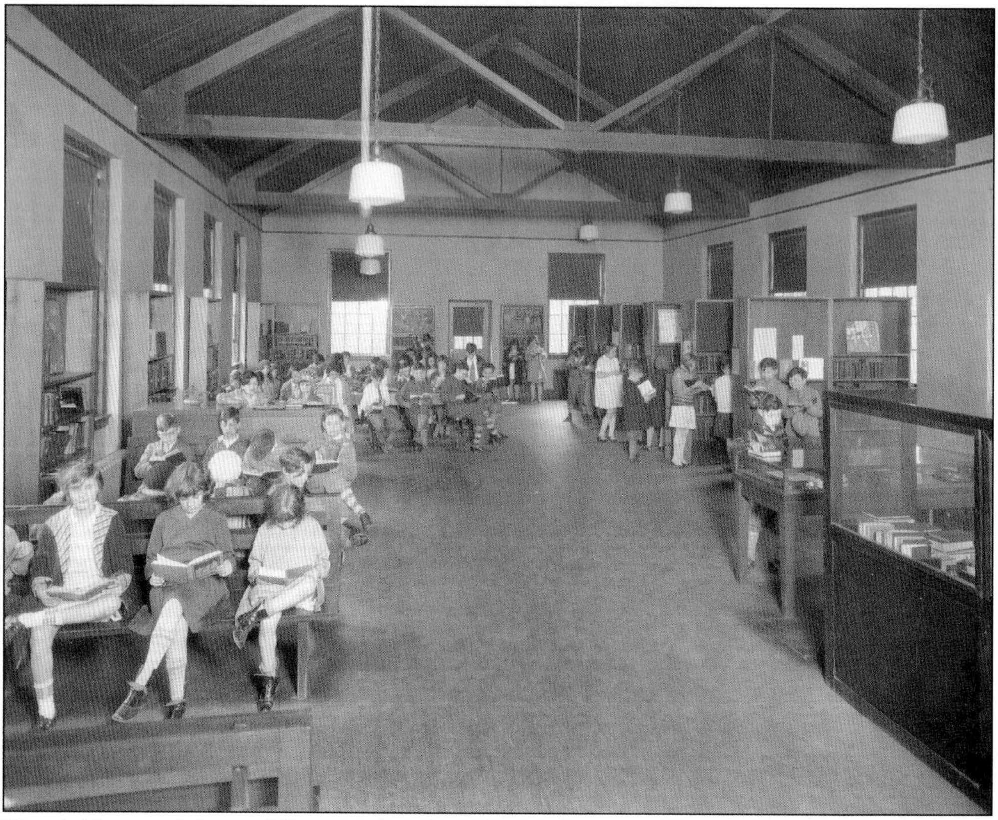

The children read fiction (57 percent) and nonfiction (40 percent). They also used various kinds of reference resources for their homework. Some of them belonged to the Boy Scouts or the Girl Scouts, both of which encouraged their members to use the branch. The Children's Aid Society and the Child Guidance Workers were big supporters.

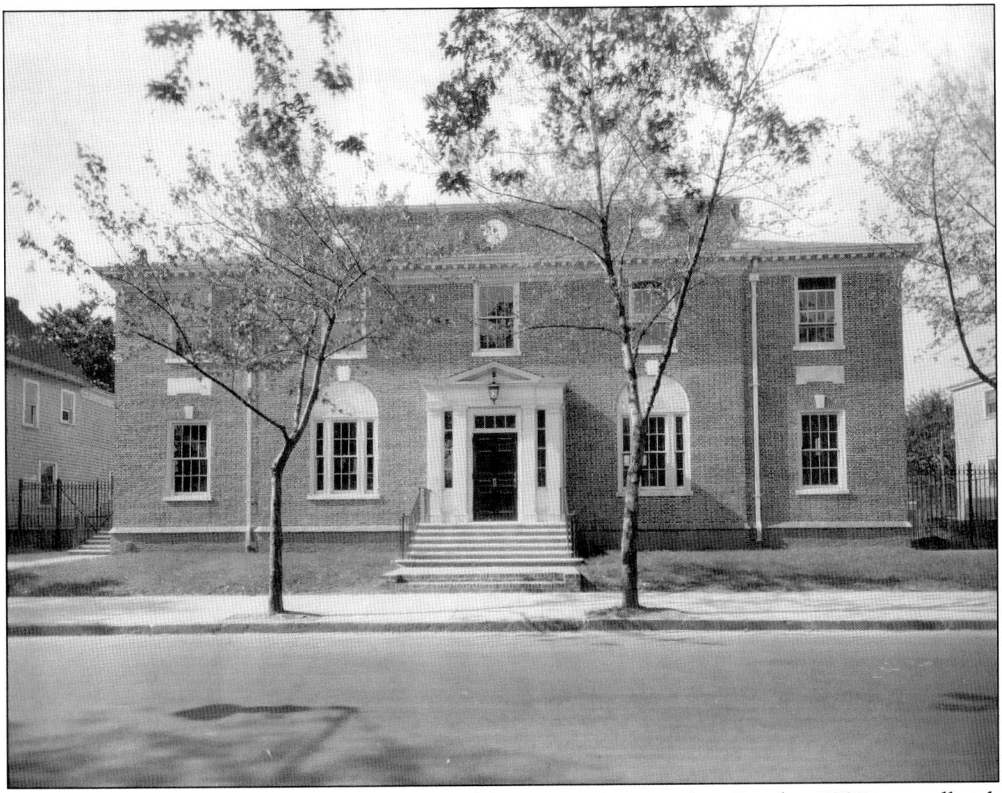

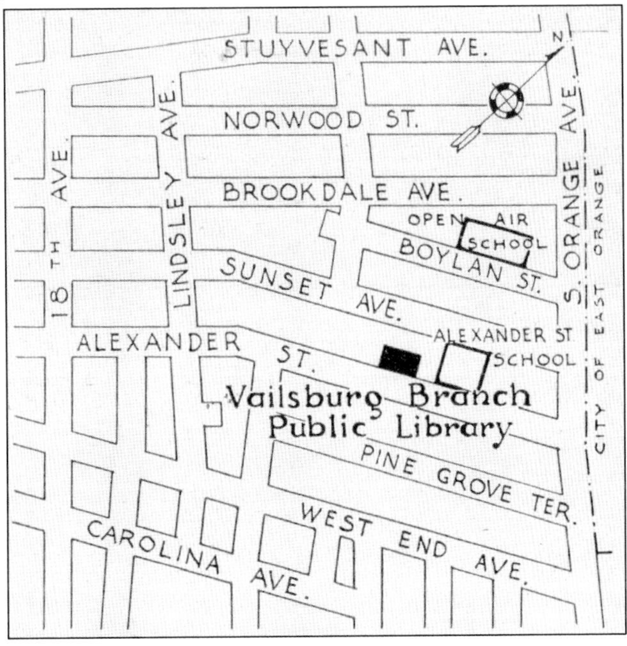

Designed in a modified Georgian style, the Vailsburg Branch opened in October 1927 in a redbrick building with white trim. Its interior was cream and white, making the first-floor adult room and the second-floor children's room appear very bright, as sunlight flooded the rooms. Four staff members and one part-time clerk kept the branch functioning.

Air-conditioning was added in 1970, but a complete renovation had to wait until 2002. At that point, an addition was built in the back increasing the size of the sections for both adults and children. A meeting room with seating for 80 visitors was included, and it has since become popular with homework clubs, community groups, and day care centers.

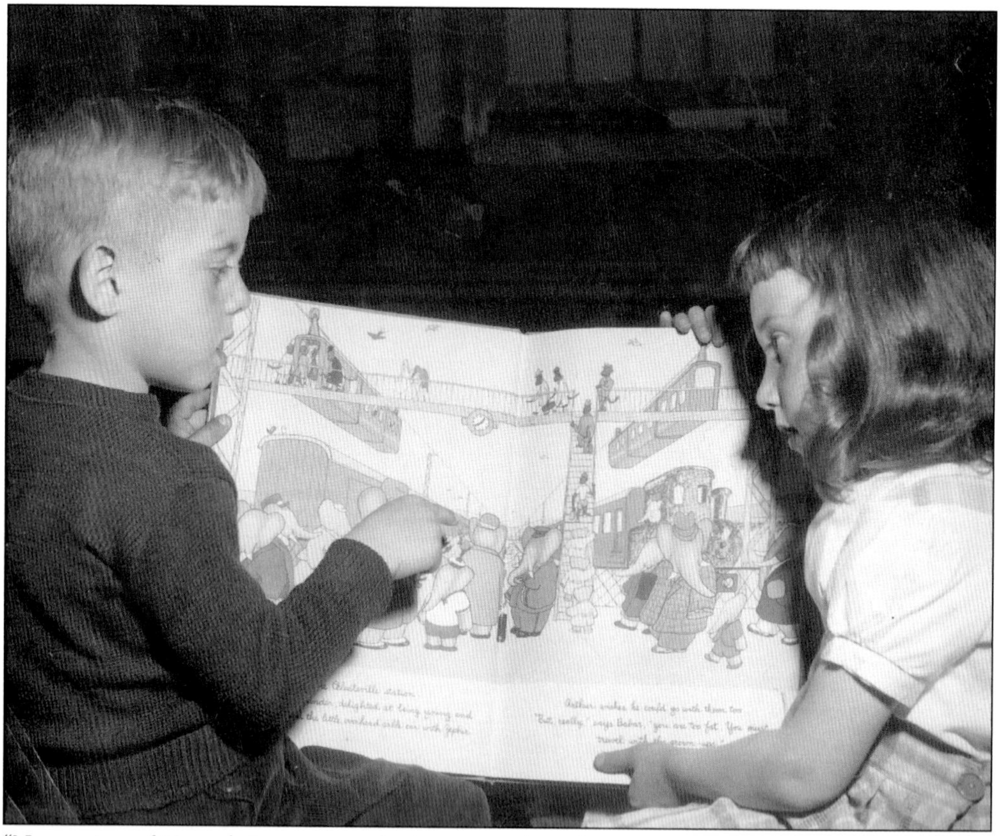

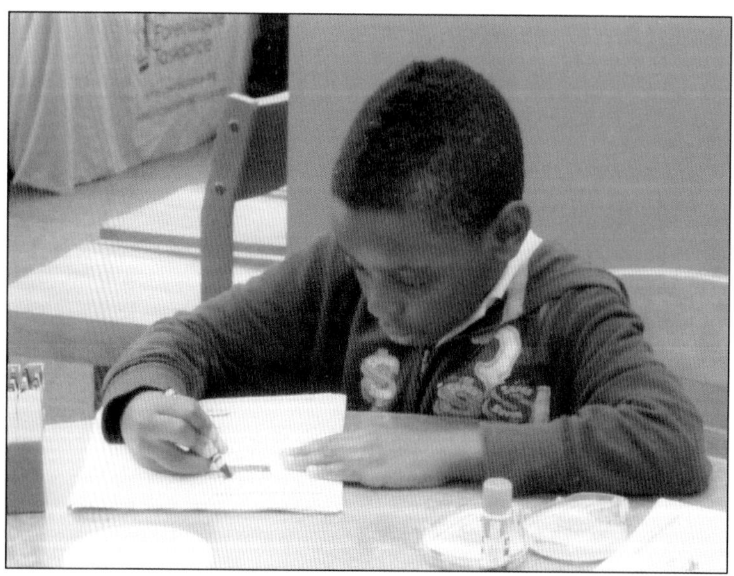

"No section of Newark is more purely American than this one," stated the author of the 1930 pamphlet on the branches. By this term, she meant second- or third-generation German, Scottish, or Irish Americans, who belonged to Lutheran, Presbyterian, or Catholic churches. They lived in a residential neighborhood with small shops and no factories.

Today, the neighborhood is predominantly African American with a large Haitian immigrant population, and this branch now has a large collection of African American novels and African American video recordings. Its current programming reflects the identity of its community. Here, a youngster concentrates on a project for the Family Financial Fair of 2012.

Children from one high school, five elementary schools, and two parochial schools visited this branch regularly with their teachers, parents, or on their own. One school sent their sixth, seventh, and eighth graders to this branch on a regular basis for book talks, which were very popular. The library assistant frequently visited third, fourth, and fifth graders at other schools.

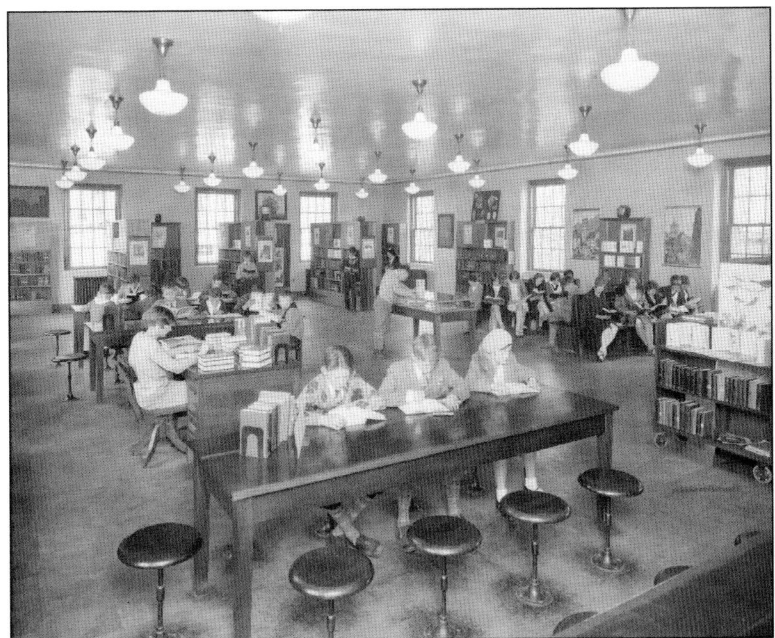

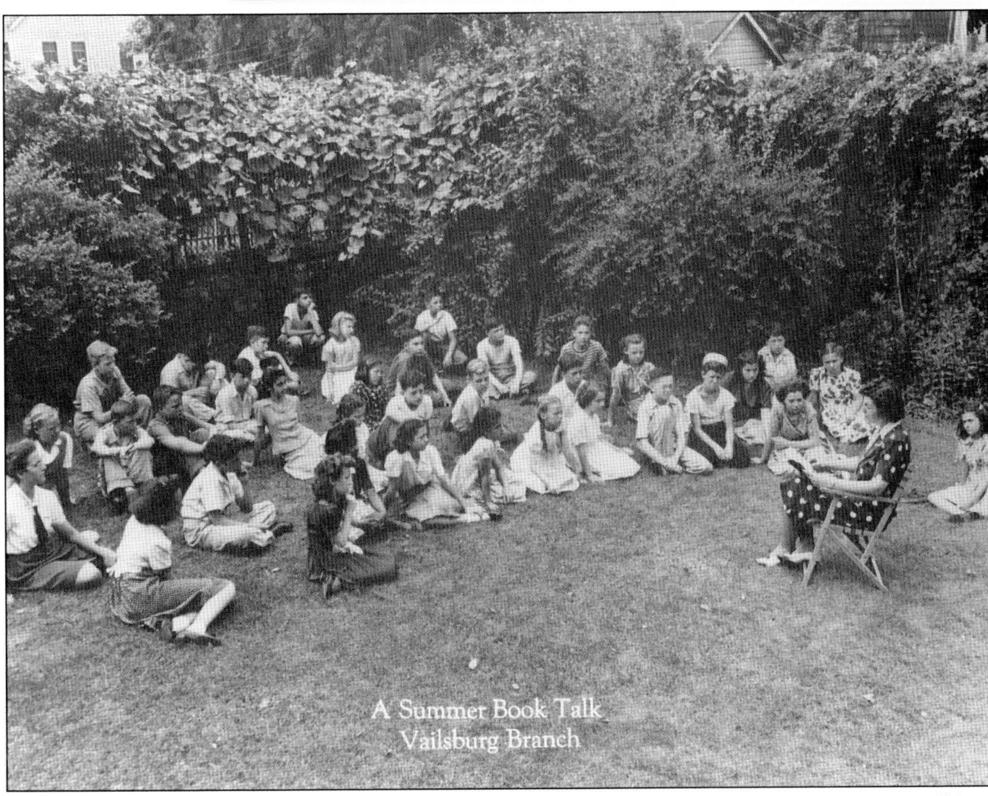

A common feature of all the neighborhood branches was the garden ("green lawns and well-kept trees"), which became popular places for book talks during the summer, like this one to a group of children in Vailsburg. Sometimes, the volume of use during the summers required additional full-time or part-time assistants in some of the branches.

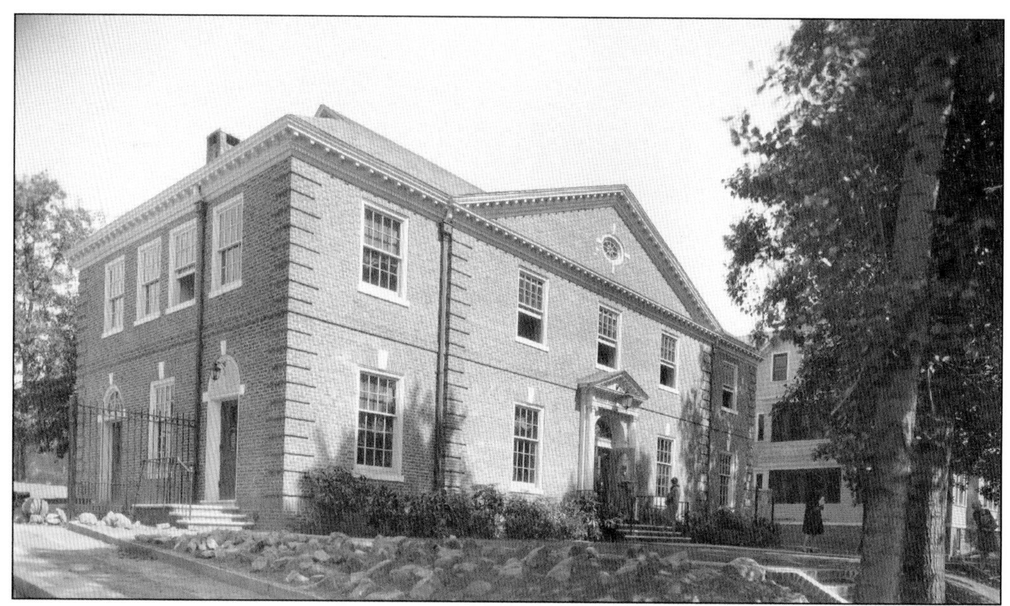

Another branch in the Georgian style, this two-story redbrick building opened in May 1929 in the Weequahic section of the city, a predominantly Jewish neighborhood. Beth Israel Hospital was its major business with other smaller stores catering to this residential community.

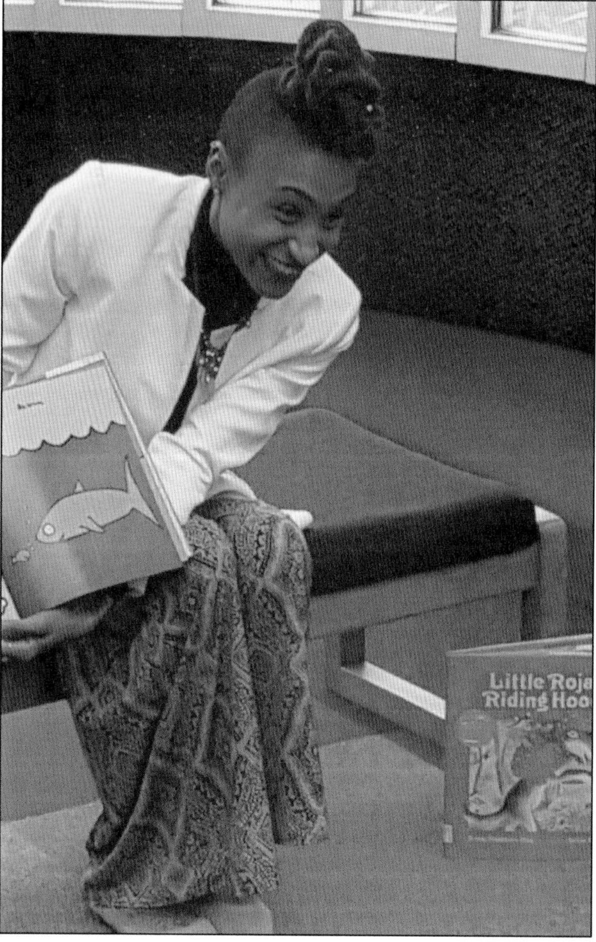

In 1992, the branch underwent a major renovation. Lighting was improved, air-conditioning was installed, an elevator was added, and a "story pit" for children was constructed (left). A new meeting room for 85 visitors allows space for community-sponsored programs and exhibitions in this now largely African American neighborhood.

As described in the
1930 pamphlet,
"an enthusiastic
clientele" checked
out 4,000 books in
the first four days
of its existence.
Children read
stories (57 percent),
nonfiction studies
(41 percent), and
magazines (2
percent); adults
perused novels (83
percent), books in
the arts and sciences
(14 percent), and
popular newspapers
and journals
(2 percent).

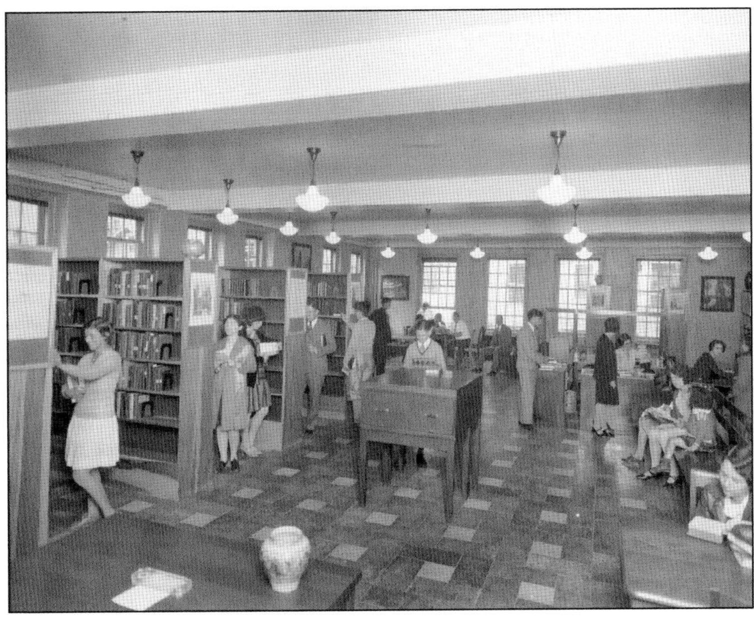

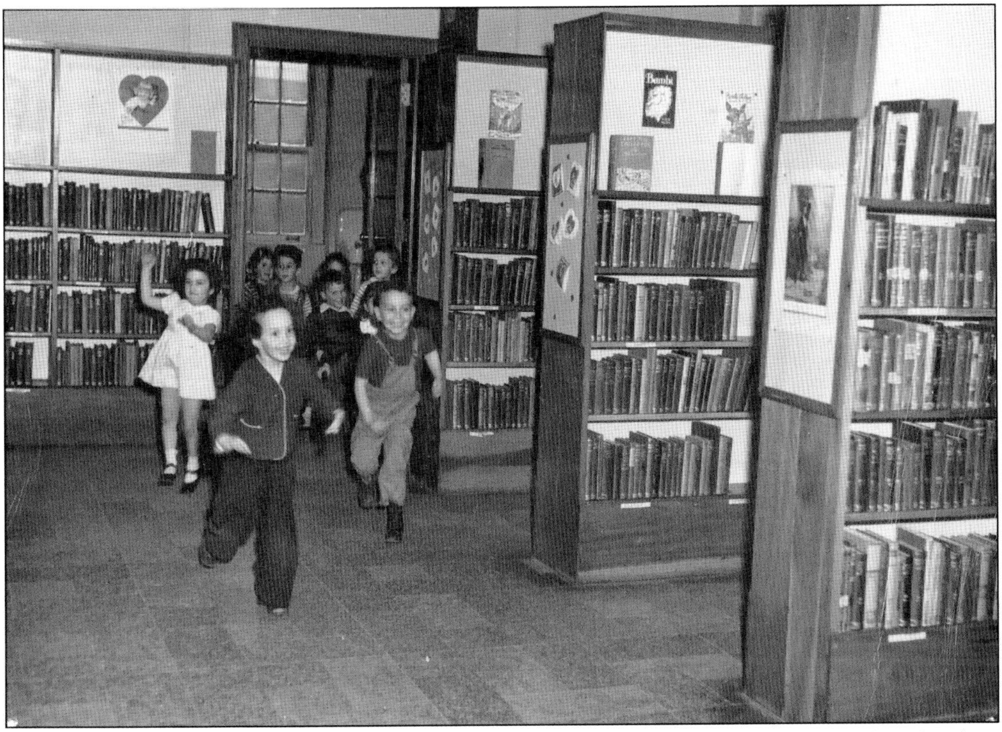

An active parent-teacher association, described as "a group of citizens desirous of the best for their
children," encouraged the use of this branch by schoolchildren. In this undated photograph, a
group of eager young readers run to get books at the Weequahic Branch. (Henningsen's Studio.)

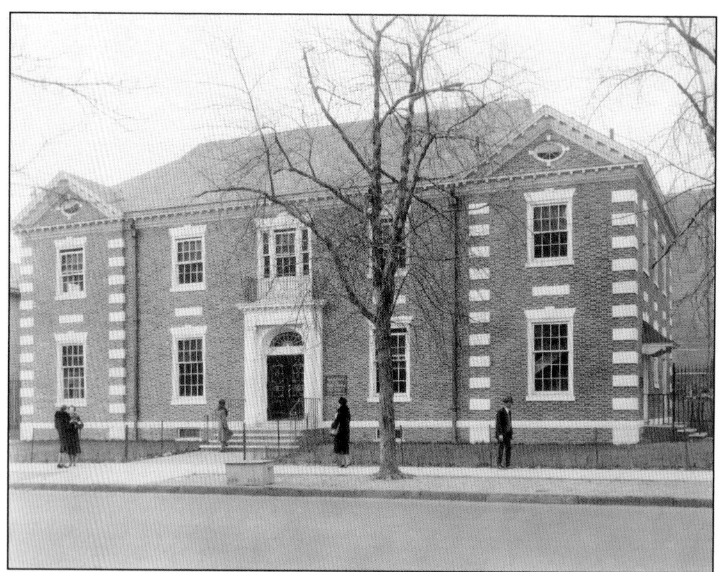

With a lawn in the front and on the side, the North End Branch opened in 1930 to serve the affluent residents of Forest Hill and Woodside, two areas that had become increasingly cut off from downtown because of changing traffic conditions. Parents and students enthusiastically welcomed the new addition to the neighborhood.

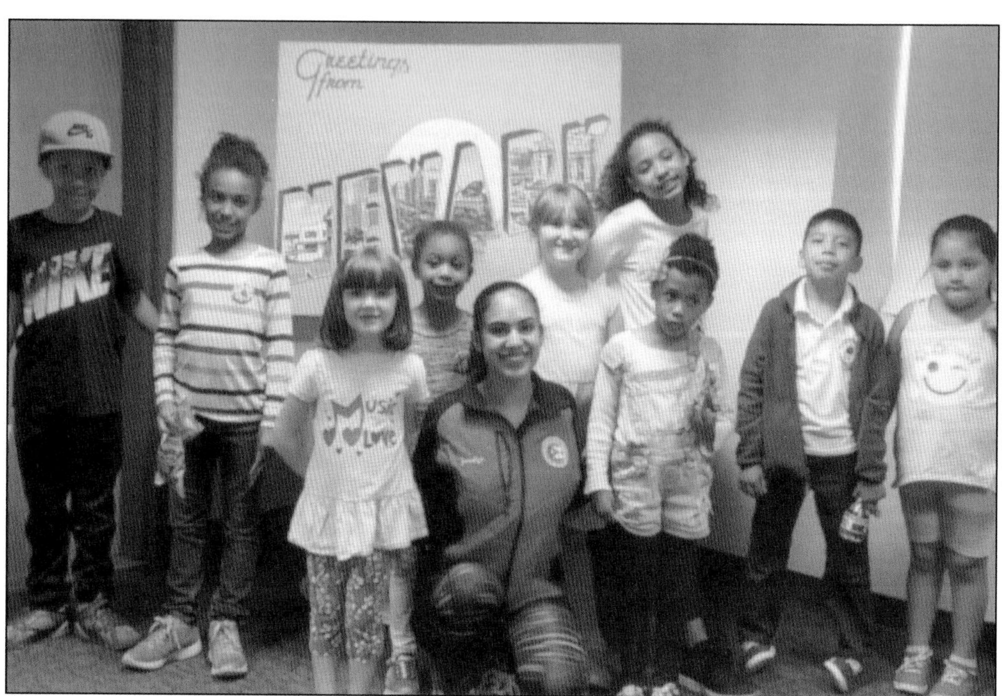

This branch was renovated in 1992. A handicapped-accessible ramp and an elevator were installed, and a new meeting room for community organizations was constructed. The children's room was designed to include a "story pit," which has become very popular. The branch now serves as a clearinghouse for community information, especially for jobs and cultural events.

As in the other branches, residents both young and old checked out novels and short stories mostly, along with books in the arts, humanities, and sciences. Popular newspapers and magazines were heavily used. As in the other branches, adults stayed on the first floor, whereas children went up to the second floor.

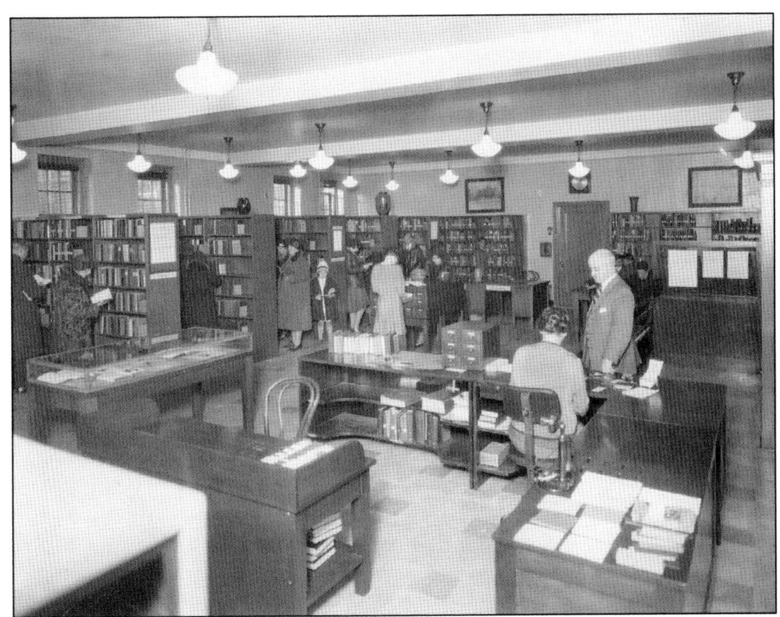

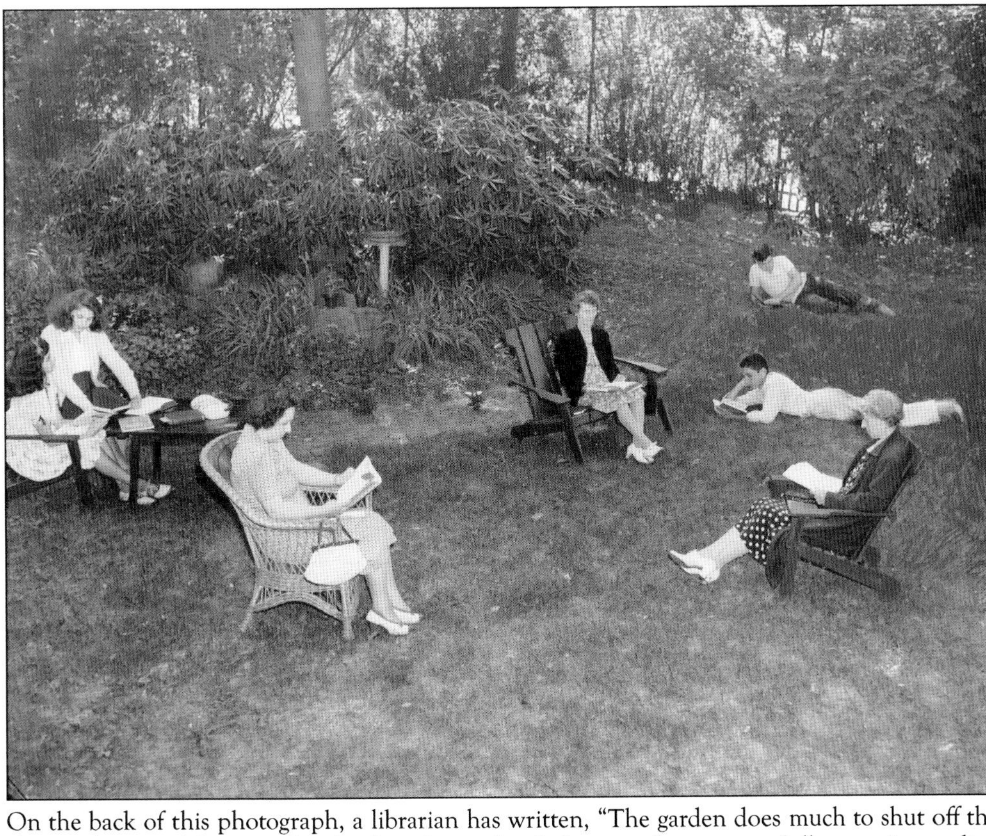

On the back of this photograph, a librarian has written, "The garden does much to shut off the glare and noise of the street." Indeed, in this undated photograph, patrons of all ages enjoy reading a good book, whether a novel, a collection of short stories, or a serious study in the arts or the humanities. (Handy & Boesser.)

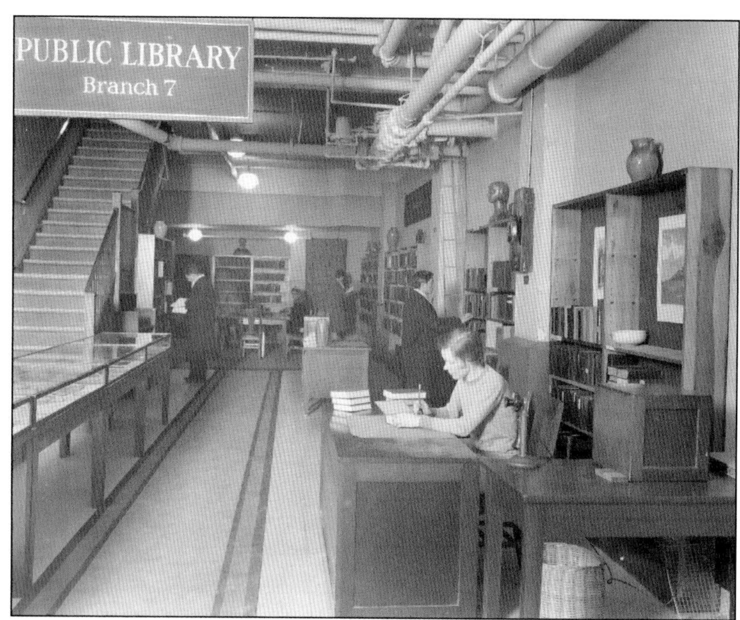

The original Branch 7 opened in 1914 in a church on Eighteenth Avenue in West Side Park, but it, too, closed during World War I. In November 1928, it reopened in "an advantageous corner in the basement" of Bamberger's department store. It was convenient for shoppers, store workers, and office workers in downtown Newark.

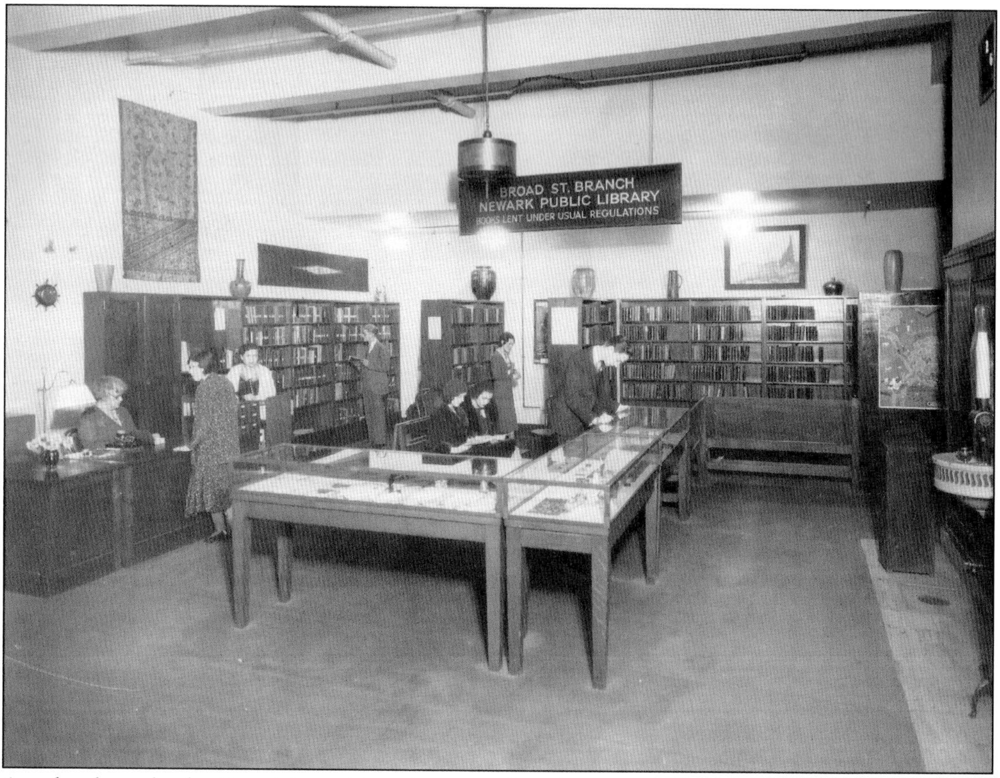

Another branch, the Broad Street Branch, opened in the same year in another department store, Kresge's, just down the street. Both branches had modest collections of best-selling novels and some nonfiction, but they did not contain periodicals or reference works. For those kinds of resources, patrons had to go to the main library on Washington Street.

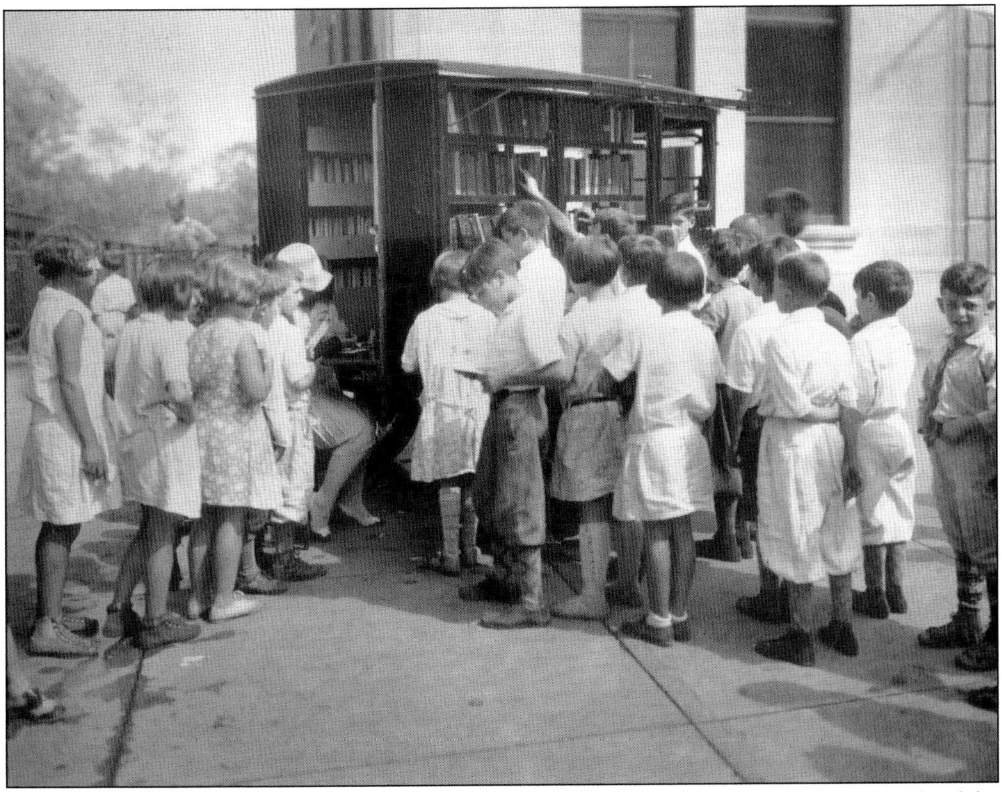

The first bookmobile was established in 1930 as another means of furthering the outreach of the library to an increasingly mobile public. It traveled to schools, playgrounds, factories, firehouses, and street corners, lending books and registering users. Unfortunately, because of the financial constraints of the Depression, it was discontinued in 1932.

The bookmobile was reinstated in 1958. This large van moved from neighborhood to neighborhood, and its interior included shelves of books and even a card catalog. It, too, was discontinued in 1992 but only after 34 years of service. The interior was spacious enough for children to browse and check out various kinds of books.

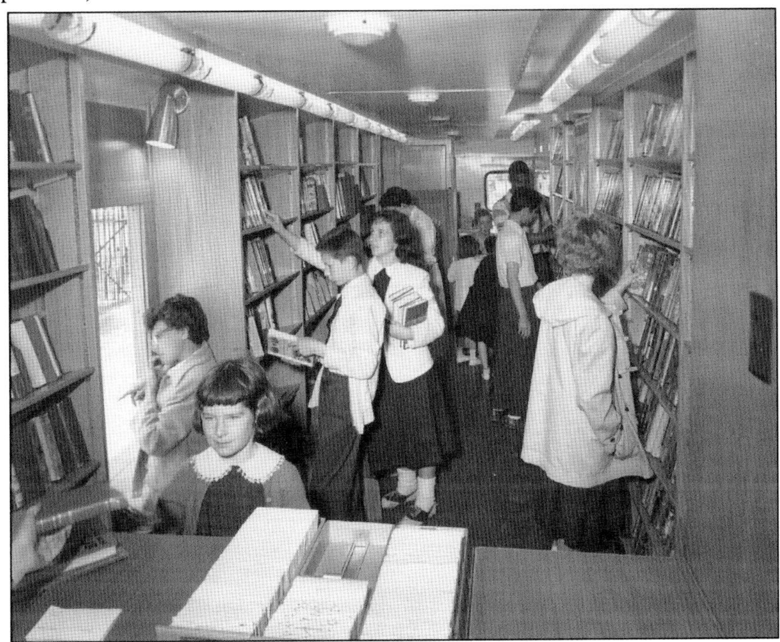

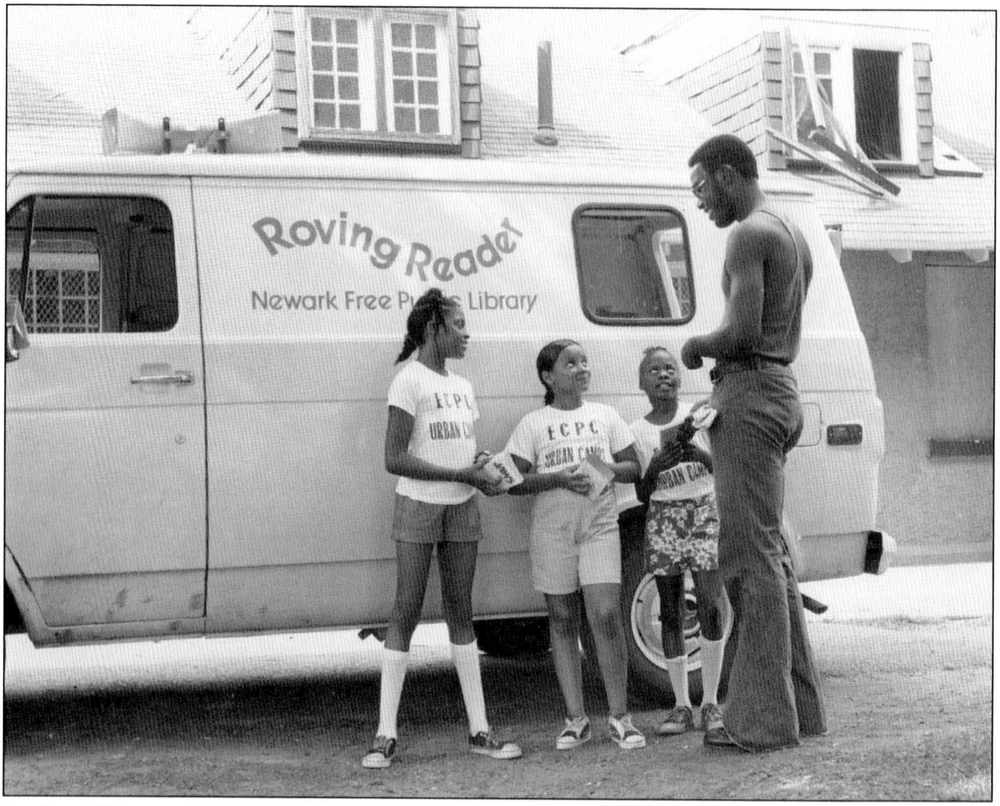

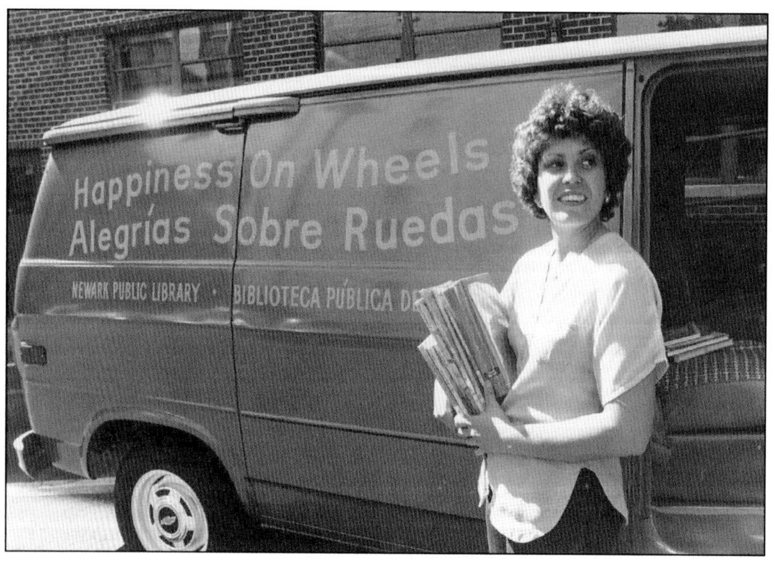

In the 1970s, smaller vehicles were purchased. The driver of this "Roving Reader" discusses the books that these three young urban campers have checked out.

In 1980, Gricelida Rivera, a bilingual specialist in the Children's Department, was transported on "Happiness On Wheels," or "Alegrías Sobre Ruedas" to one of the Spanish-speaking neighborhoods in the city.

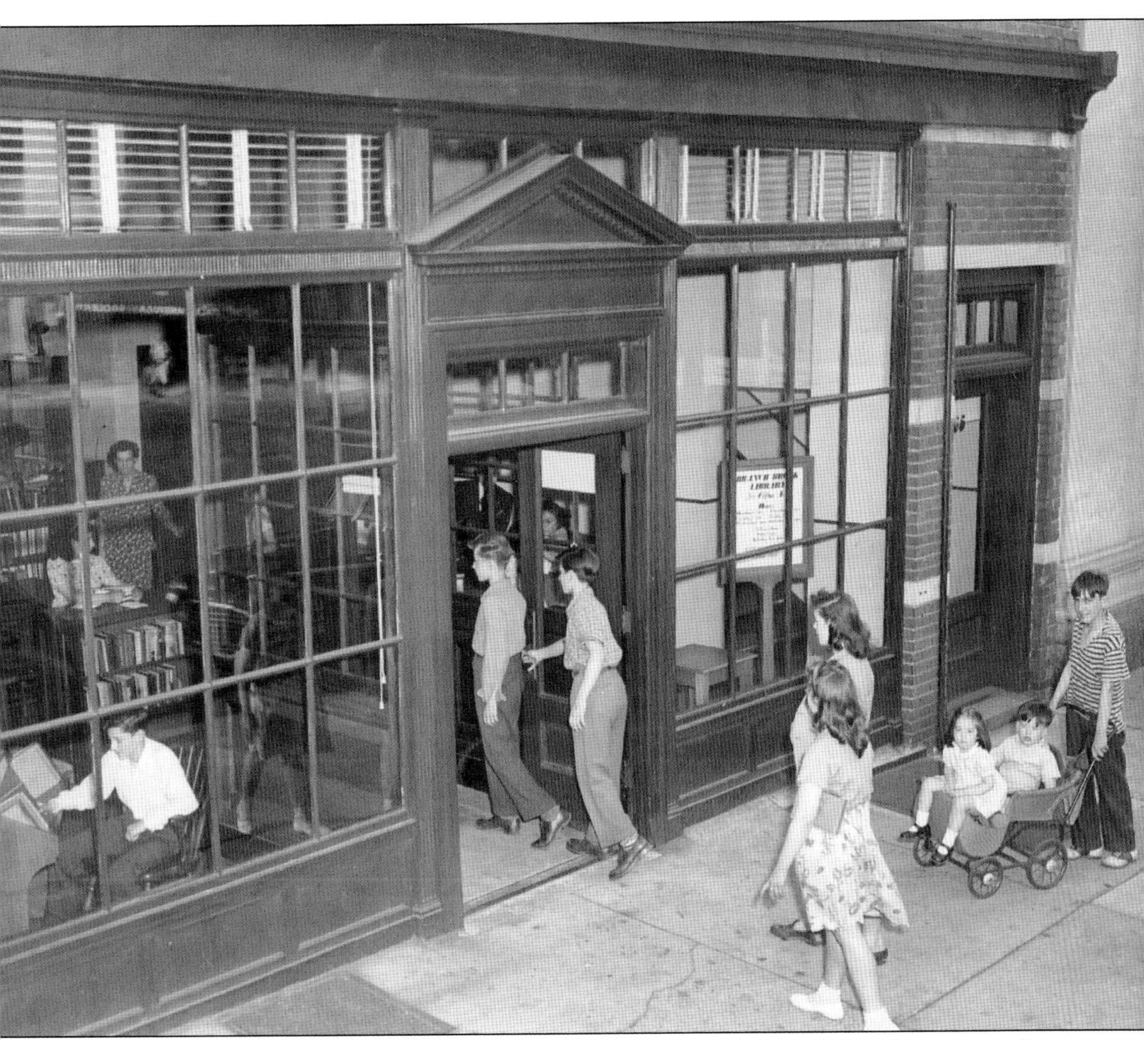

In 1946, two new branches opened: one on Clinton Avenue in the South Ward known as the Madison Branch and another one on Clifton Avenue in the North Ward known as the Branch Brook Branch (above) near Sacred Heart Cathedral and Barringer High School. In 1974, the Madison Branch expanded into another storefront next door, and another storefront branch opened on First Avenue in the North Ward. The Madison Branch and the First Avenue Branch both closed in 2010, but the Branch Brook Branch continues to serve elementary and high school students and neighborhood families in a new location. (Handy & Boesser.)

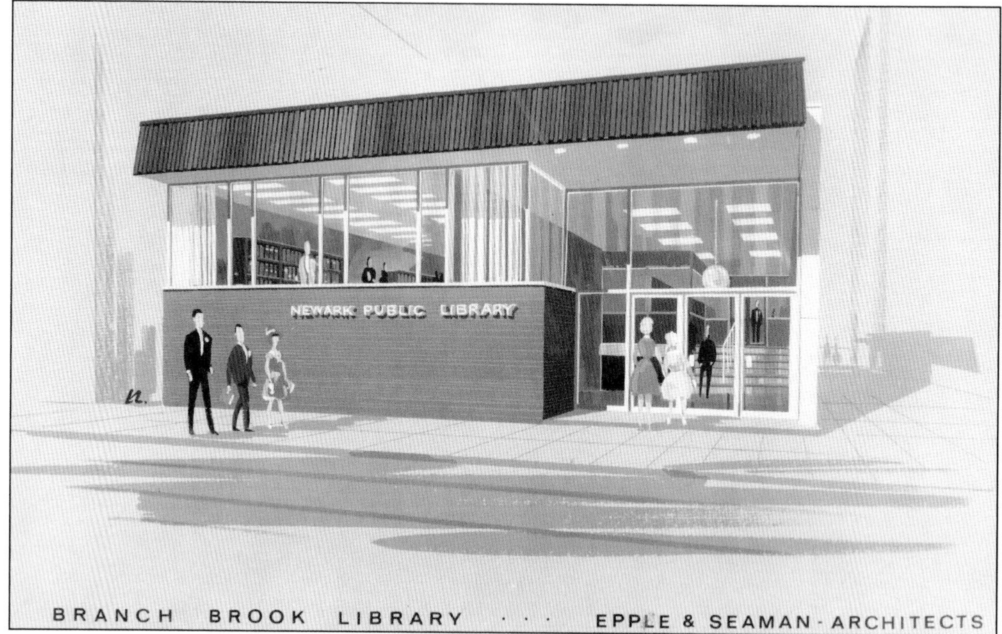

By the 1960s, the Branch Brook Branch had outgrown its original building. A new refurbished building, this modern split-level one, opened on Clifton Avenue in December 1966. With space for 36,000 volumes for adults and children and seating for over 100 people, it also included a meeting room that could accommodate up to 40 individuals.

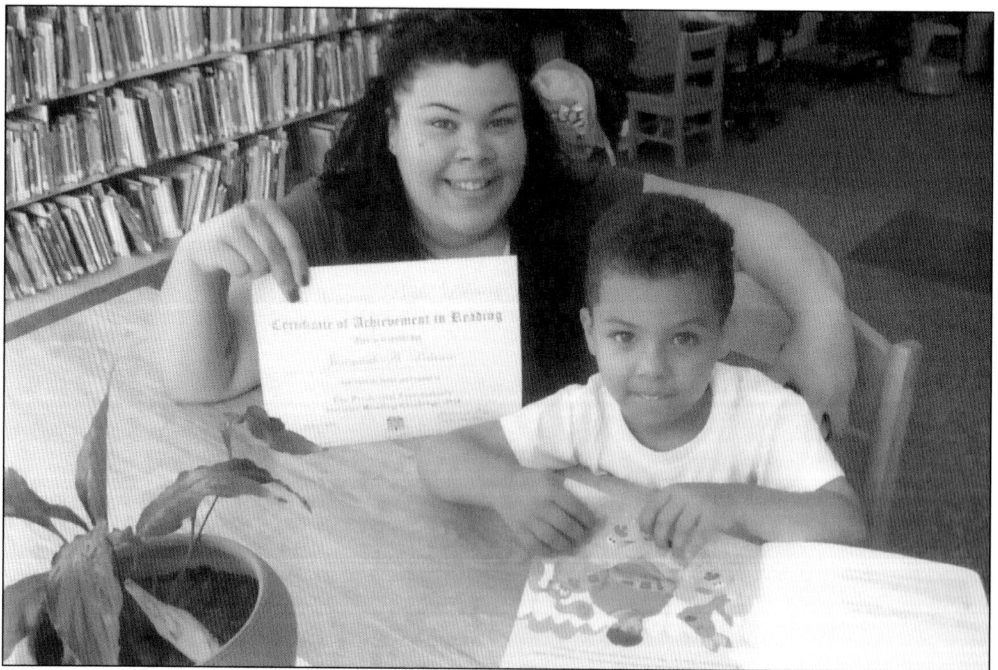

Today, in addition to its book collection, the Branch Brook Branch offers a wide range of popular video recordings for families; age-appropriate novels, including graphic novels for young adults; and special activities for children. Internet access is available to all, and the Summer Reading Challenge (pictured here) is particularly popular among the youngest users of this branch.

Six

LEGACY

In 1889, when the Newark Public Library opened its doors, Newark was a city of immigrants and their children, mostly from southern, central, and eastern Europe. A small but active community of African Americans was growing in numbers and importance. The elites—the lawyers, businessmen, and politicians, predominantly from old colonial stock—were intent on making sure that these children and adults became productive workers and responsible citizens. Toward that end, they established the Newark Public Library, but despite their paternalism, they founded an institution that catered to the needs of its users. It provided reading materials in foreign languages so readers could access information quickly and easily; it encouraged the study of American art, literature, and history so that they could make the transition to citizenship more smoothly; it provided business literature to the factory owners, store owners, insurance agents, and other professionals as well as technical information to the workers so that they could enhance their skills; but perhaps more importantly, it stocked its shelves with novels and short stories that inspired, entertained, and provoked questions.

Today, the city is more than 50 percent African American and more than 35 percent Hispanic or Latino. A third of the city's residents are foreign-born. The board of trustees and the staff of the Newark Public Library reflect this diversity, and instead of taking a top-down approach to programs, services, and collections, the library is engaging with people of all ages, abilities, beliefs, classes, colors, ethnicities, genders, and shapes to create a hub of knowledge and community, a space for learning, exploration, or connection, where individuals delve into the vast world of literature, history, the arts or the humanities, the natural sciences or the physical sciences, where young and old engage in serious research, quick fact-checking, or leisurely entertainment, where all citizens may attend a wide range of programs, exhibitions, or meetings. The Newark Public Library continues to be a place to explore rich resources, discover new stories and new ideas, and embrace the joy of lifelong learning.

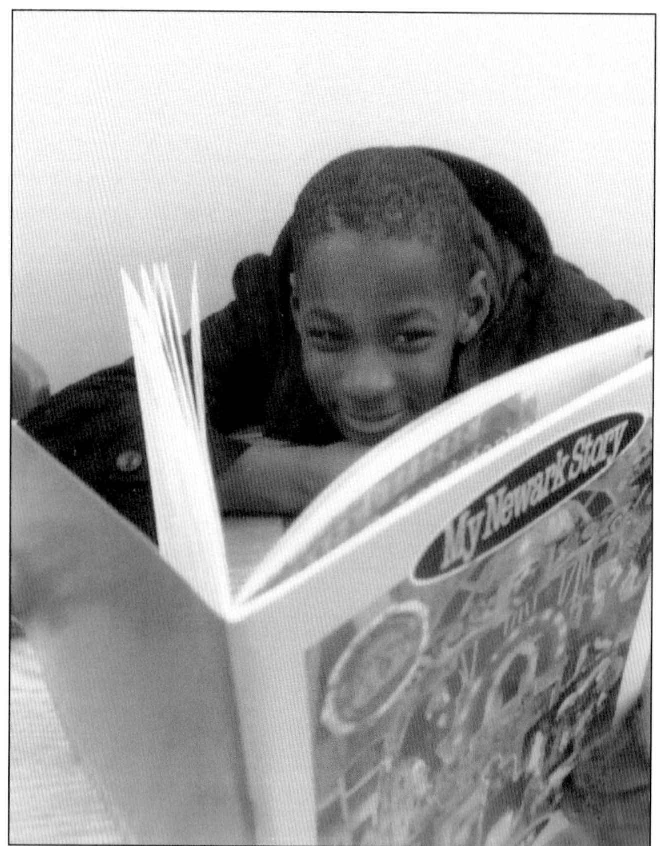

The 21st century has brought new challenges and new opportunities, but the library remains committed to expanding print and digital collections to encourage a lifelong love of reading and learning and to providing access to learning opportunities and experiences through old methods and new technologies.

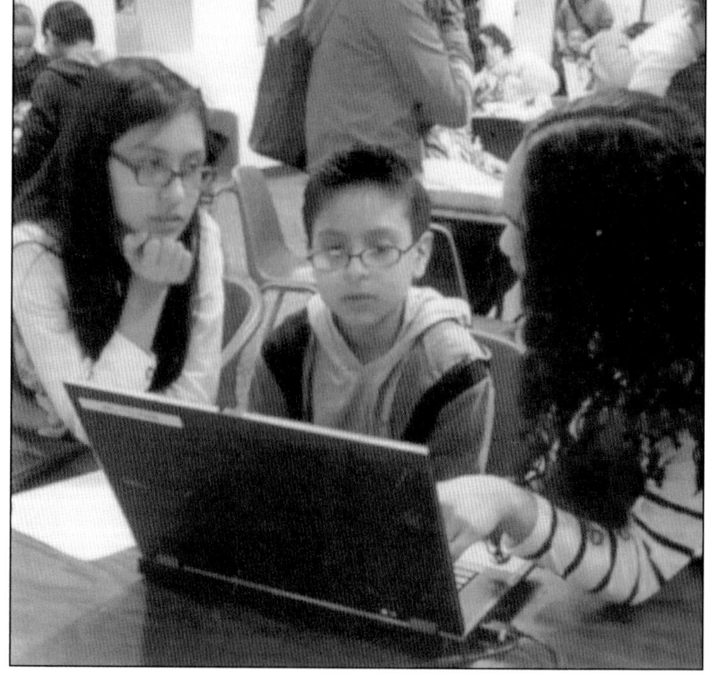

Specifically, the library assists all residents in building essential technology skills by reducing barriers for traditionally underserved populations, providing access to current and relevant technologies, and promoting new and emerging technologies that enhance learning.

In this photograph, Nell Irvin Painter relaxes after speaking about her new book, *Old in Art School*. After a brilliant career as a historian at Princeton University, the author of a biography of Sojourner Truth and *The History of White People*, the Newark resident talked about starting over as an artist in her retirement.

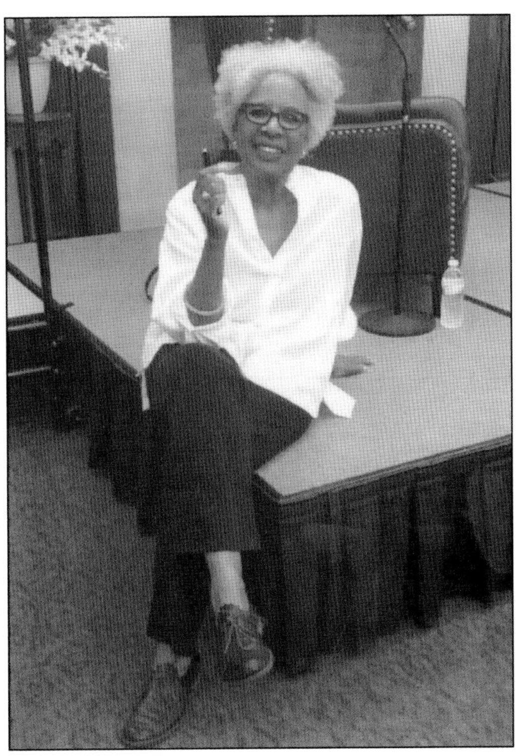

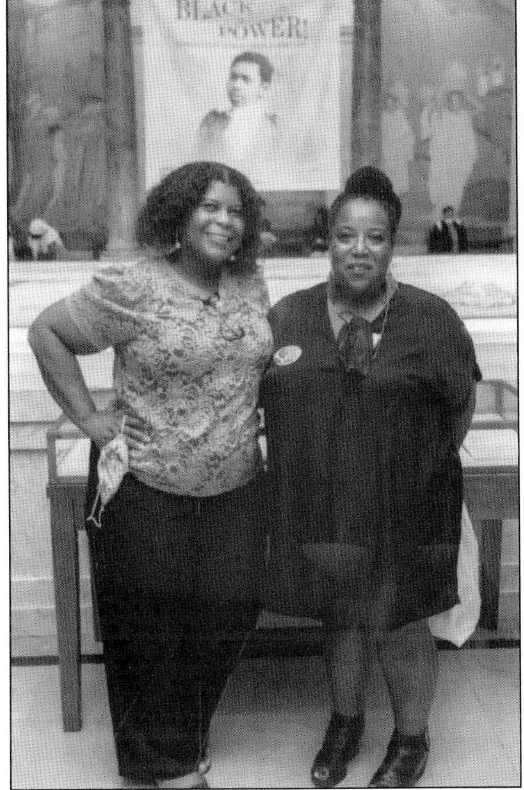

Joslyn Bowling Dixon, director from 2020 to 2022, meets with artist, historian, and activist Noelle Lorraine Williams at the opening of her exhibition *Black Power! 19th Century: Newark's First African American Rebellion* in 2020. This was the latest of many exhibitions about the history of Newark since the first one in 1905.

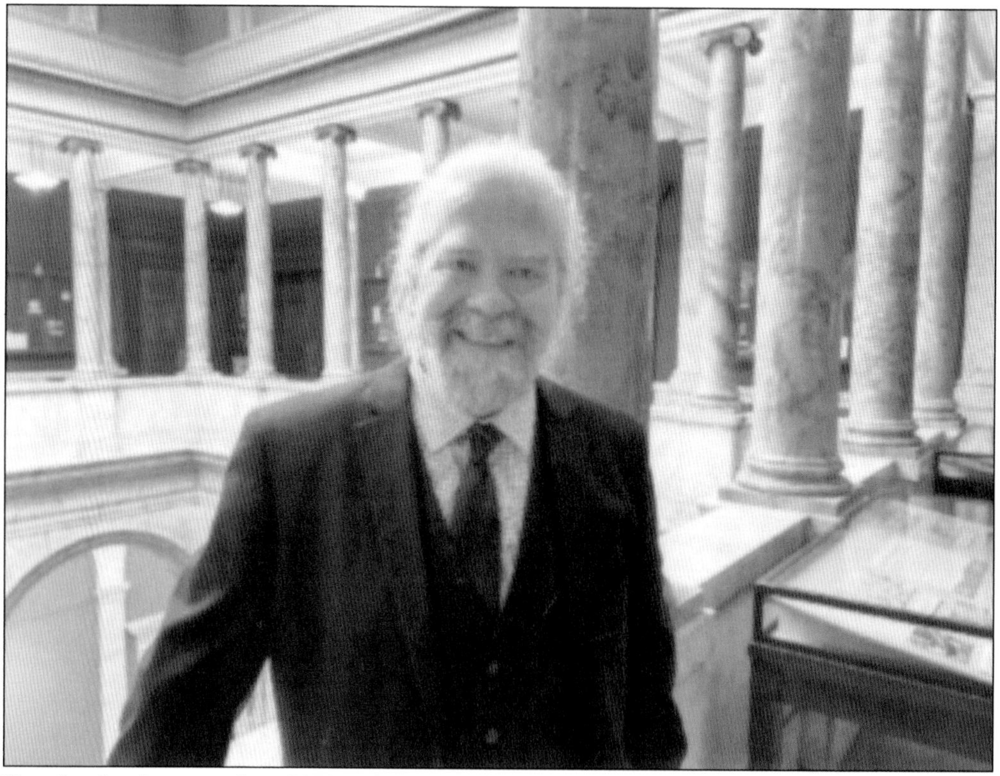

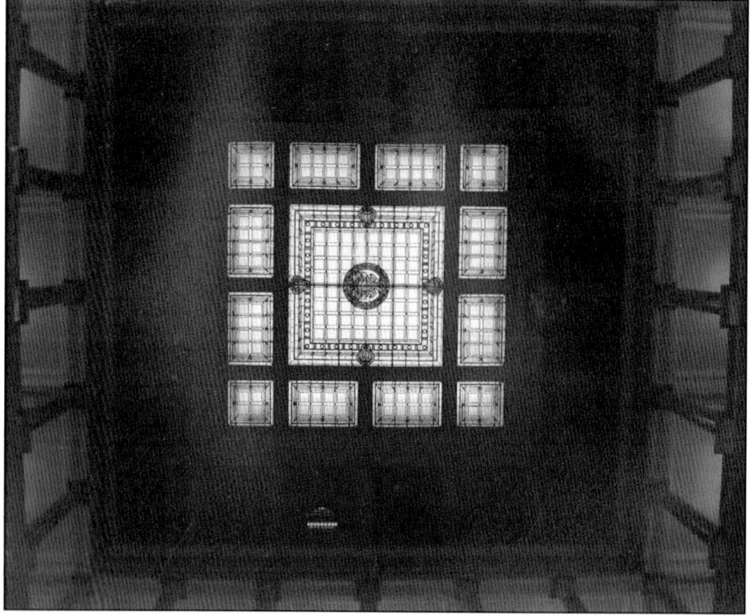

Shortly after his arrival in 2023, Christian Zabriskie, the 13th director of the Newark Public Library, stated simply, "I find something astonishing about the Newark Public Library every day. Our dedicated and innovative staff engage with the public so deeply; our collections and materials are so unique; and our facilities offer so much welcome and comfort to people throughout the city of Newark."

Together with the new director and knowledgeable staff, the current board of trustees, headed by Dr. Lauren Wells, is creating new spaces for programs and services based on unique collections that will educate, elevate, and delight the communities in and around Newark, all under the skylight of the central atrium of the main building on Washington Street or in its six active branches.

BIBLIOGRAPHY

Bryan, James E. *Newark Public Library: History.* Unpublished manuscript. Newark, NJ: Newark Public Library, undated.

Duncan, Carol G. *A Matter of Class: John Cotton Dana, Progressive Reform and the Newark Museum.* Pittsburgh, PA: Periscope, 2010.

Ford, Bruce E. "The Newark Public Library." In *A History of New Jersey Libraries, 1750–1996.* Edited by Edwin Beckerman. Lanham, MD: Scarecrow Press, 1997.

Newark Public Library. *Fifty Years, 1889–1939.* Newark, NJ: Newark Public Library, 1939.

Sabine, Julia E. *Antecedents of the Newark Public Library.* PhD dissertation, University of Chicago, 1946.

Shales, Ezra. *Made in Newark: Cultivating Industrial Arts and Civic Identity in the Progressive Era.* New Brunswick, NJ: Rutgers University Press, 2010.

Shane, Eleanor. *The Nine Branch Libraries of the Public Library of Newark, N.J.* Newark, NJ: Newark Public Library, 1930.

Discover Thousands of Local History Books Featuring Millions of Vintage Images

Arcadia Publishing, the leading local history publisher in the United States, is committed to making history accessible and meaningful through publishing books that celebrate and preserve the heritage of America's people and places.

Find more books like this at
www.arcadiapublishing.com

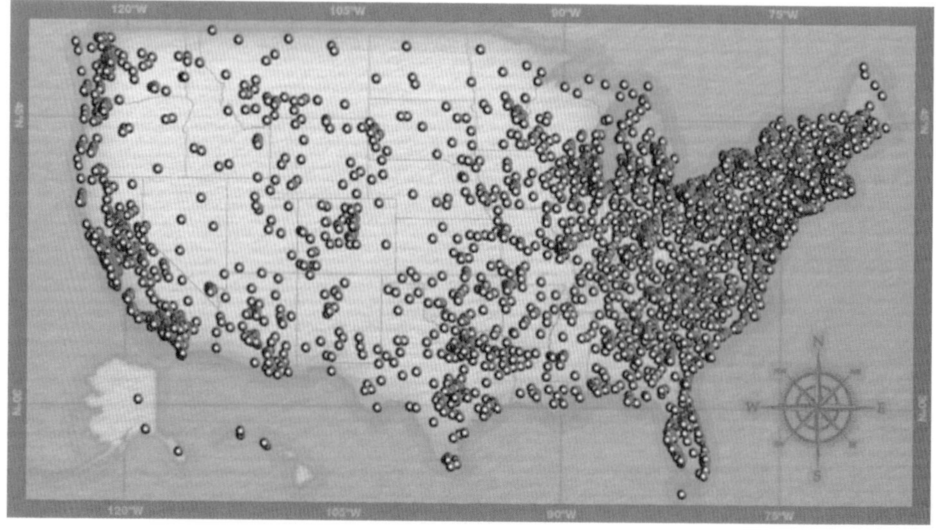

Search for your hometown history, your old stomping grounds, and even your favorite sports team.

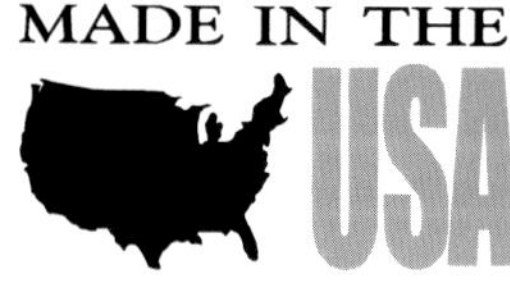